Charles Whiting was born in 1926 and was educated at the University of London, Leeds, Cologne and Kiel. He volunteered for the army at the age of 16 and served with the Reconnaissance Corps in NW Europe between 1944 and 1947. Since then he has been an Assistant Professor at the universities of Bradford, Maryland, Saarbrücken and Trier.

He is a prolific author of war fiction and has sold some 3 million copies in the UK alone and has been translated into most European languages. He was a correspondent for the *Times Educational Supplement* and his books include *Bloody Aachen* and *Patton*.

Charles Whiting is married with one son and lives in Germany.

By the same author

CHARLES WHITING

Siegfried

The Nazis' Last Stand

PANTHER
Granada Publishing

Panther Books
Granada Publishing Ltd
8 Grafton Street, London W1X 3LA

Published by Panther Books 1984

First published in Great Britain by
Leo Cooper in association with Martin Secker &
Warburg Limited 1983

ISBN 0-586-06070-7

Printed and bound in Great Britain by
Collins, Glasgow

Set in Times

Illustrations

Maps

'SOLDIERS OF THE WEST FRONT! I expect you to defend the sacred soil of Germany . . . to the very last! Heil the Führer!'

Field Marshal Gerd von Rundstedt, 1944

'The whole art of war consists of getting at what is on the other side of the hill.'

The Duke of Wellington

Contents

Introduction

'They are the men who, with their flesh and blood, buy victory. You can smash from the air, pound to rubble with artillery, thrust through with armor, but always these men on foot, the men with the rifles and bayonets and the steady slogging courage, must go on. Without them all else is in vain.'

R. W. Thompson, March 1, 1945

It was boasted that the new National Socialist Empire, founded on January 30, 1933, would last a thousand years. In fact it lasted a mere twelve years, four months and five days. Behind it, Hitler's vaunted '1,000 Year Reich' left hardly anything tangible, apart from the geographical and political consequences of the most terrible war in history. With one exception. A lasting monument in concrete and steel: the great wall built by Hitler – *Der Westwall*, which the Western Allies came to call 'the Siegfried Line.'

Even today, forty years or more since that evil genius in Berlin ordered it to be constructed, the wall crawls across the German countryside from the Swiss border to the flat plains of Holland, past France, Luxembourg, Belgium, on and on for hundreds of miles like some obscene gray reptile. All its parts are still there, in spite of efforts made by the various Allied nations to destroy it during the war and in the years that followed. The holed military roads, the dragon's teeth, the wrecked bunkers, the grotesquely twisted steel spars beneath the hedgerows – stark weathered monuments to a terrible past, they will still be there when the last survivor of that impossible dream, the 1,000 Year Reich is long, long dead.

In the late thirties when it was being constructed, at tremendous expense and with a massive recruitment of labor from all over the Third Reich, Hitler's wall was regarded by some as the Führer's great white elephant. For, they asked themselves, what useful purpose did it serve?

In Britain and America, this new gray concrete wall that had appeared so startlingly in the center of Europe was thought so amusing that it was made the subject of a comic song, which became one of the hits of 1939. For a long time afterward, first British and then American soldiers went to war singing that funny ditty about how they would soon hang their 'dirty washing' on the Siegfried Line, if the 'Siegfried Line's still there.' It was, and it is. Ironically, tragically, over a hundred thousand of those brave young men – British, American, Canadian and French (for the ditty was translated into French too) – marching so gaily away to war with that song on their lips, were fated to die before its steel and concrete defenses.

But whatever others might think about his new fortification line, Hitler knew it gave him the freedom of action in the East that he needed. For the first time in German history, due to the protection the Wall offered in the West, Germany did not have to fear a war on two fronts: the reason for her military downfall so often in the past. Thus the West Wall played a significant role in the events in Czechoslovakia and Poland in 1938/39.

The new Siegfried Line continued to deter the Western Allies through the winter and spring of 1939/40 while Hitler dealt with Poland, and when in the autumn of 1939 his peace offensive against the West failed, the Wall gave him time to plan the great attack westwards, which destroyed the French Army and sent the British reeling back to Dunkirk.

In 1940, Hitler no longer needed the Wall. Now, like Napoleon before him, he was master of all of Western Europe. For the next three years he extended that great empire of 300 million people until it stretched from Norway to North Africa and from the Channel to the Urals. The West Wall was abandoned to the wild life and the local farmers, its bunkers locked up and their keys lost, the guns removed to arm the new wall that Hitler was building on the Atlantic coast, the one that would stop the Western Allies dead if they ever attempted to invade his precious empire.

In September 1944 the West Wall came into its own again. Now, for the first time since it had been constructed, it was going to be tested as the khaki-clad tide of the advancing Allied armies who had already overcome the Atlantic Wall, swamping it with their strength, swept up against Germany's long frontiers. It would prove itself to be the impregnable fortification that Hitler had always maintained it was, even when manned by third-grade 'ear-and-nose' battalions and 'stomach' regiments – all those 'Christmas Tree soldiers,' as one of the first German defenders of the Wall, General von Schwerin, called them contemptuously. It stopped the Allied armies dead. For seven long months, British, Canadians, Americans and French, they all tried to break through it on four different national frontiers until the West Wall was finally swamped under sheer weight of numbers. It had prolonged the war by six months and the cost in Allied dead and wounded was higher than that suffered by the US Army in the Korean and Vietnam Wars combined.

* * *

In a way it was Charlemagne, the great Frankish Emperor of the ninth century, who had caused all the trouble. Not in the way he lived, but in the way he died.

In spite of the fact that he was crowned Emperor by the Pope in Rome on Christmas Day 800, Charlemagne was still a pagan Frank in many ways. He could not read, he loved war and women (many of them) and he would not accept the ordained method of succession to his great empire stretching from Holland to Italy. The Church wanted him to leave it to his eldest son and thus keep the empire together. Charlemagne wanted his inheritance to be divided, as was the Frankish custom. Thus, when he died and was buried (according to legend, sitting upright on his great throne in Aachen), his son Louis the Pious was troubled for the rest of his days by his sons wanting a share of the Empire.

When Louis died the Frankish tradition triumphed. In 843 at the French city of Verdun, his three sons signed a treaty that was one of the most memorable documents of European history. By this treaty the great empire of their grandfather was divided into three parts. Charles the Bald gained the kingdom of the West Franks, which one day would be France. Louis the German acquired the East, which would develop into Germany. For his part, the eldest son Lothar retained the title of Emperor and a narrow strip of territory starting in Belgium and running down north-east into Burgundy. This barrier between the other two became known as Lotharingia. The uneasy frontier between the future France and Germany which would trouble Europe for the next thousand-odd years had been created.

From that day onward only two men would ever again rule over the combined territory of the Franks as Charlemagne had once done. Each would do so for only a short time and each would achieve his ambition by force of arms. One was a Frenchman, who wasn't really a French-man, for he was born of Italian stock in the island of Corsica: Napoleon Bonaparte. The other was a German, who wasn't a real German, for he only accepted German nationality in 1928 when he was already forty. His name was Adolf Hitler.

For over a thousand years the history of that unhappy frontier country, the one-time Lotharingia, could be com-pared to the working of an accordion. When France was strong, which was most of the time, the pressure was *inward*. When Germany was strong, less frequently, the pressure was *outward*.

In the second decade of our own century, however, these bloody migrations of the one-time West and East Franks back and forth across the ancient kingdom of Lotharingia finally reached their climax. For four long years in World War One, Frenchmen and Germans fought each other all along the uneasy frontier, dying in their millions to establish who would receive Charlemagne's heritage. In 1916 in the course of this epic struggle, the bloodbath of Verdun occurred which was to harden French military thinking for the next thirty years. There, on those same grim chalk heights where Charlemagne's heirs had divided his kingdom, the French lost 315,000 men and the Germans 281,000 in an area less than ten square miles.

The Battle of Verdun brought France to its knees. Mutinies followed. For a whole year, the French Army was incapable of launching a major offensive. Indeed it was only through the efforts of Marshal Pétain, the defender of Verdun who had been summoned from a Parisian brothel to take command (at the age of sixty-nine!), that the French Army survived the shock. Verdun, where even today the poison gas seeps through the earth on wet days and a true compass reading cannot be obtained because of the amount of rusting metal still in the earth, became the crucial experience for many Frenchmen who were going to determine the course of events after the victorious war. André Maginot was one of those men. He had volunteered as a Parisian deputy for the Army. As a sergeant in the infantry, the huge politician had had his leg shot away at Verdun. Now, between 1930 and 1932 when he died from eating poisoned oysters at a New Year's banquet, the new Minister of War – for such he was – pushed the building of 'the Maginot Line,' a great defensive work to stretch from the Swiss frontier on the Upper Rhine to Longwy in the French Ardennes, on the border with Belgium. After Maginot's death, the work continued. Great bunkers of steel and concrete began to appear on every dominating hilltop and height along France's long frontier with Germany.

By 1935 the Line was completed. The French generals, for the most part, and the French public were happy with the new defensive feature. If the Germans ever came again, they would be halted and broken by the guns and traps of the Maginot Line, in which the *poilu* would be able to fight without danger to himself. There would be no more great blood-lettings on that frontier. It appeared that at last the age-old immigrations back and forth across Charlemagne's old empire had come to an end.

In March 1935 there was a major debate in the French Chamber of Deputies on the subject of military policy. Paul Reynaud, one day to be France's premier, stood up – armed with figures supplied by a certain Colonel de Gaulle, who himself had been wounded and captured at Verdun – and argued that the French Army needed more armor, just in case the Germans swung around the Maginot Line and entered France through Belgium. War

Minister General Maurin was not impressed. He replied: 'How can anyone believe that we are still thinking of the offensive when we have spent so many billions to establish a fortified frontier? Should we be mad enough to advance beyond this barrier – on I don't know what sort of adventure?'[1] That was that. Five short years later, as leader of his beaten country, Reynaud would learn just how right de Gaulle had been.

It seemed that the French Government, and with it the Army, had given its final official seal of approval to the Maginot Line. Next day General Maurin was undoubtedly astonished to hear that in Berlin the new German leader Adolf Hitler had torn up the Treaty of Versailles. He had announced that Germany would immediately replace the 100,000-man professional army established under the terms of the *Diktat* – as the Nazis called the treaty – with a vast conscript force of 500,000 men. What Hitler didn't announce was that the Third Reich was soon going to have her own Maginot Line. The concept of the West Wall had been born already. Hitler wanted to build a wall of his own.

In May 1938, the great undertaking commenced. Hitler had ordered that the whole length of Germany's frontier with France, with Luxembourg and with Belgium should be fortified within eighteen months. The man who was given the task of supervising construction work was Dr Todt, an engineer from an upper-class southern German family, who had little contact with politics and the National Socialists but who was well liked by Hitler.

Now Todt set to work with his usual energy, drawing on the huge sources of cheap or even free labor still available in a Germany just barely recovering from the Depression. There was the *Arbeitsdienst*, the Nazy Labor Force, which every able German boy and girl had to join for six months as soon as they reached the age of seventeen. Their free muscle provided the labor for digging the foundations and the anti-tank traps. The cities provided plenty of skilled labor too, for carpenters, bricklayers and engineers who were only too glad to have a job again, even if they now found themselves in the remote border areas where time had stood still for centuries. And finally there were the natives of this traditional backward and depressed border who were happy to supplement the miserable incomes they received from their pathetic little farms, still organized in the strip system of the Middle Ages.

In the end Todt had 100,000 military engineers, 350,000 men of his own outfit known as *Organization Todt* and the many thousands of the *Arbeitsdienst* working for him. From May 1938 to August 1939, these busy workers used eight million tons of cement, over a million tons of steel and iron and nearly a million tons of wood to construct 14,000 bunkers and pillboxes, over thirty-five per mile, along a line of four hundred miles in length. The cost was estimated to be 3.5 billion marks. It was the greatest construction program ever undertaken in Germany's history.

Der Westwall, as Hitler called the defensive feature of which he was so inordinately proud, was very different from the Maginot Line (the bunkers of which were in some cases only a couple of hundred yards away from the new German ones). Unlike the Maginot, which was really a thin line of forts, the West Wall was built in depth – averaging two and a half miles – of hundreds of mutually supporting pillboxes, observation and command posts, linked by concrete roads, with troop shelters and bunkers. If the Maginot Line could be regarded as a prestige item, with underground railways, air-conditioning, sun-tan rooms for the garrison, underground cinemas, fully equipped hospitals, reversible gun turrets, and even mushroom farms, then the West Wall was typically Germanic – hard, lean and spartan.

Todt's fortifications were much simpler. The typical Todt bunker was about twenty-one feet wide, eighteen feet high and forty-two feet deep, with walls and roofs of reinforced concrete up to nine feet thick. At least half the structure lay underground. Each contained web-bottomed beds arranged in tiers to sleep the usual fourteen-man garrison. Most had two firing holes. Though these holes provided only limited fields of fire, the pillboxes were arranged in clusters so that the guns in one – mostly machine guns and 37mm cannon – could cover the approaches to several others.

Now, on the eve of World War Two, the fortification line with its 'dragon's teeth' (the anti-tank obstacles) lay along the whole length of Germany's uneasy frontier like some ugly gray snake, waiting, ready to strike. It would take much longer than Hitler had estimated for it to catch its prey, but when it did, its bite would be deadly . . .

This book is about what happened when finally the Allied armies ran into this 'Devil's Garden,' as Brigadier Essame has called the West Wall. This is not a story of generals and their tactics and decisions, but simply of the 'doughs,' the 'Canucks,' the 'PBI' (Poor Bloody Infantry) who slogged it out that long murderous winter with Hitler's Wall, and those 'stubble-hoppers,' as they liked to call themselves, who defended it.

It is, in essence, a story written in blood . . .

Book One: 1944

'Believe me, General. I am the greatest builder of forti-fications of all time. I built the West Wall.'

Hitler to Colonel-General Guderian, January 1944

September

'Maybe there are five thousand, maybe ten thousand Nazi bastards in their concrete foxholes before the Third Army. Now, if Ike stops holding Monty's hand and gives me the supplies, I'll go through the Siegfried Line like shit through a goose!'

General Patton, September 1944

1

Panic reigned!

During the first week of September 1944, all along that frontier with the '1,000 Year Reich' – from French Lorraine in the south, through Luxembourg, the Belgian Ardennes, and right into the Dutch Province of Maastricht – all was confusion and panic.

One month earlier, the Allies had finally made their breakout from Normandy after seven weeks of slogging it out with the *Wehrmacht*. Now the British, the Canadians, the Americans, and all the minor allies they had brought across the Channel with them on that fateful June 6th – the Poles, the Czechs, the Dutch, the Belgians, the French – were streaming eastward, joyful and triumphant.

The Germans tried to stop them on the Somme. To no avail. It was the same on the Seine. Paris fell. The beaten *Wehrmacht*, its corps reduced to divisions, its divisions to regiments, its regiments to battalions, tried to halt that victorious advance on the Meuse. Again they failed. The Americans under General Hodges would brook no delay. They crossed the last natural bulwark before the German frontier itself at Namur and half a dozen lesser points and swept on. Nothing seemed able to stop them now.

'We have no vehicles or guns left,' US Intelligence men read in a letter found on the blood-stained corpse of a German tanker, 'and whoever is still alive will have to fight as an infantryman. But I won't stay with them very long. I really don't know what we are still fighting for. Very soon I shall run over to the Tommies if I am not killed before I get there.'[1]

The 3rd US Armored Division did him that particular favor, as they did another nameless 'stubble-hopper,' as the hard-pressed German infantrymen called themselves. On his body sprawled out in the unnatural posture of those who had been put to death violently on the field of battle, they found a note which began, 'My total estate now fits into my breadbag. I have lost everything else. The words "hot meal" sound like a foreign language. We are gaining ground rapidly – but in the wrong direction.'[2] The would-be humorist never finished his epistle. His own dark-red blood obscured the next words.

'An orderly retreat became impossible,' wrote General Speidel, Rommel's Chief-of-Staff, who would soon be arrested himself for his part in the plot to assassinate Hitler that July. 'The Allied motorized armies surrounded the slow and exhausted German foot divisions in separate groups and smashed them up . . . There were no German ground forces of any importance that could be thrown in, and next to nothing in the air.'[3]

Karlludwig Opitz, a soldier with an infantry division, recorded the details of that great retreat back to the Reich: 'Vehicles pile up. Cars, heavily laden with officers' gear, honk a way through the jam, twisting past lorries in their effort to make better time. Guns are abandoned and blown up. Heavy tractors stop for the lack of fuel: a couple of grenades in the engine and that's that. The huge

Mercedes diesels of a workshop company are hit by rockets. The soldiers on the tanks cannot make out where these powerful, ultra-modern machines can suddenly have come from. The men have never seen their like before. Christ, we should have had them earlier! . . . And the fighters are having a field day; they hedgehop along the road, the engines screeching. Empty ammunition belts fall from them, rockets, grenades, machine-gun bullets, bombs, everything is thrown at the stream of vehicles.'[4]

A few of the diehards turned that first week of September and attempted to make a stand. One of them was Kurt Meyer, known as 'Panzermeyer,' the youngest general of the *Waffen-SS*. He had seen his division, the 12th SS 'Hitler Youth,' wasted away at the Battle of Caen, with 10,000 casualties among his seventeen- and eighteen-year-olds and 21 of his commanders dead, wounded or captured. Now, with his remaining 600 panzer grenadiers and a handful of vehicles, he attempted to halt the pursuing Americans on the far side of the last waterway, the Meuse, at the little Belgian hamlet of Durnal.

On the night of September 6th, after successfully stopping the 'Amis,' as the Americans were contemptuously called by the SS, for thirty-six hours, Meyer heard that they had turned his flank. He ordered an immediate withdrawal. At the edge of the village, however, the boys of the *Hitlerjugend* ran into trouble. A Sherman rumbled around the bend in the road, firing as it rolled towards the stalled Germans. Captain Heinzelmann in the first looted jeep took a direct hit; he disappeared in a burst of flame. Meyer, behind him, knew he couldn't turn in the narrow village street. He dived from his jeep right over a stone wall and pelted for the nearest farmhouse, pursued by machine-gun fire. But there he realized with a sense of shock that he had run into a trap. There was no back way out of the farm; it had been built with its rear dug into solid rock!

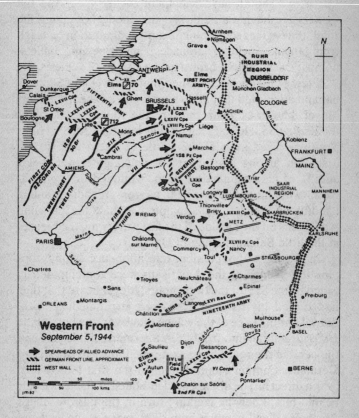

Western Front
September 5, 1944

→ SPEARHEADS OF ALLIED ADVANCE
⫻ GERMAN FRONT LINE, APPROXIMATE
⫶⫶⫶ WEST WALL

10   50   miles   100
10   50   100 kms

JM 82

Another dark gasping shape joined him: Major Max
Bornhoeft, an old comrade. Now it was *sauve qui peut*.
The survivors of the 12th SS were running for their lives.
But Meyer, a veteran of five years of war in two continents
and a dozen countries, didn't lose his head. Together with
Max, he hid in a chicken-coop, the general who had been
received by the Führer countless times. The Americans
passed on, but they were replaced by the partisans of the
ruthless Belgian resistance, the White Army, so-called
because of the white overalls which the British had
dropped them as uniforms. But now it began to rain and
Meyer reasoned that the partisans were fine-weather
soldiers; the heavy rain would drive them indoors.

Together the two SS officers left the cover of the
chicken-coop. A graveyard. Rain dripping off the ornate
crosses. A sudden cry of alarm. The two men went to
ground. Panzermeyer drew his pistol and waited. Two
policemen, their capes streaming with rain, came running
into the churchyard, weapons at the ready. Meyer didn't
wait to fight it out with them; he ran for the nearest wall.
Up and over – the drop was fifteen feet! His legs felt as if
they were being driven deep into his stomach. Sick with
shock, he ran on through the rainstorm. Slugs cut the air.
A cry of pain. Behind him Max slammed to the *pavé*,
wounded. Panzermeyer pumped off a couple of angry
shots at his pursuers. They went to the ground, and then
with the last of his strength the SS general swung into the
cover of a wooden barn.

'Once,' he recalled after the war, 'there had been a time
in Russia when we had all sworn we would never be taken
alive by the enemy. Now I was faced with the moment of
truth, what was I to do? I raised my pistol to my temple.
But each time I was tempted to pull the trigger and finish
it all, the picture of my family flashed in front of my
mind's eye.'[5]

Suddenly there was a shout A young boy, armed with a carbine which was much too big for him, had spotted the fugitive in the barn. The wooden door was splintered by a couple of shots.

'Come out!' someone yelled.

Meyer let his shoulders slump in defeat. This was the end of the road for him. His meteoric career as the youngest SS general was over. With his hands raised above his head General Kurt Meyer, commander of the elite 12th SS Panzer Division, surrendered to a middle-aged Belgian farmer turned partisan and his fourteen-year-old son.

There were few 'Panzermeyers' along that 120-mile border with Germany as the first week of September 1944 gave way to the second, one to be even more terrible for the beaten German Army fleeing eastwards than its predecessor. Everywhere the fugitives in field-gray were deserting. In the neighborhood of the great Lorraine city of Metz in Northern France, three deserters hid in one of the many bunkers that dominated the area. Engineers blew up some ammunition outside and the three were trapped by a huge block of concrete which filled the entrance. For seventy-two hours the three men tried to dig themselves out by means of their eating utensils, the only tools they had. When local farmers found the would-be deserters, two were blind and one died a few days later in hospital due to total exhaustion. At the other end of the escape corridor, Dutch Dr Frans Huygen of the village of Lent near Nijmegen saw German soldiers begging for civilian clothing from the local villagers, while in Nijmegen they demanded clothes at gun point.

Now all discipline started breaking down. Officers and NCOs began to lose control, even in elite formations. Soldiers stole carts, bicycles, horses, cars – anything that would convey them away from the Allied steamroller descending upon them. Everywhere the civilians of the border area watched as the once victorious field-grays fled eastwards, now a rabble of dirty, frightened men out to save their skins, some of them even pushing pram-loads of loot filched from France and Flanders. 'Scenes were witnessed,' wrote Walter Goerlitz, post-war military correspondent of the German newspaper *Die Welt*, 'which nobody would ever have deemed possible in the German Army. Naval troops marched northward without weapons, selling their spare uniforms . . . They told people that the war was over and they were going home. Lorries loaded with officers, their mistresses and large quantities of champagne and brandy contrived to get back as far as the Rhineland and it was necessary to set up special courts-martial to deal with such cases.' That second week of September, in one border city alone, the old Roman town of Trier, special officer patrols rounded up 42,000 soldiers, *the equivalent of two and a half infantry divisions*, who had fled or been separated from their outfits in France and the Low Countries, and sent them back to the front.

That week, the Intelligence Summary of General Eisenhower's Supreme Headquarters stated that the German Army was 'no longer a cohesive force but a number of fugitive battle groups, disorganized and even demoralized, short of equipment and arms.'[6] Even General John Kennedy, the conservative director of military operations at the British War Office in London, noted on September 6th that 'If we go at the same pace as of late, we should be in Berlin by the 28th.'

Behind them came the triumphant Allied soldiers, mobbed and feted by the almost hysterical crowds they had now liberated from four years of Nazi domination.

'As long as I live I don't guess I'll ever see a parade like that,' Private First Class Verner Odegard of the US 28th Infantry Division told the press that week. 'Most of us slept in pup tents in the Bois de Boulogne the night before and it rained like hell and we were pretty dirty, so they picked out the cleanest guys to stand up in front and on the outside. I had a bright new shiny patch so they put me on the outside. It was a good place to be, too, because every guy marching on the outside had at least one girl on his arm kissing and hugging him. We were marching twenty-four abreast down the Champs Elysées and we had a helluva time trying to march, because the whole street was jammed with people laughing and yelling and crying and singing. They were throwing flowers at us and bringing us big bottles of wine. The first regiment never did get through. They just broke in and grabbed the guys and lifted some of them on their shoulders and carried them into cafés and bars and their homes and wouldn't let them go. I hear it was a helluva job trying to round them all up later.'[7]

It was no different for the British. Crossing the border of Belgium into Holland, the 6th Battalion of the King's Own Scottish Borderers of the 15th Scottish Infantry Division was similarly 'assaulted' by the enthusiastic locals. After the war, Company Commander Captain Robert Woollcombe recalled: 'All semblance of orderly movement became hopelessly lost. Tilburg was now a mass of wild humanity and chaos swallowed us up. The entire population must have been packed along our route. We entered the older part of the town and all these delirious people still cheered and cheered. They showered fruit on us. Men, young and old, ran up to shake us by the hand. Many stood at the curb wringing the hand of every soldier who passed. Women with tears on their cheeks lifted little children to be kissed by "Tommy" as though the act was a dispensation that could formally dispel the shadows of tyranny . . . The occupation was ended!'[8]

At that bright highpoint of the campaign in Europe, neither PFC Verner Odegard nor Captain Woollcombe could know that the good days were about over and that they were both heading with their divisions for a great blood-letting on that remote frontier, which would leave the one shattered and the other reeling with shock from the losses it suffered.

For now as the first little groups of men in khaki began to feel their way to the German frontier in the wake of the fleeing, broken *Wehrmacht*, a change was beginning to take place, not only in the terrain, which had become rugged and hilly, with dense fir forests marching up the slopes like regiments of spike-helmeted Prussian guardsmen, but also in the character of the civilians.

Here the national flags of the newly liberated countries were absent, as were the cheaply colored, highly flattering portraits of Churchill, Roosevelt and de Gaulle which had decorated every house in the plains below. No crowds cheered here; the victorious troops were greeted with silence, even sullenness. Most of the citizens of these remote towns and villages along the frontier were German-speaking, and many of them, Lorrainers, Luxembourgers and Belgians from the so-called 'East Cantons,'[9] had menfolk serving in the German Army; indeed the two last groupings had been German citizens since 1940. And among them were many Germans who had been evacuated from the bombing of the great cities of the Rhineland to this remote rural area.

The GIs started to feel a change of mood too. After the heady enthusiasm of the last weeks, the cheering, the kissing, the drinking, they began to sense that here they were no longer liberators but conquerors; and before them loomed the green mysterious heights which were Germany. What, they started to wonder as their vehicles rolled ever closer to the 1,000 Year Reich, climbing and climbing all the time, lay ahead for them up there?

Lieutenant Vipond, Executive Officer of Troop B, 85th Reconnaissance Squadron of the US 5th Armored Division, had told Staff Sergeant Warner W. Holzinger that if he wished to claim the credit of being the first enemy soldier to enter Germany since the time of Napoleon nearly 150 years before, he'd better hurry. On this afternoon of September 11th, 1944, other US outfits were hurrying toward the mountain frontier at half a dozen spots.

Now as the shadows started to race down the tight valley of the River Our, dominated by the great height on the east bank, which remained ominously silent, young Sergeant Holzinger and his little patrol decided to stick their necks out.

The little stone bridge located between the village of Stolzemburg on the Luxembourg side and the tiny hamlet of Gmuend, just around the loop in the Our on the German side, had been blown by the retreating field-grays, but the water was shallow and sluggish. The four Americans and the Frenchman crouching in the cover of a bunch of trees could see the bottom easily.

Holzinger went in first and started to wade across. Soon Corporal Ralph Diven, T-5 Coy Locke, PFC George McNeal and their French interpreter Lieutenant Lille joined him, their eyes fixed apprehensively on the wooded slope that rose steeply to their front. But nothing happened. All was silent save for the steady rumble of the heavy guns of the permanent barrage, the background music to the war.

They clambered out of the water and crossed the narrow road running along the bank on the German side. Almost immediately they stumbled across the first concrete bunker, built at the side of the road to cover the bridge. It was empty. They ventured a little further through the firs and found another three, also empty. In the end they clambered almost to the top of the height, with the Our a silver ribbon far below in the valley, finding some nineteen or twenty concrete pillboxes, all empty, their equipment long gone, with dust thick on the floor. Around one some local farmer had built a chicken coop. Holzinger and his little patrol had unwittingly entered the *Westwall*, that 'Siegfried Line' on which the British Tommies had boasted in 1939 that they would hang out their 'washing, mother dear!'

But now it was getting dark and Holzinger felt no desire to linger on this steep height with its *Westwall* fortifications. Together with his men he stumbled down the slope, the sun sinking behind the hills on the Luxembourg side and night beginning to poke long black fingers into the valley of the Our, waded the river at the double and hurried to the parked scout-car. Thirty minutes later Holzinger was excitedly relating his discovery to Lieutenant Vipond. Sixty minutes after that the information was on its way to no less a person than General Courtney Hodges, the commander of the half-a-million strong US First Army to which the 5th Armored Division belonged. That night First Army issued a statement, couched in the dry unemotional prose of the Army. It read:

At 1805 hrs on 11 September, a patrol led by S. Sgt. Warner W. Holzinger crossed into Germany near the village of Stolzemburg, a few miles north-east of Vianden, Luxembourg.

For the first time since 1814, an enemy soldier had set foot on German territory during wartime. Staff Sergeant Holzinger had returned to the land of his forefathers as a

conqueror; and the Great Wall of Germany was un-
manned. It seemed nothing could stop the Allies now.

That evening and the following morning, more and more
American outfits started to slip over the border into a
strangely quiet and undefended Germany the whole
length of the frontier between Echternach in Luxembourg
and Veals in Holland. A reinforced company of the 109th
Infantry, 28th Infantry Division, crossed the River Our
between the Luxembourg village of Weiswampach and
the German village of Sevenig. Almost at the same time a
patrol from Colonel Lanham's 22nd Infantry of the 4th
Division crossed the Our near the village of Hemmeres.
Men of the patrol spoke to the first German civilians they
had met and in order to prove that they had actually
crossed into the Third Reich brought back with them a
peaked German cap, some marks and a symbolic packet
of German earth, which perhaps to this very day holds
pride of place in some suburban front parlor – if its
possessor lived to take it back with him.

Ernest Hemingway, big and bearded, looking like 'a
khaki teddy bear' in his correspondent's uniform and
enjoying himself hugely with Lanham's 22nd to which he
had attached himself, entered Germany the following
morning, following a tank and some halftracks through
Schirm and Maspelt.[10] Far ahead 'Papa' Hemingway and
his companions watched a halftrack 'scuttle like an
animal' out of the edge of the forest. Two planes, their
bombs gone, strafed the ground at tree-top level. Hemingway and his group climbed the height ahead of them
and then suddenly, Hemingway wrote later, 'There was
Germany spread out before us!'

Later that same Tuesday afternoon, Hemingway
watched two German tanks racing up the road to his front
with American artillery blasting yellow clouds of smoke

and road dust in their path. The infantry, Hemingway with them, crossed into the village of Hemmeres, where 'ugly women and squatty ill-shaped men' came sidling toward the Americans bearing bottles of schnapps, drinking some themselves to prove it was not poisoned. Others held up their hands in token of surrender as if they were soldiers, or carried white flags. All the houses in the tiny Eifel village were empty and in one Hemingway found the warm remains of some hastily departed German officer's meal.

While Lanham's infantry went ahead to secure the high ground to the east, 'Papa,' obviously reminded of his own stomach, set about organizing a dinner. He shot the heads off a small flock of chickens with his .45 and set a German woman to plucking and fricasseeing the dead fowls.

That night, as Allied bombers droned over their heads to plaster key spots along the frontier in order to speed up the pursuit on the following day, Colonel Lanham, a short, wiry, brown-eyed West Pointer – something of a writer himself, and just as profane and explosive as Hemingway – was invited with his three battalion commanders to a celebration dinner. Lanham thought, in retrospect, that the meal of 'chicken, peas, fresh onions, carrots, salad and canned fruit' was his 'happiest night' of the whole war. 'The food was excellent, the wine plentiful, the comradeship close and warm. All of us were heady with the taste of victory, as we were with the wine. It was a night to put aside the thoughts of the great West Wall against which we would throw ourselves in the next forty-eight hours. We laughed and drank and told horrendous stories about each other. We all seemed for the moment like minor gods and Hemingway presiding at the head of the table might have been a fatherly Mars delighting in the happiness of his brood.'[11]

2

Exactly one week before that celebration dinner at which
Colonel Lanham banished all thoughts of the West Wall,
one old soldier who in five years of war had not lost a
single battle for his Führer (although he hated the man; he
called him contemptuously the 'Bohemian corporal') was
received by Hitler at East Prussian HQ, 'the wolf's lair.'
After days of kicking his heels at a local inn, 69-year-old
Generalfeldmarschall Gerd von Rundstedt, Germany's
greatest soldier now given to overmuch French cognac,
was ushered into the presence of the man who had fired
him on July 2, 1944. That 'Bohemian corporal,' von
Rundstedt had fumed to his chief-of-staff, had used 'my
age and ill health as an excuse to relieve me in order to
have a scapegoat.' Back in July when he was commanding
the Western Front, von Rundstedt had wanted a slow
withdrawal to the German border, 'exacting a terrible
price for every foot of ground given up.' Hitler had
disagreed. As always he had wanted to direct operations
himself so that, as von Rundstedt often complained, the
only authority he had as Supreme Commander in the
West was 'to change the guard in front of the gate.' Now
this September afternoon von Rundstedt was greeted by
Hitler 'with unwonted diffidence and respect' and offered
his old job back. As von Rundstedt sat 'motionless and
monosyllabic,' Hitler and his staff swiftly sketched in the
horrific details of the situation on the Western Front,
which he was to take over, if it still could be called a front.

It had been ripped apart. In the north, British Field
Marshal Montgomery's tanks had slashed their way
through Holland and could well turn the left flank of the

vaunted West Wall. In Belgium General Hodges's First Army was hurrying for the German frontier; and to the south General Patton's Third Army was barreling across Lorraine for Metz and the German Saar Basin. In short, the situation of von Rundstedt's new command was disastrous.

But, as always, Hitler was the great optimist. He confidently expected that the Allied drive across the great plain of northern France and Belgium would soon end, when the British and Americans ran out of supplies – for most of their ammunition, fuel and food was still coming from the Normandy beaches, conveyed to the front by the famed 'Red Ball Express': a one-way system up to the front and then back, to be crossed by no other vehicles under whatever circumstances. In addition, the Führer thought that the weather would soon worsen and that when winter came Germany would regain the initiative. Besides, Hitler reminded the stony-faced Field Marshal, there was always the great fortification system he had ordered to be built nearly a decade before. Germany still possessed the *Westwall* . . .

On September 12, 1938, Hitler had addressed over a quarter of a million people at the annual party rally at Nuremberg and revealed the secret of this strange construction project which was currently employing nearly a million of their fellow citizens on the border with France. 'I ordered the immediate building of our fortifications in the west,' he bellowed at the rigid ranks of the Brownshirts and the teenagers of the *Arbeitsdienst* bearing their burnished shovels over their young skinny shoulders as if they were rifles. 'I can assure you that since May 28th, the most gigantic fortification work of all time has been constructed!'[12]

Once they had overcome their first stunned reaction to

Hitler's speech, the intelligence services of Holland, Britain, France and Belgium attempted to pierce the secrets of this new wall that Hitler had boasted about.

The French Deuxième Bureau had been first off the mark. After all, the French felt themselves most threatened. 'Zero C,' otherwise known as Group-Captain Fred Winterbotham of the British Secret Intelligence Service, later recalled how they fitted an 'enormous and ancient wooden camera into a very old aeroplane,' which was flown up and down the Rhine between the Maginot Line and the West Wall, the camera being 'operated by a splendid old man with a flowing beard who was normally a portrait photographer in Paris.' Thus the French managed to keep track of the German plans.

The British Secret Service followed the French example. Hungarian film magnate Alexander Korda, Colonel 'Uncle Claude' Dansey of the top-secret Continental branch of the SIS melodramatically entitled the 'Z Organization,' and of all people the staid British 'Jewish Board of Guardians' smuggled questionnaires to the large Jewish communities in the border area. These they filled in with whatever details they could gain of the West Wall and despatched through the forests of the Eifel-Ardennes by means of professional smugglers.

Other amateur Jewish agents managed to fool the Gestapo by pretending to be smuggling out valuta (forbidden to Jews). As a result they were subjected to the usual dose of castor oil at border check-points so that the Gestapo could ascertain whether they had swallowed gold coins or jewels. Naturally they hadn't. They had another kind of much more valuable contraband hidden about their persons: information about Hitler's new wall.

In Berlin young Major Kenneth Strong, the British assistant military attaché, also puzzled out the problem of when the Line would be completed and what kind of troops manned it. Strong, who one day would be Eisenhower's Chief-of-Intelligence, struck lucky in June 1939. That month there was a parade held in honor of Prince Paul of Jugoslavia and the night before it was scheduled to start, Strong received a telephone call from a friend in the German War Office. He suggested in a roundabout way that Strong should take a walk, since it was a fine evening.

'I thought this a curious message,' Strong recalled much later,[13] 'but I decided to go. To my astonishment I found the Germans had marked on the pavements the names of the units which were to assemble that evening and take part in the parade on the morrow. It was a real bonanza!' Later the young officer was confronted by 'an army of cleaning women with buckets and mops . . . to wash away the secret information. Someone in authority had discovered the blunder. But I already knew now what units manned the Siegfried Line.'

The Dutch even got a handsome young agent to seduce the secretary of a general in charge of the section of the West Wall around Aachen, one of its most formidable parts, in order to find out its secrets from her.

All the same, in the autumn of 1944 when the Western Allies prepared to attack through Hitler's Wall, they knew as little about it as their forerunners had known back in 1939/40.

Yet the Americans of General Hodges's V Corps who would launch the first attack against the West Wall were confident it would provide little hindrance to them. On the night of September 11th, the same day that Sergeant Holzinger had made his first foray into enemy territory, Colonel Thomas Ford, G-2 of V Corps, predicted that the attackers would meet only the battered remnants of the three divisions which the Corps had recently chased across Belgium and Luxembourg. 'There seems no doubt,' he concluded his briefing to the Corps staff that night after V Corps had just received permission to attack, 'that the enemy will defend the Siegfried Line with all of the forces that he can gather.' Colonel Ford smiled and added that what the enemy could gather was 'very much to be questioned.'

From the German side that day, it seemed Ford was right. 'Today, I was transferred to the 42nd Machine-Gun Fortress Battalion as messenger,' a young German soldier wrote in his diary that day (the diary was taken from his dead shattered body some time later), 'destination West Wall. This battalion is composed of Home Guard [*Volkssturm*] soldiers and half-cripples. I found many among them who were quite obviously off mentally. Some had their arms amputated, others had one leg short, etc, etc – a sad sight. "We're the V-2 and the V-3," they jokingly call themselves. A bunch of fools!'

Field Marshal von Rundstedt had no alternative but to mobilize these 'fools' in order to defend the vital Wall, while the battered remnants of the armies beaten in France and the Low Countries re-formed.

Alarming reports were being filed at von Rundstedt's new headquarters in Koblenz, seventy miles behind the Wall, that the Americans were already in possession of some of the West Wall bunkers. But as the troops of the 1st SS Corps – four divisions which had been so badly depleted that their commander General Keppler had merged them into two divisions – started to occupy the West Wall bunkers, it was discovered that the American preparations had been the work of reconnaissance patrols. Von Rundstedt was able to heave a sigh of relief.

The race for the West Wall was over. Technically the Germans had won it. But as Charles MacDonald, the war historian who as a young captain occupied one of those same West Wall bunkers back in 1944, has written: 'So soon were the Americans upon them [the Germans] that the end results looked very much like a dead heat.'[14]

3

General Norman Cota's 28th Infantry Division was the first to kick off V Corps' attack on the West Wall. It started to cross the River Our in strength on the night of September 12, 1944.

The leading infantrymen began to wade the knee-deep river with the rifles at the high port against only very light small-arms fire. For a while the first companies at point crouched on the little road that runs along the river on the German side, waiting for the Germans to attack. But all they received was sporadic rifle fire, although German flares were hissing urgently into the night sky everywhere as the defenders of the Wall reported the American crossing.

An order was given and the first wet soldiers began to advance cautiously on the line of dragon's teeth which ran up and down the green dark hills ahead like the knobs on a crocodile's spine. Again their progress was halted merely by frightened bursts of tracer and the odd lone mortar bomb.

By dawn they had seized a whole length of the anti-tank defenses. As the first white light of the new day flushed the sky to the east, the GIs of the 28th Infantry Division found themselves everywhere confronted with the enemy's main defense line – the squat low silhouettes of the bunker line. This was it!

Early that morning, September 13th – an unlucky thirteenth for the 28th Division – the infantry commenced their attack on the first of the concrete pillboxes. Immediately they ran into trouble. Several German machine guns opened up, and as the startled GIs went to ground seven hundred yards away from the fortified line, the frightening howl of the enemy six-barreled mortar, 'the screaming meemie,' ripped the morning air apart. Huge holes appeared everywhere abruptly like the work of gigantic moles. Frantic company commanders asked for artillery support. Towed 57mm anti-tank guns rumbled into the line. But not for long. Enemy gunners, endowed with superior observation from the heights, made sudden death of their efforts, even before the Americans had unlimbered their pieces. Indirect artillery fire was called for. It proved useless and did little to damage the thick roofs of the concrete pillboxes, still spitting fire, save to 'dust off the camouflage,' as one participant in that first attack recalls.

The next day the 28th Division attacked again. At heavy cost they seized a section of pillboxes a mile wide in front of the village of Roscheid. The first German prisoners, many of them over-age and ill, told of the High Command's frantic attempts to man the line; in some cases, the would-be garrisons had been unable to find the keys to open the bunkers! A forty-year-old cook told his interrogators bitterly that he had been at the front only two hours when he was captured.

The quality of the opposition did not encourage the hard-pressed Americans very much, who had now made two small impressions in the West Wall at such great cost. As Major James Ford, S-3 of the 28th's 110th Infantry, pointed out, 'It doesn't much matter what training a man may have when he is placed inside such protection as was afforded by the pillboxes. Even if he merely stuck his weapon through the aperture and fired occasionally, it kept our men from moving ahead freely.' One of Ford's men phrased it more pungently: 'I don't care if the guy behind the gun is a syphilitic prick who is a hundred years old – he's still sitting behind eight feet of concrete and he's still got enough fingers to press triggers and shoot bullets.'

General Gerow, commander of V Corps, was not too unhappy with the progress of the 28th. He reasoned that the first punctures in a fortified line were always the toughest. He ordered the 5th Armored Division to stand by for the breakthrough and encouraged the 28th to 'redouble' its efforts.

Cota of the 28th knew what 'redouble' meant; heads would undoubtedly roll if his men did not achieve a significant breakthrough soon. Therefore he in turn encouraged his regimental commanders to 'redouble' their efforts.

At six-thirty on the evening of September 15th, ten unarmed engineers, each carrying a 50 lb load of TNT, inched forward through the fog to a roadblock which was holding up a mixed force of infantry and tanks, ready to attack Hill 555, one of the most strategic points in this sector of the West Wall. Feeling very naked out there in no man's land, the engineers hurriedly placed their charges under the steel beams emplaced in concrete that made up the roadblock. Activating the charges, they pelted back to the waiting infantry, going 'like hell to the rear,' as the young lieutenant in charge phrased it later. Next instant the TNT exploded. The roadblock disintegrated in a flash of ugly red. Immediately the Shermans opened up with 77mms at the pillboxes behind the roadblock. At that range they couldn't miss. Great chunks of concrete started to fly from them. Hastily the infantry doubled forward, bayonets fixed. In forty-five minutes it was all over. Seventeen pillboxes were taken and fifty-eight prisoners. After three days of frustration and mounting casualties, the 28th Division had finally captured a significant objective in the West Wall. Hill 555 was theirs.

That night Captain Schultz of the 110th Infantry's F Company penetrated even further into the Wall, capturing a nest of pillboxes and fifty more prisoners. But his men were too weary to go on. They bedded down in the pillboxes so recently captured, heavy with the smell of German soldiers, that unmistakable odor of coarse black tobacco, unwashed bodies and their sour black bread, the *Kommissbrot*.

It was a long night. For the first time it started to become clear to the hundred-odd men in the German pillboxes that they were the tip of the spearhead; of all the million-strong US Army in Europe, they were the deepest into enemy territory. It was not a pleasant feeling. On guard outside one of the pillboxes, Private Roy Fleming thought he heard the sound of tracked vehicles somewhere in the gloom to his front. 'Suddenly,' as he recalled later, 'everything became quiet. I could hear the clank of these vehicles . . . I saw a flame-thrower start and heard the sound of a helluva scrap up around Captain Schultz's position.'

A few minutes later the whole company was alerted by the sudden angry snap-and-crackle of a small-arms fight. Instantly the darkness ahead was cut by the white morse of tracer bullets. Red and green signal-flares shot into the sky, illuminating the ground below with a glowing, sickly, unnatural hue.

'*King Sugar to anybody!*' Radio operators belonging to another company of the 110th picked up the frantic message from Captain Schultz's company, the urgency of the operator's voice coming through even the metallic distortion of the radio link. '*King Sugar to anybody. Help!*

We are having a counterattack – tanks, infantry, flame-throwers . . .'

Colonel Seely, commanding the 110th, was informed immediately. He hesitated to throw more troops into a hasty attack in the pitch darkness. He decided to give Schultz artillery support. But Schultz's radio could only send, not receive, and thus an anxious Seely waited out that long night until dawn flushed the sky over the Eifel a dirty white. But morning brought no sign of Captain Schultz's F Company. They seemed to have disappeared from the face of the earth. Only one thing was clear. The Germans were once again in possession of the pillboxes that he had captured the previous evening.[15]

Two days later Corps Commander Gerow, not so confident now, personally visited General Cota to order him to call off the divisional attack. The 28th Infantry had lost 1,500 men, nearly one tenth of its strength and it had still not penetrated the West Wall effectively. The 28th Division would take a long time to recover from its first encounter with the Great Wall of Germany. General Cota's 'high hopes' of 'bouncing the Siegfried' had vanished. Now it would be a long hard slog; indeed it would be another six months before the 28th Infantry Division finally passed through those grim gray pillboxes for good.

Further north, General Raymond Barton's 4th Infantry Division, nicknamed 'the Ivy League,' had probed the woods around the little German village of Bleialf successfully enough on September 14th. Now before them lay the hills of the Schnee Eifel, that part of the wooded hills where the snow lay longest in winter, and the West Wall.

At ten o'clock that morning, two regiments of the Division started to advance through a gray cold drizzle that made the infantrymen hunch their shoulders, the raindrops dripping from the rims of their helmets like tears.

The leading battalion of Colonel 'Buck' Lanham's 22nd Infantry was nearing the fir woods east of Bleialf when the familiar, frightening sound of a 100 lb 88mm shell startled them into action. Ripping the morning stillness apart as if a great piece of canvas was being torn, it slammed into one of the Shermans covering the advance, rocking it back on its haunches. The crew bailed out immediately. Privately American tankers called the Sherman 'the Ronson lighter' because even a shell hitting its sprockets would often ignite its gas tank; the tankers didn't want to be burned alive as so often happened in the Sherman. The other tanks started to take evasive action, flinging up great clods of mud and turf as their tracks flailed the ground. Behind them the riflemen panicked. They thought the tanks were abandoning them. '*They're bugging out!*' they cried to each other and started to fall back.

Colonel Lanham and his officers took over hurriedly. Armed only with a Colt .45, Lanham cried, 'Let's get up over this hill and get this place taken!'

As if to make up for their initial fear, the riflemen charged at the run. In twenty minutes they were through the woods and into the pillbox line. Tank destroyers rumbled up and started firing with their great 90mm cannon. 'You never saw such a mess,' Captain Howard Blazzard of the 22nd Infantry reported later. 'The tank destroyers had worked up behind the German bunkers, firing point-blank at doors and embrasures. Every one of the Germans was wounded in five or six different places, from pieces of concrete and steel . . . All the time inside there was the most piteous moaning and screaming . . .'

It seemed as if the 4th Division was going to be luckier than its neighbor the 28th.

On September 18th, 'Papa' Hemingway returned to his favorite regiment. That night he was invited to a steak and cognac dinner at Colonel Lanham's command post not far from the village of Brandscheid (which, by the time the fighting was over in February 1945, would have changed hands at least ten times).

'The meal was just being served,' recalled Colonel Lanham long afterward, 'when an 88 crashed through the wall which Hemingway was facing. It went out of the other side without exploding. The 88 traveled at almost the speed of sound, so there was never any warning of its approach. In a matter of seconds my well-trained people had disappeared into a small potato cellar . . . I was the last one to get to the head of the stairs. I looked back. Hemingway was sitting there quietly cutting his meat. I called to him to get his ass out of there into the cellar. He refused.'[16]

Later Hemingway told Lanham, 'In the next war, I'm going to have the Geneva Convention tattooed on my ass in reverse so I can read it with a mirror.' But in an after-dinner letter that he wrote to his new love Mary Walsh (one day to be his fourth wife), the grimness of his experiences in the Eifel is clearly expressed. 'This country is all a succession of wooded hills and rolling country with some bare heights from which you can see everything that moves . . . Sometimes there is thick forest like home or in Canada and it seems as odd to be killed as it would be in Upper Michigan.' A little poem he wrote for her at that time, too, exemplifies the gravity below the superficial banter and mock heroics.

> So now
> Losing the three last night
> Taking them back today
> Dripping and dark the woods . . .

'Can't write poetry from too much talking,' he added, 'it started to come out as chickenshit Hiawatha.' But on the

back of the letter to Miss Walsh, Hemingway wrote his
address and the instruction: '*Please Deliver In Case of
Casualty*.'[17]

That shelling by the German 88mm seemed to herald a
change in fortunes for the 22nd Infantry, indeed for the
whole 4th Infantry Division. A new force had entered the
line opposite them – the black-clad troopers who wore the
tarnished silver skull-and-crossbones and runic double
letter of the SS. General Heinz Lammerding's 2nd SS
Panzer Division had arrived.

The 2nd SS, 'Das Reich,' was not the division it had been
in the old days when it had raced across France or deep
into the heart of Russia. Now it was reduced to about
2,500 effectives, many of whom were ethnic Germans –
or, as they were called behind their backs by real Germans, 'Booty Germans' – and foreigners from a dozen
different countries. Nor was scar-faced General Lammerding a particularly brilliant commander. His main claim to
fame in World War Two was that he would be held
responsible for the infamous massacre of Oradour-
sur-Glane in July 1944. But he was an energetic officer
in the ruthless SS tradition and he set out immediately
to contain the penetration made into the Eifel by the
'Amis.'

On the same day that Hemingway ate his steak dinner
under shellfire, Lammerding had succeeded in establishing a stop line in front of the 22nd Infantry, at a point
where the main road leading to the nearest town, Prüm
(Lanham's new objective), started to climb at the village
of Sellerich and where the terrain tended to funnel
dangerously for any attacker.

The advance got off to a bad start. The shelling by the
SS guns so unnerved the leading companies that several
officers broke down and had to be evacuated on account

of what was politely called 'combat exhaustion.' Still those officers who took over from the ones who had broken down carried on the advance, mounting the height beyond Sellerich. Now the infantry plodded forward behind the tank and tank-destroyer screen, like farmers coming home after a long day's work in the fields, shoulders bent, rifles carried at the port, eyes grave.

A teller mine exploded beneath one of the tank destroyers. Its trail came off like a severed limb and it rumbled to a stop. Almost at once SS gunners hidden on both sides of the road opened up. Solid shot thudded into the tanks. They broke and scuttled back to the safety of the village. The infantry were not so fortunate. Mortar and artillery fire sealed off their escape route as the SS prepared to counter-attack.

Colonel Lanham was informed. He called off his attack on Brandscheid and rushed tanks and infantry to help the scared GIs trapped near Sellerich. More and more of them were being hit. Two of their officers were severely wounded. As the remaining officers started to lose control, here and there individual soldiers started to sneak off on their own. Not many of them made it. Eventually Lanham authorized the withdrawal of the survivors. After dark, the ugly flashes of the German guns still stabbing the night angrily, they started to trickle back into Sellerich. In the end only two officers and sixty-six men of the leading company which had been trapped on the height made it; their casualties had been over fifty percent.

That same night the Ivy League's assistant divisional commander General Taylor went to see Gerow at V Corps HQ to explain the 4th Division's situation and ask for the offensive to be called off. He had no trouble convincing General Gerow. The sallow-faced Corps Commander, who would be soon handing over his corps in order to return to the States, had already decided to stop

V Corps' attack into Germany. In confidence he told Taylor of his decision, and thus the 4th's drive for Pruem came to an inglorious end. It would be another four months of bloody combat before Colonel Lanham's 22nd Infantry finally managed to capture that objective.

That week, General Hodges's aide-de-camp noted in his diary, 'It is not improbable that we shall have to slow up, even altogether halt, our drive into Germany – and this in the very near future.'

4

The Siegfried Line at Aachen seemed the most unlikely place for the Americans to achieve any success. Yet that was where the dynamic General 'Lightning Joe' Collins (he had gained the nickname in the Pacific), Commander of VII Corps and Hodges's favorite general, proposed to make his attack that second week in September. Back in 1938 the builders of the *Westwall* had ensured that the old Imperial city, where Charlemagne was buried, was defended more strongly than any other of the larger cities that lay close to the frontier. They had erected two bands of defenses about five miles apart and increased the density of the pillboxes appreciably. The first band along the frontier was named the Scharnhorst Line, after the great Prussian general of the Napoleonic Wars. The second, even stronger and thicker, was called the Schill Line and covered the two 'corridors' of the small towns of Stolberg and Monschau, which Collins intended using for his drive into the Reich. In essence Collins was not intent on capturing Aachen; he wanted to breach the Wall and push on to the Rhine less than forty miles away, and he gave instructions accordingly to the two divisions concerned:

the 1st US Infantry, 'the Big Red One,' and the 3rd
Armored, 'the Spearhead.' All the same, he knew that the
enemy would fight like the devil to hold the West Wall and
prevent the fall of 'the holy city of Aachen,' as Propaganda Minister, Dr Josef Goebbels, the undersized club-
footed media genius of the Third Reich, was now calling
the border city. In the final analysis, events in Aachen
would determine to what degree Collins's two divisions –
one of them the 3rd Armored, now only a thousand yards
away from the Siegfried Line this night of September
13th, 1944 – would be opposed.

But it seemed that events were in the cocky little
General's favor that night, for unknown to him chaos and
naked panic reigned in the old Imperial city.

General the Count von Schwerin, commander of the
116th Panzer Division, drove past the long column of
civilians, old men, women and children, their carts piled
high with their pathetic possessions, frowned glumly and
then swung into the courtyard of the Quellenhof,
Aachen's most expensive hotel.

The man who commanded the 'Greyhound Division,' as
his Westphalians called it, was remarkably like the man
who at this moment was planning to attack the line at
Aachen only a dozen miles or so away to the west. He had
the same high forehead, hair slicked to one side, and the
same pugnacious jaw. He could have been General Collins's big brother. But the big German general, whom
Hitler thought 'a splendid battlefield commander who
unfortunately is not a National Socialist,' was not feeling
particularly brotherly at that moment. Indeed, he felt
decidedly angry.

The local Party bosses had implemented Berlin's order
that the 'Red Zone' should be evacuated before the
advancing Americans. Then those same brown-shirted

'golden pheasants,' as they were called behind their backs on account of their love for gold braid and decorations, had hurriedly fled to nearby Juelich to save their own skins, leaving the citizens of Aachen to their fate. Not only that, but the Party had ordained that the city, already shattered by thirty-eight air raids, should be defended to the 'last round and the last man.'

'With what?' von Schwerin asked his waiting staff assembled in the nineteenth-century hotel famed for its thermal baths in which once Roman legionnaires had bathed.

They told him. Apart from his own battered panzer division, the defenders of Aachen consisted of over-age men, Hitler youths, 'stomach and eye battalions' (men suffering from stomach and eye complaints) and whatever stragglers had not managed to escape the cordons of the 'chaindogs,' as the common German soldier called the MPs.

'A lot of Christmas Tree soldiers!' von Schwerin snorted and made his decision about the 'Greyhound Division.' He would fight *north* of the city, leaving it to the 'Amis.'

The first rounds of American artillery were fired by men of the 'Big Red One,' living up to their reputation of being the first in everything; in World War One they had been the first US outfit to fire at the Germans and now in World War Two they would be the first to fire their artillery into Germany proper. As their shells started to land at the little crossroads of Bildchen, just outside the city, von Schwerin penned a hasty note in English. It read:

I stopped the absurd evacuation of this town; therefore I am responsible for the fate of its inhabitants and I ask you in the case of an occupation by your troops to take care of the unfortunate population in a humane way. I am the last German Commanding Officer in the Sector of Aachen.

                                                    Schwerin.[18]

Von Schwerin handed the note to an employee of Aachen's main post office, telling him to give it to the first American officer entering Aachen, knowing that he had just signed his own death warrant if anything went wrong. Since the July 1944 attempt on his life, Hitler had felt no compunction whatsoever in having his generals strangled to death slowly with chicken wire if he felt they were traitors – and von Schwerin was already under suspicion. Then he was on his way back to his battered Greyhound Division. Aachen, Charlemagne's historic city, had been saved and the West Wall, or at least the Scharnhorst Line with its handful of 'Christmas Tree soldiers' defending it, had been handed to Lightning Joe Collins on a silver platter.

The man to whom Collins gave the job of making the decisive breakthrough in the Siegfried Line was Maurice Rose, commander of the 3rd Armored Division; and it seemed fitting that the first US General to set foot in Nazi Germany was a Jew.

The son of an East European rabbi, Rose had worked his way through the ranks from private to general in spite of prejudice against Jews in the pre-war US Army. A tanker who had learnt the business from General Patton himself in the pre-war 2nd Armored Division, he was a strict disciplinarian, inclined to threaten senior commanders with a court-martial if they did not meet with his expectations in combat. Unlike many of his fellow divisional commanders he was not an easy man to know; his former commanding officer, the barrel-chested General Harmon, described him as a 'cool, able soldier, distant and removed in temperament.' He was also inclined to command from the front, against which General Harmon warned him more than once; and in the end this would be his undoing. For within six months General Maurice

Rose, the first American senior officer to enter Nazi Germany, would be shot while involved in a confused night ambush by a bunch of young SS men, riding at the point of his division, to become the only divisional general to be killed in action throughout the whole of the ETO in World War Two.

On September 13th, the commander of the 3rd's Task Force X, a lieutenant colonel with the fittingly heroic name of Leander – Leander Doan to be exact – had discovered a small cart track leading through the Scharnhorst Line. Apparently in the four years since the West Wall was cleared of troops in 1940, a local farmer had built a small track through the dragon's teeth covering the pillboxes in order to take his cattle back and forth to his fields more conveniently. That same night General Rose ordered Lieutenant Colonel Leander Doan to attack over this track, although it was blocked by a Sherman flail tank used for clearing mines earlier in the day.

First the stricken tank had to be removed. Thus it was that Sergeant Dahl and his platoon commander Lieutenant John R. Hoffmann found themselves directly in front of the West Wall, furiously trying to tow the flail tank away while German 88mms thundered and filled the fields all around them with fist-sized pieces of flying shrapnel and great clods of wet earth. Finally the two sweating anxious men had done it. The flail tank was out of the way and the armored advance could commence.

Not that Colonel Doan was very sanguine about his chances. Darkness was approaching rapidly and at night the Sherman with its high silhouette was extremely vulnerable. Even one of von Schwerin's 'Christmas Tree' soldiers armed with the one-shot German equivalent of the bazooka, the *panzerfaust*, could easily knock out 20,000 dollars' worth of expensive machinery and four or five highly trained specialists with very little risk to

himself. Still, General Rose's orders could not be dis-
obeyed.

So the Shermans started to clank along the cart track,
one by one, until twenty of them had vanished into the
gloom, heading straight for the West Wall.

It happened just as Doan had feared. On both sides of
the track, German soldiers sprang up. A dry crack. An
ugly spurt of yellow flame. The first pot-shaped hollow
charge hurtled through the darkness, trailing fiery red
sparks after it, straight for the leading tank. Metal struck
metal with a hollow boom. A fleeting glow of molten
metal. A thick crump – and next instant the stricken lead
tank lurched to a halt.

In the next few minutes Doan lost four Sherman tanks
to the Germans armed with their *panzerfaust*. High on the
narrow track with no room to maneuver, they were like
sitting ducks. Soon they were burning, guns lowered like
the snout of some dying primeval monster, with their
crews pelting for the rear pursued by the angry zip-zip of
tracer.

There was worse to come. To the right of the stalled
column of Shermans there came the rumble of heavy tank
tracks. Doan knew they couldn't be American; there was
no US armor up there. Should he withdraw while he still
had chance, in spite of General Rose's orders? Before he
could make up his mind, the first Ferdinand SP gun of the
34th Assault Gun Brigade loomed up out of the glowing
darkness, its great 90mm cannon hanging down low.

Cannon thundered. Number Five Sherman trembled
violently as if struck by a sudden hurricane. It started to
blaze immediately. Another self-propelled gun crawled up
and went into action. Against them Doan was virtually
powerless. The Germans easily outgunned the Shermans
and their armor-piercing ammunition was much superior
to the solid-shot US ammo. Helplessly he watched as the

Ferdinands turned his column into a charnel-house. One after another six more of his remaining sixteen Shermans were picked off.

In the end, Doan gave in. Within fifty minutes he had lost half his tanks. Only ten remained. On this grim Wednesday night, the West Wall had beaten the 3rd Armored Division. Angry, sad and frustrated, Colonel Leander Doan gave the order for his men to stop their advance and dig in. To his front, the Shermans continued to burn . . .

5

Now it was the turn of the 'Big Red One.' Cocky and self-opinionated, often a law unto themselves, even the greenest replacement among their ranks, the doughboys of the United States Army's premier infantry division launched their first attack on the Scharnhorst Line on September 14th – with surprising success. The leading infantry battalion of the 16th Infantry reported back to regimental headquarters that the pillboxes located at the point of attack were hardly worthy of the name. They had penetrated them easily. They pressed on gleefully. Next morning they advanced even deeper and broader into the first belt of the vaunted Siegfried Line.

By nightfall on September 15th, the 1st Infantry Division had completed its mission. Aachen was ringed on three sides, though the Schill Line had still to be breached. As they always boasted, there was the 'Big Red One and then the rest of the US Army.' Now it was up to the 'rest of the US Army' in the form of Rose's 3rd Armored Division to fulfill its duty too.

*   *   *

That Friday morning, as Rose's tankers took up the challenge of the West Wall once more, the Party and with it the Gestapo returned to Aachen. They immediately started to arrest those town officials who had remained in office, thereby disobeying orders that all citizens in the 'Red Zone' should be evacuated in accordance with Hitler's plan to turn the whole of the Eifel into a wasteland, offering no succour to the enemy.

A very worried von Schwerin rescinded his order that Aachen should become an open city. He had heard all about generals being hung on butchers' hooks in the cellars of Gestapo headquarters at Number 10 Prinz Albrecht Strasse in Berlin, photographed for Hitler's sadistic pleasure as they writhed and died in excruciating agony with the cruel hooks biting ever deeper into their jaws. Von Schwerin was a brave man, who had been wounded several times and won Germany's top decorations for bravery in the field, but he didn't want to suffer that fate.

While, only miles away, Rose's Shermans rumbled into the attack again, this time supported by armored infantry, von Schwerin sweated out that long day, half hoping that the 'Amis' would break through before the inevitable happened. They did not. Then on the next morning, Saturday, September 16th, he received a telephone call from his Corps Commander General Schack. His compromising note to the Americans had been discovered.

'Schwerin,' Schack told him sadly, 'it can only be a matter of hours now before you are relieved of your command. Place yourself at my disposal, please.'[19] Without another word he hung up.

But Count von Schwerin, scion of a long line of German aristocrat-soldiers who had served their state loyally for generations, did not yet know how bad his situation really was as he brooded in the isolated farmhouse that served as the headquarters of the 'Greyhound Division.' The post office employee to whom he had entrusted the note had driven straight to Cologne and reported its contents to the Gauleiter Grohé, who promptly passed on the shocking information to the Führer at the 'Wolf's Lair' in East Prussia. The reaction had been explosive. Orders had been rushed out that von Schwerin was to be tried as traitor by a court-martial to be set up by the German Seventh Army – and *SS Standartenführer* Przybilski was ordered to drive immediately to the Eifel and bring back the General, 'dead or alive.'

Even as von Schwerin was taking that fateful telephone call from General Schack, Rose's 3rd Armored Division was making its attack on the West Wall.

With the 3rd was Task Force Loveday up at point, led by a tall colonel of that name. In spite of his name, Loveday was no altruistic dreamer; he was a hard-driving officer who got his combat command moving. He pressed the Germans relentlessly, sweeping through the 'Christmas Tree' soldiers and heading hell-for-leather for the Schill Line. Nothing could stop him, it seemed.

During the night of Friday, September 15th, the third-class troops holding the first line of bunkers melted away before Loveday's Shermans. As soon as daylight came on the Saturday morning, the Americans advanced once more, triumphantly sweeping past empty pillboxes, their guns abandoned and silent. Ahead lay open country. Task Force Loveday was all the way through the vaunted West Wall.

Hard-pressed Corps Commander Schack summoned his last reserve – what was left of the shattered 9th Panzer Division. He radioed General Mueller commanding the Division to 'attack the enemy and throw him back behind the West Wall. There is no time to lose!'[20]

Now Loveday's point was advancing along the highway
and fields between the villages of Mausbach and Gresse-
nich, both lying in a shallow valley bordered by wooded
heights. The tankers were confident but careful. Radios
hummed as they kept contact with each other, the tank
commanders with their turrets 'buttoned up' searching the
ground to their front and flanks the best they could
through the calibrated glass periscopes, sweating in the
green-glowing gloom of the 30-ton Shermans. Were they
walking into a trap? It looked all too easy. The first line of
Shermans reached a point half-way between the villages
with their timber-and-stucco houses grouped around the
typical slate-roofed churches of the area. There was no
sign of life. Had the Germans abandoned the villages too?
They rumbled on.

Then it happened. From both flanks came the hurrying
white blob of AP shells, gathering speed by the instant as
they raced toward the Shermans, whose crews were
spurred now to frantic action as the squat German Mark
IVs and lumbering SP guns came scuttling out of their
hiding places. A series of hollow booms. One Sherman
reeled back on its rear bogies like a horse being put to
saddle for the first time. Another ground to a halt, a
gleaming silver hole skewered in its turret, its crew all
dead as the deadly German AP shell exploded inside,
throwing razor-sharp pieces of metal everywhere. A third
Sherman skidded out of control, thick white smoke pouring from its shattered engine. Frantically the crew bailed
out and started to pelt to the rear. An ambulance raced up
to evacuate the casualties; the big red crosses on its boxlike sides were clearly visible, but the German gunners
didn't hesitate. It disappeared in a thick ball of exploding
smoke. When the smoke had cleared there were dead and
dying men sprawled on the battle-littered cobbled road.

With seven Shermans knocked out and one tank

destroyed, Colonel Loveday had had enough. Hastily the Task Force pulled back to the cover of Mausbach. He radioed an angry General Rose and reported that he had only thirteen tanks left, less than forty percent of his authorized strength. He asked permission to halt for the night. Reluctantly Rose gave it. His 'Spearhead' had finally done what Lightning Joe had asked it to do; it had broken through the West Wall, and in doing so had helped the troops of the US 9th Infantry Division to make an effective penetration further south too. But the cost had been high in both men and material. Already the casualty clearing stations back in Belgium were beginning to fill up with his wounded, and as always in an advance it was the boldest, the best and the bravest who were being hit; they were men Rose could ill afford to lose. That Saturday night it was not only General von Schwerin on the other side of the line who finally went to bed a troubled and worried man.

That same Saturday night, *General der Panzertruppe* Erich Brandenberger, an earnest somewhat pedantic officer who commanded the Seventh German Army defending the Eifel, issued an order of the day from his headquarters at Munstereifel. It read: 'The Seventh Army will defend its position . . . and the West Wall to the last man and the last bullet. The penetrations achieved by the enemy will be recaptured. The forward line of bunkers will be regained.'[21]

For a week now Brandenberger's forces had held off the enemy. Many of his shattered formations were reluctant heroes, badly demoralized; others were composed of sick over-age men, the 'Christmas Tree' soldiers; and those such as von Schwerin's Greyhounds were plain traitors. But they had held the Americans; although there had been some penetrations through the West Wall, these were not yet large enough for the Americans to exploit successfully for their drive to the Rhine, their primary objective. Now, Brandenberger reasoned at his head-quarters in that idyllic little Eifel town, once a pre-war tourist trap and honeymooners' paradise, if the 'Wild Buffaloes' could reach the front in time, he might well achieve what had been thought impossible one week before – throw the 'Amis' back and stabilize the front on the West Wall.

The 'Wild Buffaloes' were the men of the German 12th Infantry Division, which had gained the nickname back in 1941 when it had marched deep into Russia right to the source of the River Volga, 'sweeping everything in front of it like a herd of wild buffaloes.' Three years later, although its divisional sign was a raging buffalo tearing down a fence, the old fire had gone. Few of the original 'Wild Buffaloes' of 1941 were left. Now the division's ranks were filled with young inexperienced soldiers, though as always under the German system there was still a nucleus of highly trained veteran NCOs and officers to lead them.[22] Above all, the 'Wild Buffaloes' were fully up to strength. Moreover the 12th was commanded by Colonel Engel, 36 years old, brave, bold and somewhat arrogant, who had once been Hitler's adjutant and, as Colonel von Gersdorff noted at the time, 'probably was on the telephone to Hitler all the time.' Gersdorff, Chief-of-Staff to the Seventh Army, might well have been right; for of all the divisions present on the Western Front that Saturday, September 16, 1944, the 'Wild Buffaloes' were the best equipped. Indeed, when they started to clamber from their troop trains at Dueren and Juelich that night, the fit healthy young men in well-pressed uniforms made such an impression on the local civilians, so used now to the bedraggled mutinous survivors of the great débâcle of the West, that they cheered.

6

As the 15,000 young men of Engel's 12th Division started to leave their railheads in the Eifel that night, several things happened that would affect the campaign against the Great Wall of Germany and turn it from a 'reconnaissance in force,' as General Collins had over-optimistically called it, into a hard bloody slog which would last well into the spring of 1945.

Far away in England, three Allied airborne divisions, the 1st British, and the 82nd and 101st US, were preparing for the great drop across sixty miles of enemy-held countryside in Holland. They would carry out Field Marshal Montgomery's bold plan to 'bounce' the Lower Meuse and the Rhine, where they would be joined by the land forces of his Second British Army, which would then barrel into the Reich and turn the flank of the West Wall. From thence Montgomery would thrust into the power-house of German war industry, the Ruhr, and bring the war to a speedy end.

When General Omar Nelson Bradley, the lantern-jawed, bespectacled commander of all American ground forces, heard of the bold plan he was astounded: 'Had the pious teetotaler Montgomery [Monty was a bishop's son] wobbled into SHAEF with a hangover, I could not have been more astonished than I was by the daring adventure he proposed! For, in contrast to the conservative tactics Montgomery ordinarily chose, the Arnhem attack was to be made over a sixty-mile carpet of airborne troops.'[23]

But Bradley knew that his own attacks on the West Wall might well be reduced to the status of a side-show, possibly even superfluous, if Montgomery's plan succeeded. He protested to Eisenhower, but Ike silenced his objections, describing the plan as 'a fair gamble' and adding, 'It might enable us to outflank the Siegfried Line, perhaps even snatch a Rhine bridgehead.'[24]

Bradley had to give in, though he didn't like the plan one bit, nor the fact that Montgomery would be given priority in supplies. Indeed, after the war some American writers would maintain that Bradley's attack on the Wall fizzled out because the supplies of ammunition and fuel he needed went to Montgomery instead. (In truth, none of those supplies started reaching the British Second Army until the first day of the great airborne operation.) All the same, commanders in the US First Army were beginning to wonder that wet Saturday, why keep up the pressure on the West Wall when Montgomery might well sneak around the flank?

Von Schwerin made a personal decision that same Saturday. He would not report to Corps and allow himself to be tried and perhaps slaughtered like a dumb animal. For the time being he would go into hiding under the protection of his loyal fellows of the 116th's reconnaissance squadron; his 'Greyhounds' were just itching to tangle with the *SS Kommando* reportedly on the way to arrest him.[25] Thus, the only senior officer on the Aachen front who might have succeeded in opening the gates to the West Wall for the Americans disappeared from the scene; and in his passing he symbolized the resurgence of a new will to resist, based primarily perhaps not on patriotism, but on fear.

And as the fog started to sweep in that rainy day, the eager young men of Colonel Engel's 'Wild Buffaloes' started to enter the line, straight from their trains, directly ahead of the US 3rd Armored. Their orders were stark and brutal in their simplicity. They were to drive forward in a two-pronged thrust, fling the 'Amis' out of their positions and restore the Schill Line. The West Wall had to be retaken *at all costs*.

The German guns opened up with a hoarse exultant scream. Abruptly the silence was ripped apart by shells hissing toward the 3rd Division's positions, bursting with a mighty antiphonal crash around the foxholes of the American infantry. They went to the ground immediately, some of them quaking, holding their hands over their ears like frightened children. The multiple mortars joined in, sending great stabs of fiery-red flame slamming into the sky. The noise rose and rose. In its fury it was almost Wagnerian: a great elemental frenzied counterpoint.

Hardly had the barrage died away, leaving the GIs ashen-faced and shocked, than the men of the 27th Fusilier Regiment of the 12th Infantry Division began to charge the American positions in disciplined waves, bayonets fixed. They might have been practicing on some peace-time training ground.

The GIs forgot their shock, their fear. Whistles shrilled. Orders were bellowed. Radios crackled. Everywhere they started to pop their helmeted heads above the rim of their foxholes and prepare for battle, staring at this new steaming lunar landscape and the figures of field-gray running toward them.

Far to the rear, in some cases as far as five miles back, the divisional artillery took up the challenge. Closer to the front the heavy mortar companies cracked into action, filling the sky with their fat-bellied bombs. Great gaps appeared in the waves of the running *Fusiliere*. Still they came on, goaded by strange freaks of fancy as men are at such moments, or carried away by a wild unreasoning blood-lust.

Now the firing line erupted into violent action. The *Fusiliere*, fewer of them by this time, came running heavy-chested toward the GIs, stumbling under the impact of the machine guns, toppling forward, faces twisted in agony, clawing the air, trampled like a fleshy carpet by those who followed, who in their turn fell writhing among those already dead or dying.

Perhaps a couple of dozen of them reached the American line. None of them crossed it. Only dead and wounded sprawled now in the open, while little groups cowered in ditches or gullies, or against the banks packed with their own dead, as the 'Ami' machine guns chattered and the tracer cut their bent heads. They came again and again. But in the end they'd had enough. Like beaten animals they crept back the way they had come, leaving their dead sprawled there like bundles of blood-stained rags. The total cost to the defenders: two dead and twenty-two wounded.

It was no different for the 48th Grenadier Regiment, Engel's other formation. Its attack ground to a halt with terrible casualties, while US artillery pounded the cowering Germans. This was not war, but slaughter. When the smoke from the artillery bombardment had drifted away to reveal the stark brutality of that terrible field, even the hard-bitten defenders were shocked. American officers later estimated that of the first two attack companies, perhaps some 250 riflemen, only ten had managed to escape.

It was the same with all Colonel Engel's regiments thrown piecemeal into the attack. He was forced to ask for a truce to collect his wounded from the battlefield, although this was specifically forbidden by the Führer. It was an act of disobedience that might well have cost him his post. He called off his attack for the coming day. High command urged him not to procrastinate, but Engel was not one to be impressed by local brass; was he not a personal favorite of Hitler?

Thus Seventh Army Chief-of-Staff Colonel von Gersdorff met him just after that blood-letting, drinking coffee and eating cake and whipped cream under American artillery fire. Von Gersdorff asked anxiously, 'Where's the cellar?'

Engel, the hero who had long ago 'cured his throatache'[26] and whose neck was now adorned with the Knight's Cross of the Iron Cross, laughed and answered that 'Amis always shoot at the very same target.' There was no danger from the Americans, he said, unless their 'gun-layer makes a mistake.' So the two senior officers ate their home-made *Torte und Schlagsahne* while, outside the little forward CP, mud-splattered ambulances with cracked, bullet-shattered windscreens rumbled by, bearing their cargoes of broken-limbed young men.

The Wild Buffaloes' attack was a bloody failure, but the appearance of this division and other new formations that von Rundstedt was pumping into the line to reinforce the West Wall in the Aachen area convinced Lightning Joe Collins that, like his fellow corps commander General Gerow, he wasn't going to succeed in breaking through the Siegfried Line in any depth this month.

'A combination of things stopped us,' Collins recalled later. 'We ran out of gas – that is to say, we weren't completely dry, but the effect was much the same – we ran out of ammunition and we ran out of weather. The loss of our close tactical air support because of the weather was a real blow.'[27]

But the attackers had also run out of steam. In the tank and rifle regiments which really did the fighting, losses had been high and the enemy held, as Collins himself admitted, 'really beautiful' positions in the West Wall. Behind the lines the little hospitals at Verviers, Eupen, St Vith started to fill up with men suffering not only from gunshot wounds but also from 'combat exhaustion' and trenchfoot, thousands of them lying on their beds with their swollen purple toes exposed, wads of iodine-soaked cottonwool between each sausage-like member, hoping against hope that they weren't going to lose their feet.

The cost of the First Army's first 'reconnaissance,' as it was called at General Hodges's headquarters, had been high: some 10,000 casualties of all kinds. Now as September 1944 gave way to October, new plans were dreamed up and discussed. They had to break through the Siegfried Line and win the war so that the doughs could be home for Christmas.

'Home for Christmas' became the ruling slogan as confidence started to return to the downcast corps staffs. This time, they told each other, when they had all the gas, all the ammo and all the doughs they needed, they'd make it for sure. Optimism flourished everywhere, from the smallest divisional staff near the frontier right up to First Army headquarters located in the elegant surroundings of Spa, the Belgian watering place where in 1918 the Kaiser had finally acknowledged defeat and surrendered to the Allies. This time, the West Wall would not stop them!

Little did they know, those confident planners housed in chateaux and elegant hotels, that it would cost the US Army 130,000 casualties (79,000 battle and 51,000 non-battle) – more than the whole total of the long Vietnam War – to fight the Battle of the West Wall over the coming three months. And even then they would not succeed. For in that coming December a whole US Army, 80,000 strong, would be reeling back from the Wall in defeat, shocked by the impact of the great German counter-offensive. Soon it would seem to the planners that the Great Wall of Germany, running mile after mile along the hills of that remote frontier, was impregnable.

October

'Silent cannons, soon cease your silence. Soon unlimber'd to begin the red business.'

Walt Whitman, *Drum Tap*, 1865

1

Now it was nearly winter. The wooded ridges of the Eifel were continually wreathed in mist or obscured by a steady rain, gray and cold, the raindrops dripping mournfully from the gloomy firs often the only sound. For now the fighting along the length of the West Wall had died away, save in the north where the 'Big Red One' and General Hobbs's 30th Infantry Division launched set-piece attacks through the pillboxes in an attempt to capture Aachen; and in the south where General Patton despaired of ever being able to capture the Lorraine city of Metz. He'd been trying for nearly a month now.

Tours 'in the line' were reminiscent of those in a quiet section of the trenches in World War One. Captain C. MacDonald, one day to become a military historian himself, recalls 'going up' on October 3, 1944: 'Our truck convoy wound its way back through the thick forest into Schoenberg the next morning and out again over the highway leading east. As we neared the German border, the road began a steep ascent into the mountains to our front. A big white signboard with glaring letters told us what we were near: "*You are now entering Germany, an enemy country. Be on the alert!*"[1]

Once at the top of the heights, Captain MacDonald's company got out of the trucks and started to march. Their guide from the company they were relieving told MacDonald to hide his captain's bars quick, or they might attract snipers. Then he saw the *Westwall* for the first time. 'We crossed a slight knoll and the antitank wall of the Siegfried Line came suddenly into view. It looked like a prehistoric monster coiled around the hillsides; the concrete dragon's teeth were like scales upon the monster's back – or maybe headstones in a kind of crazy cemetery.'

The new company passed the first pillboxes now in American hands, the ground around pitted with black holes where shells had exploded, and then their guide said urgently, 'We'll have to run again here.' He pointed up the hill to their right where there was another row of pillboxes. 'That's *theirs*!'

Finally the new boys reached their position, a little farmhouse set right inside the Wall. 'We found the company commander, a first lieutenant, in a small low cellar illuminated only by a dim kerosene lamp that needed its shade washed. There were men in every conceivable sleeping position all over the floor . . . When we reached the light of the first floor I saw the lieutenant's eyes were bloodshot and a half-week's beard covered his face. His voice trembled when he talked and he would start at the slightest noise.' Captain Charles MacDonald's Company I, 23rd Infantry, 2nd Infantry Division, was 'in the line.'

Some of the men did not have a farmhouse roof over their heads as did that frightened lieutenant. That October a BBC correspondent recorded an interview with an angry private stuck in a waterlogged foxhole in the line.[2] 'Do *you* know what it's like?' he asked. 'Of course you don't. You've never slept in a hole in the ground which you've dug while somebody tried to kill you . . . a hole dug as quick as you can. It's an open grave but graves don't fill up with water. At night the infantryman gets some boards or tin or an old door and puts it over one end of his slit trench; then he shovels on top of it as much dirt as he can scrape up nearby. He sleeps with his head under this. Did I say "sleeps?" Let's say, *collapses*. You see, the infantryman must be awake half the night. The reason is that one half of the troops are on watch and the other half are resting, washing, shaving, writing letters, eating or cleaning weapons; that is if he's not being shot at, shelled, mortared, or if he isn't too exhausted to do it. When he's mortared or shelled he's deathly afraid and in the daytime he chain-smokes, curses or prays, all this time lying on his belly to lessen the pain from the blast . . . A trench is dug just wide enough for the shoulders, as long as the body and as deep as there's time.'

As the BBC man commented, obviously impressed, 'The next time you are near some muddy fields after the rain, take a look in a ditch. That's where your man lives!'

But a spell in the line was not usually as bad as that. The veterans had come to terms with their grim wet environment. They had weatherproofed their foxholes, covering the roofs with thick logs and earth just as the Germans had done a couple of hundred yards away. They shared the earthen pit with a buddy and five minutes each day they stripped off their boots and massaged each other's unwashed feet to restore the circulation and ward off the feared trenchfoot. They stuffed paper in between the outer and inner layers of their clothing in the fashion of Depression hoboes. When they were in the rear, they stole the little cast-iron stoves from abandoned houses and heated their foxholes with these. Wood there was enough of in the shattered forests of the Eifel-Ardennes.

They ate better than the greenhorns did, too. Game was plentiful in those dense woods and many a GI went hunting for deer that October when his company commander wasn't looking. Venison stew, even if the dead animal was not properly hung, tasted great after the monotony of K-rations.

The veterans organized their week or so in the line, giving themselves a fixed timetable. Day would start with a general stand-to, for dawn was the Germans' favorite time of attack. Not that the unwashed, unshaven GIs expected an attack, for combat-wise as they were, they knew the Germans had noted their timetable and wouldn't select this particular time to launch an attack when everybody was alert. But it was useful for their officers and non-coms to check that everybody was on his feet and that all weapons were sited correctly for any action that might take place that day.

Breakfast would follow, always a relief, even if it was only K-ration coffee and fried spam. Now the men could relax and chat for a while, though as one ex-GI recalls, 'The language sure wouldn't have passed muster in anybody's drawing room.'[3]

Mess kits washed in chlorinated water or rubbed out with dirt if there was no water available, the men would then be detailed for the tasks of the day. Mostly they would be the mundane sort of job, harmless if back-breaking: stringing new wire, filling sandbags, digging drainage ditches, strengthening their foxholes, keeping watch on the silent heights where lay the enemy. Warlike activity was reserved for the night.

Captain Robert Merriam of the Army's Historical Division rode up that October to visit the front not far from the Luxembourg frontier town of Wiltz. As he and his driver rolled along the ridge line above the River Our, he asked the GI where the Germans were

With a dramatic flourish the GI said, 'See that ridge line over there just across the valley?'

Merriam nodded.

'That's it.'

'What?' Merriam enquired naively. He later described the scene thus: 'We were riding along the top of a huge ridge, silhouetted in plain view of an enemy no more than eight hundred yards away, guns of the West Wall supposedly bristling behind every bush and nothing happened. "Have to be careful at night," my talkative guide continued. "Krauts like to sneak over patrols, just to make a social call. Ambushed a jeep in daylight the other day and got a new battalion commander. Hell, he didn't even get a chance to report in! But the only shelling we get is when a Jerry goes to the latrine; seems like they have a machine gun and a mortar there and each one fires a burst – hope they don't get diarrhea!" '[4]

Night was the really worrying time for the veterans. Not even they could quite adapt to the long winter nights in those cold spooky mountain forests. Night was silence, isolation, fear. The long freezing hours in the pillboxes and foxholes would creep by with leaden feet, so that sometimes it seemed to the nervous riflemen holding the line that time itself had died. With maddening obstinacy the night hours would linger, reluctant to yield to the blessed relief of dawn. In the darkness the men were prey to all sorts of unreasoning fancies and fears. A shell-shattered tree stump, a hummock of earth, a coil of rusting barbed wire, a wrecked tank from the fighting of the previous month – every half-seen object could take on new and menacing forms, and in the light of the signal flares and star shells periodically flushing the darkness with their eerie unnatural hue, could even seem to be moving toward the tense, apprehensive GIs crouched wide-eyed in their damp holes.

Night, too, could be violent activity. It might come in the form of a sudden artillery bombardment or a mortar barrage, when the darkness would be riven by the ugly stabs and slashes of 88mms and the spine-chilling howl of the six-barreled German mortar, which when it ended left behind a loud, echoing, nerve-racking silence that seemed to go on for ever.

Then there were the patrols, the fighting ones often composed solely of volunteers. None of them bore badges of ranks. Faces were blackened, not for camouflage purposes but to tell friend from foe, and everyone had his personal choice of weapon: blackjack, sock filled with sand, trench knife, bayonet honed to a deadly cutting edge, haversack full of grenades. Each night they'd sneak out into the darkness, the return password burnt indelibly on their minds – at night sentries in the line shot first and asked questions afterward – creeping toward the German positions looking for prisoners who could be sent back to intelligence.

Leslie Atwell, a medic with the 67th Infantry, recalls that in his battalion a volunteer patrol group had been formed called the 'Tiger Patrol.' 'They were to go out on highly dangerous scouting missions into enemy territory, and in exchange for this they were to work only every other day. In their free time they were to have no duties, the best possible food, and were to be quartered indoors.' One of the first volunteers was a man called Braaf from C Company. As he told Atwell: 'What the hell – it's only every other day. Back in the company, I was out *every* day on patrol, every night, too. Ran my f---ing ass off, so I might as well be down here.'[5]

Atwell didn't like the members of the Tiger Patrol; he thought them 'tough little exhibitionists.' A lot of other men in the line didn't like them either. The nights were scary enough without their own patrols blundering about in no man's land, alarming the Germans and probably bringing down fire on their own positions, or even a local counter-attack. By now the veterans had adopted the attitude of all soldiers who had been in the line for a long time: let sleeping dogs lie. You play ball with me, and I'll play ball with you.

When blithe daylight came again, they would get together and tell tall stories. Staff Sergeant Henry Giles of the 291st Combat Engineers at Steinfort, Luxembourg, that month, working on a bridge across the Our for the 4th Armored Division, wrote in his diary for October 1st: 'Some of the wildest things can happen. I didn't have the Sgt. of the Guard last night. Think Loftis did. Anyway it was set up and security posted. Then a work detail had to go out and repair a culvert. They either didn't know the password or had forgotten or something went snafu. Anyway, some kid got excited, thought they were Krauts and started shooting off his rifle. Today we heard practically the entire artillery of the 4th Armored was alerted . . . And there's a weird story about one of the artillery gun crews. Seems they have their own private dame. One of the boys swears it's the truth. Says she visits them every two or three days and they "queue" up. Asked him why he didn't join the line. He said, much astonished, "Hell, them artillery boys'd murder you!" He's a sort of mild fellow, quiet type, doesn't talk much and just the way he said it sent us into convulsions.'[6]

And they griped – *how* they griped! About the war, the food, the line, the officers, the mail-call, but above all about the 'canteen commandos' – the great infrastructure that had grown up behind the line to support them, those healthy young men in immaculate clean uniforms, who were all 'downgraded,' it seemed, who had all the girls, the good chow and the smokes that were in perennially short supply. '*One* man in the line,' they sneered to each other contemptuously, 'and *five* to bring up the Coca-Cola!'

Indeed the 'Com Z,' the supply system, the Red Cross, the USO, the SOS, the APO and half a score of other organizations which supported the dirty, bearded handful of riflemen holding the line, had spread their tentacles throughout liberated Europe by now. There was hardly a village or hamlet back of the line in Northern France, Luxembourg, East Belgium or Holland which did not contain some of these 'support' people.

The primary task of the organizations was to supply the front and maintain the morale of the fighting soldier when he came out of the line. They established rest camps just behind the line where riflemen could be sent for forty-eight or seventy-two hours to take a warm shower, sleep in a real bed and get some rest, and where they could be entertained by the Red Cross and the USO. Sometimes all this entertainment amounted to was a cup of coffee and a doughnut to go with a sing-song or even the long forgotten 'spelling-bee' (the American soldier of 1944 was much more easily satisfied than his counterpart one generation later in Korea: no geishas and mixed bathing, let alone the drug-parties of Vietnam's R and R's). Sometimes, however, they struck lucky. Marlene Dietrich, for instance, entertained GIs at the little border town of St Vith that October, within the shadow of the West Wall, although she knew that as a 'German renegade' she was on Hitler's black list and might well be executed if she were captured. Bob Hope and Bing Crosby completed the same circuit too.

All the same, the hard-bitten veterans didn't like the canteen commandos one bit; they envied them the girls and the easy living. It was not too difficult for unscrupulous soldiers in the Service of Supply, for example, to make a small fortune, especially if they could get their hands on cigarettes and gasoline. That October Staff Sergeant Giles wrote in his diary, 'Wish to hell I had a smoke. Haven't even got the makings. Don't understand to save my life why we're so short.'[7] Soon he found out why.

In Paris a scandal erupted when it was discovered that there was a flourishing black market in gas and cigarettes, conducted by men of the SOS. Eisenhower hit the roof when he heard about it. 'That some men should give way to the extraordinary temptations of the fabulous prices offered for food and cigarettes was to be expected,' he wrote after the war. 'But in this case it appeared that practically an entire unit had organized itself into an efficient gang of racketeers and was selling these articles in truck and car-load lots. Even so, the blackness of the crime consisted more in the robbery of the frontlines than it did in the value of the goods. I was thoroughly angry.'[8]

Eisenhower wasn't the only one to be angry. When the story burst in the Friday edition of *Stars and Stripes*, October 13th, an irate Giles wrote in his diary, 'It's a black Friday all right. For a long time we have been hearing rumors about a big blackmarket gang operating in and around Paris. Today it was in the S & S. They say it's mostly AWOLs and that there are about 17,000 of them running loose,[9] highjacking and stealing stuff to sell to the French. Everything from cigarettes to gas to food, tires, jeeps, all the stuff we need so bad. But there are some SOS people in on it too. And that burns the hell out of us. As if they didn't have the softest jobs of anybody, sitting on their fat asses in their big plush headquarters in Paris, they have to go stealing from their own troops. There is one whole railway battalion involved. One damn major has sent home over thirty thousand dollars. It's the dirtiest low-down thing I ever heard of. They're up for courtmartial and I hope to hell they all get life at hard labor. They *ought* to be shot!'[10]

The brass to the rear – Eisenhower with his 5,000-strong staff, his pet dogs, his mistress, his personal PR man established at Versailles; Hodges, lodged in the imperial nineteenth-century splendor of Spa's Hotel Britannique; Bradley in his eighteenth-century Belgian chateau just outside Namur – wanted the frontline soldiers to be entertained when they were 'resting.' As Eisenhower later wrote, 'Morale of the combat troops had always to be carefully watched. The capacity of soldiers for absorbing punishment and enduring privations is almost inexhaustible so long as they believe they are getting a square deal.'[11] He encouraged subordinate commanders to set up clubs and coffee-and-doughnut wagons, to provide as he put it 'an occasional hour of homelike atmosphere for the fighting men as far as was possible in an area thousands of miles from America.'

But that was not what the men coming out of the line wanted. Their lives were short and brutish. Coffee and doughnuts were not enough. Neither was Bob Hope and his wisecracks, nor the 'Old Groaner' dreaming perpetually of that sentimental 'White Christmas.' Even Miss Dietrich's attraction palled, her celebrated legs usually clad in ill-fitting olive drab these days. What the men from the line wanted was women. General Patton (also living 'high on the hog,' as he would have put it, in his Nancy headquarters) expressed it in characteristically forceful terms: 'A man who won't fuck, won't fight.'

As soon as the war settled into the autumn stalemate, leave-men started to stream back from the Wall to enjoy forty-eight or seventy-two hours of hectic activity in the big cities to the rear: Liège, Brussels, Maastricht, and above all 'Paree.' Pockets full of backpay – they had not

had much use for money during the last three months –
haversacks heavy with goods to sell on the black market if
they ran out of cash, drunk already, or soon to be in that
happy state, they descended upon 'Pig Alley' (Place
Pigalle) looking for one thing and one thing only.

It wasn't hard to find. Paris was alive with whores, just
like the other cities to which the leave-men went. Dressed
in skimpy frocks, rabbitskin furs draped around skinny
shoulders against the autumn cold, bare legs (silk stock-
ings cost a fortune on the black market) above their high-
heeled, cork-soled wooden shoes, the women would loiter
in doorways offering themselves to each potential *chéri* in
khaki who passed. When the blackout descended, they
flashed little blue-disked flashlights at the men in uniform
or pressed the light against their stomachs provocatively
to make their offer quite clear.

There are no figures available on the VD rate among
GIs, but as the 'social disease' was endemic in British
frontline divisions by the end of the war, it can be assumed
that things were no different in the US Army. There were
constant warnings about the risk of catching the disease –
indeed in Germany, Eisenhower imposed a death penalty
on any German woman transmitting VD, though it is
doubtful whether the sentence was ever carried out.
Green Cross stations were everywhere, usually set up by
the Canadian Army for some reason, where soldiers could
treat themselves after intercourse; by the time curfew had
begun to descend for the civilians, the places would be
filled with mostly drunken GIs standing at long troughs,
bathing their organs with purple solutions from thin
rubber tubes and doctoring them with all kinds of white
and yellow ointments.

They weren't particularly pleasant young men, these
leave-men from the front. They got drunk, they whored,
they fought, they got sick. Their tempers were short and

they were quick to take offense. The ubiquitous white-helmeted MPs – 'Snowdrops' as the civilians called them – would give trouble-makers short shrift. They clubbed them over the head and dragged them off to the nearest jail, though they weren't kept there long. Riflemen were in short supply; they were needed too urgently at the front to be kept in prison for the sake of upholding military discipline and the public prestige of the US Army. The line would dampen their high spirits soon enough.

Hemingway invited four of Lanham's battalion commanders to visit him and his new love Mary Walsh, also a correspondent, at the Hotel Ritz in Paris (it seems that *Time-Life* correspondents fought the war only from the best of hotels). At first the young officers were very restrained. Politely one of them asked Marlene Dietrich, who was also present, whether she would pose with him on the bed for a photo he'd dearly love to send home. She agreed and the 'blushing officer warily arranged himself as stiff as at attention beside her.'[12]

But by the time they all went to eat (on black-market US rations), 'eyes were becoming a bit glazed and speech a bit slurred.' One of the officers found himself in conversation with Congresswoman Clare Boothe Luce, wife of the owner of *Time-Life* and Mary Walsh's employer. She told him she was impressed by the work of the Army Air Corps in the campaign and suggested that in Belgium and Germany the infantry must surely be of some use.

'You're darned right, babe,' one of the 4th Division officers snarled, 'and don't you put your mouth on it!'

'The infantry, they pinpoint an advance, don't they?' asked Mrs Luce.

'*Pinpoint it? Sweet Jesus!*' the drunken young officer exploded. 'You ought to read a book, you dumb broad!

What are you doing here anyhow?' He didn't listen to the powerful Congresswoman's answer.

That night Mary Walsh took Hemingway to task about his guests. 'Your friends are drunks and slobs. They threw up all over my bathroom. They probably lost me my job. They drove Marlene away. They may be heroes in Germany, but they stink, stink, stink here!'

Hemingway punched her.

But the men always went back. Pay gone, heads aching, hollow-eyed and morose, or drunk, talkative and boasting, they tumbled into the waiting 'deuce-and-a-half' from Division which would take them back to the killing line. They'd leave the 'Com Z' with its whores and cheap cognac, its 'gontac' and 'pox,' its 'feather-merchants,' canteen commandos and gracious ladies serving doughnuts, and enter the cleaner air of the front. And there it would be, waiting for them in those somber, wet-dripping ridges, silent and grayly sinister – the Great Wall of Germany.

2

That October, while the Americans prepared for another attack on the Wall, saw Germany's 'Miracle on the Marne.' It was the work of two men: the brilliant technocrat Albert Speer, and the man whom von Rundstedt contemptuously called *der Bubi-Marschall* ('the Boy Marshal'), Walter Model.

Despite the Allied bombing raids the previous month, Speer's myriad war factories, some of them run on slave labor in the great underground caves of the Harz Mountains, had maintained their high production levels. It was the same in October. Germany's war industry was flourishing, in spite of everything the RAF and the USAF attempted to do. The production of SP guns was doubled, and although tanks were more difficult to manufacture, Speer managed to produce enough to replace half of those lost in the débâcle of France, the shortfall made up with mobile assault guns, which were more suitable in defense anyway.

By October 8th, when Colonel-General Jodl presented details of his draft plan for the top-secret offensive that Hitler had dreamed up at the peak of the September crisis, he could offer the Führer thirty-two divisions, twelve of them panzer or panzer-grenadier, all armed and motorized – thanks to the efforts of the man whom Hitler regarded as an artist and his spiritual son, Albert Speer. It was a tremendous achievement, an act of technical genius. But the man who was to use those new forces now streaming into the Rhineland and the West Wall was no artist and definitely no genius: Walter Model. His chief, von Rundstedt, did not think very highly of his strategic ability, but perhaps that was because the 'Boy Marshal' had sold his soul to Adolf Hitler – and von Rundstedt hated Hitler.

But Field Marshal Model was exactly the commander that Germany needed in 1944. Ruthless, unscrupulous, unconcerned with politics, he rode his officers hard and was respected by his soldiers as a 'front-swine' like themselves, who more than once when the situation was critical took command of a battalion and led it in the assault. In Russia he had saved the front from breaking three times. Once, in January 1942 when the German Ninth Army had reached the end of its tether under severe Soviet pressure, Model had appeared at Army headquarters, entering without ceremony, a small tubby man with a fur-collared greatcoat that came down to his ankles, old-fashioned ear flaps over his ears and the inevitable monocle screwed in his right eye. His officers clicked to attention. The little man didn't seem to notice. He flung his coat, cap and earmuffs on a chair, polished his monocle which had steamed up immediately (the temperature outside was fifty below) and stalked over to the situation map. 'Rather a mess,' he commented after a few moments, and then started rapping out orders while the staff officers stared at him in open-mouthed amazement. Where, they asked themselves, was the little general going to get the men he needed for his bold counter-attack against the Russians?

Finally Colonel Blaurock, Ninth Army's Chief-of-Staff, asked, 'And what, Herr General, have you brought us for this operation?'

Model regarded his new Chief calmly and answered with one word: '*Myself.*'[13]

This was the man who would engage the Americans on the West Wall. Six months later, alone save for one other officer, his army vanished, a price on his head (General Bradley had offered the Bronze Star to any soldier who brought in the fugitive Field Marshal), he found himself in a remote forest, unable to run any longer. Taking out his pistol, he said wearily, 'A German field marshal does not surrender.' Then he shot himself, the only one of the dozen or so surviving Germans of that rank at the end of World War Two to do so.

Model knew he had to husband his resources. Hitler needed them for his grand plan. In essence he had to make do with second-rate troops, fortress battalions, emergency units, 'stomach and eye battalions' and all the rest of the 'Christmas Tree' soldiers. But his presence here, there and everywhere at the front inspired even these poor specimens.

At Aachen he encouraged the besieged Colonel Wilck

and his couple of thousand substandard soldiers to hold on for a little longer, although Hobbs's veterans of the 30th Infantry Division and Huebner's men of the 'Big Red One' were already well established in the old Imperial city. Further north, in the Peel Marshes on the border with Holland, Model sent the newly arrived 7th US Armored Division reeling back six clear miles and caused panic among the rear elements of Montgomery's 2nd Army supply services, for Monty's headquarters was only twenty miles away. That day Brigadier Essame of the British 43rd Infantry Division commented sardonically, 'Even the Headquarters cooks took up their rifles and, for the first and last time in the campaign in Europe, prepared to die a hero's death!'[14]

Above all, Model prepared to engage the Americans in a bloody battle of attrition in which some 60,000 men would die in the most savage fighting of World War Two in Western Europe – and following which Model would die by his own hand.[15]

The name of the place? The *Huertgenwald* – that 'Passchendaele with tree bursts,' as Ernest Hemingway called it, or, as it was known to division upon division of apprehensive GIs, 'the Green Hell of the Huertgen.'

The *Huertgenwald* lies just south of Aachen, twenty miles long and ten miles wide, riven by steep gorges, their slopes thick with tall dark-green trees so that it is still easy to lose your way in its resin-heavy confines. It is the kind of forest you read about in those old German fairy tales, stifling and not a little frightening. Indeed, an imaginative person might be inclined to drop things behind him to mark his path, as did little Hansel and Gretel trying to find their way home but finding instead that dreaded *Pfefferkuchenhaus* with its cannibalistic witch. In October 1944 there were plenty of bodies for her to eat.

The Battle of the Huertgen Forest had really started back in September when Lightning Joe Collins tried to make his first 'reconnaissance in force' through the Siegfried Line. Then one regiment of General Craig's veteran 9th Infantry Division had been given a kind of support role to the 3rd Armored Division in its attempts to break through the pillbox line.

For five solid days the 9th fought to break through that section of the West Wall to the front of the forest, taking appalling casualties in the tight confines of the packed firs, unable to maneuver, the trails and fire-breaks covered by fixed-line machine guns and thick with a new type of anti-personnel mine. Mounted in a glass or wooden container, the package of deadly steel balls could not be located by the engineers' electronic detectors. To locate the unseen killers, the hard-pressed infantry had to prod the earth for them with their bayonets, or employ the hazardous expedient of digging for them with looted, long-handled German pitchforks.

American soldiers had not fought in conditions like this since the Argonne back in 1918, and the battle was totally unlike the kind of high-speed combat in wide open spaces that they had been trained for back in the States. 'The enemy seemed to be everywhere,' one of the 9th's infantrymen recalled, 'and in the darkness of the thick trees and the confusion, the firing seemed everywhere.'[16]

'If anybody says he knew where he was in the forest,' one battalion commander later complained bitterly, 'then he's a liar!'

Overnight, in order to survive, the GIs of the 9th Infantry had to learn the new skills required for the specialized fighting of the fir forest. The usual kind of foxhole was no use when an outfit was being shelled in the trees. Here, shells didn't explode on the ground with the killing pieces of shrapnel erupting upwards; they exploded

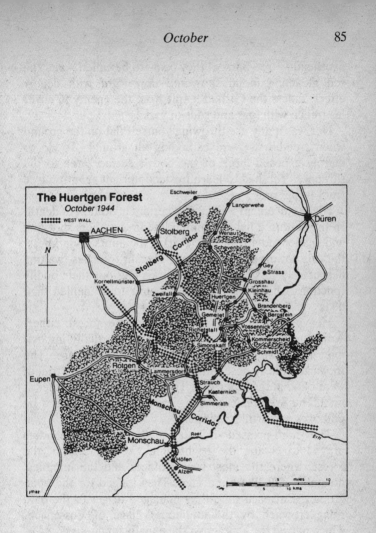

The Huertgen Forest
October 1944

WEST WALL

N

AACHEN · Stolberg · Eschweiler · Langerwehe · Düren

Stolberg Corridor

Wenau · Schevenhütte · Gey · Strass

Kornelimünster · Zweifall · Grosshau · Kleinhau · Huertgen · Brandenberg · Bergstein

Gemeter · Richelstall · Vossennick · Kommerscheid · Schmidt

Simonskaff

Rotgen · Lammersdorf

Eupen · Strauch · Kesternich · Simmerath

Monschau Corridor

Roer · ErR

Monschau · Höfen · Alzen

5 miles 10
5 10 kms

JM 82

overhead – 'tree-bursts,' they came to be called – and the red gleaming metal showered *downward* with deadly effect, unless the GI had learnt from the enemy to cover his trench with logs and sods of grass.

Nor was it any use throwing yourself flat on the ground when tree-bursts were exploding all around. To do so merely exposed more of the body's surface area to the shrapnel. You had to learn to stand upright against a tree trunk – and pray.

Night movement was tabu, a certain invitation to death. In the confused fighting among the firs, soldiers shot first and challenged afterwards. During the hours of darkness, the GIs cowered in their grave-like slit trenches, waiting desperately for dawn to come, carrying out their bodily functions where they squatted: better to be defiled than dead.

Heavy weapons were no use in the forest either. Adjusting mortar and artillery fire was virtually imposs-ible; there were thick rows of trees everywhere. The forward artillery observers, the infantryman's best friend, were blind in the Huertgen. Tanks were little use either at first. The fire-breaks and logging trails were covered by pillboxes and artillery pieces.

The hard-pressed infantry and their commanders prayed to escape the frightening vice-like grip of the forest, where the most senior officer and the humblest doughboy felt like blind men. They longed for the open ground. But each time they managed to get to the bald ridge crowned by the infamous village of Vossenack, which barred the way across the equally infamous gorge of the Kall River, leading to Schmidt, the village which was the key to the whole Battle of the Huertgen Forest, the Mark IVs and SPs appeared.

The days blurred into one long never-ending misery and fear in that green hell. No one recalled the separate days any more. Each dripping dawn among the shattered firs brought new cannon-fodder, bug-eyed replacements in their clean uniforms, complete with necktie – and new death. Many a young soldier entered combat for the first and last time in that treacherous forest, not even knowing the unit to which he belonged before he too was being brought back by the sweating litter-men, another casualty of the Battle of Huertgen Forest.

Even the Germans, more familiar with this kind of warfare from their experiences in the great forests of northern Russia, felt the horror of that killing place. Colonel Wegelein, Commander of a German battle group, *Regiment Wegelein*, was spotted by an American sergeant wandering around in the forest, not far from his foxhole, alone and unarmed. The NCO promptly shot him dead and took from his body the maps of his Regiment's planned counter-attack. But what had an experienced senior officer, with five years of combat experience behind him, who had served in the German Army since 1921, been doing wandering around like that? Was he, too, sick of the slaughter and courting death as an end to it all? Or had he simply lost his way?

Many Americans, too, would lose their way among the trees of the Huertgen and never return to tell the tale.

On October 16, eleven days after the bulk of the 9th Infantry Division had entered the Huertgen Forest, it was decided by General Hodges that they had had enough. As a young captain, Courtney Hodges had gone through a similar hell in the Argonne and he knew when an outfit was at the end of its tether. The 9th, veteran of two years of war, had not broken down like some of the outfits which would follow it. There had been no mass panic, no headlong retreat, no refusal to go into action, no summary relief of battalion commanders or even regimental ones, as was soon to come. But the 9th Infantry had suffered terrible casualties and it couldn't go on much longer, even if it did receive more replacements; after all their most strenuous efforts they were still fighting the pillboxes and bunkers of the West Wall (one infamous bunker located at the aptly named 'Dead Man's Moor' held out way into November, two months after the battle had opened).

By the time it was relieved, the 9th Infantry had penetrated the West Wall but to no great depth, capturing 1,300 Germans and killing or wounding an estimated 2,000. But the cost had been high. After nearly two weeks of bloody and ferocious combat they'd driven exactly 3,000 yards into the Huertgen Forest at a cost of one casualty per yard, a total of 4,500 men killed, wounded or missing in action. Together with the non-battle injuries, the 9th had lost one third of its effectives. Sadly General Craig took his shattered division out of the forest. Replacements wouldn't be enough, he knew. It would be a long time before the 9th was ready for action again. Now it was to be the turn of the 28th Infantry Division under its commander, the big, ruddy-faced, brave General 'Dutch' Cota.

Moving in to relieve the 9th, the National Guardsmen of the 28th found themselves immediately swallowed up by that grim dark forest. All about them lay the waste of battle. Empty ration crates, yellow shell-cases, unearthed mines, belts of used ammunition – and the somber-faced men of the Graves Registration Units still removing the rain-soaked, stinking, bloated bodies of the dead.

It was not an encouraging reception, and the GIs of the 9th now moving out did nothing to cheer the newcomers up. There was none of the usual banter of such occasions: no 'Bronx cheers,' no 'You'll be sorry, buddy,' no shaking of hands. The mud-splattered, unshaven 9th Division soldiers were nervous and morose, too haggard and worn for that. They stumbled out of their positions, glassy-eyed and staring, walking as if in a dream. They looked, the newcomers thought, like men 'who had been through hell – and worse.'

They had. As Sergeant Mack Morris wrote for *Yank* magazine that month, 'The Infantry, free from the claustrophobia of the forest, went on, but behind them they left their dead and the forest will stink with deadness long after the last body is removed. The forest will bear the scars of our advance long after our scars have healed, and the Infantry has scars that will never heal . . . For Huertgen was agony and there was no glory in it except the glory of courageous men – the MP whose testicles were hit by shrapnel and who said, "Okay, doc, I can take it." The man who walked forward, firing Tommy guns with both hands until an arm was blown off and then kept on firing the other Tommy gun until he disappeared in a mortar burst.'[17]

Dutch Cota, who had gained a reputation for great personal daring and courage in Normandy, was just as unhappy as his men. He was to attack along the Germeter–Huertgen highway to the woods line overlooking Huertgen village, while at the same time infantry and tanks were to clear the Vossenack Ridge, near the village of that name. In the coming battle, Vossenack itself would change hands at least ten times, and gain the dubious honor of being the site of the highest concentration of casualties incurred in the whole of the 1944/45 campaign.

But the terrain restricted movement badly, especially for the tanks which Cota's corps commander had attached to the 28th in large numbers. His problem was how best to use the limited freedom the forest offered him and at the same time overcome the immense supply and follow-up difficulties imposed on him by the divergent missions and the cruel rugged battleground. In the end, with a week to go before his attack was scheduled to kick off on November 1st, Cota assigned two battalions of engineers to work on supply trails through the forest, and to enlarge the existing cart track across the Kall gorge which led to the village of Schmidt, just beyond the West Wall. It had cost the 9th a thousand casualties in their failed attempt to take Schmidt. Now, for the time being, Cota was going to leave the defense of the cart track in the hands of one battalion of combat engineers, unaware that Model thought Schmidt was the key to the whole battle of the Huertgen Forest.

If Schmidt and Vossenack fell, then nothing could stop the 'Amis' from grabbing the vital road and communications center of Dueren, just behind the West Wall. The Roer River dams, which potentially provided the Germans with the means of flooding the Rhine valley as a defensive measure, would also fall into their hands. Schmidt had to be held at all costs – and the best way to ensure that the 'Amis' did not grab it, Model knew, was to cut that cart track running across the heights into the Kall gorge.

So the engineers were the first to move into 'the Green Hell of the Huertgen.' It rained constantly as they went about their mundane tasks, hewing down the shattered firs to build cordwood roads through the forest, as Cota had ordered, pushing forward steadily yard by yard behind their armored bulldozers, running for cover every time the hidden German mortars opened up on them and staring in shocked surprise when after that single dry crack, like the sound a twig makes underfoot in a hot parched summer, another of their number sank noiselessly into the mud or reeled back screaming, hand clapped to shattered head or blinded eye, scarlet blood seeping through white fingers, yet another victim of the lurking snipers.

'It was like wading through the ocean,' one of them

recalled later. 'You walk in it all right, but the water is all around you.'[18]

But they waded on, one by one overcoming the various obstacles laid by the German engineers in their path: the mines, the booby-trapped logs, and the *schuhminen*, or 'deballockers' as the Americans called them. These fiendish little objects, no bigger than an ointment box, would when trodden on produce an explosion powerful enough to blow a man's testicles off.

Whenever the hard-pressed, sweating engineers came to a grove, a clearing or a fire-lane on their way through that grim dripping forest, they would loop primer cord onto a rifle grenade and fire the grenade. As it lobbed forward the primer cord snaked open behind it, the length of the opening. Then it was touched off, and a whole row of the deadly *schuhminen* in their glass and wooden cases would explode in an ear-splitting roar. Or the engineers would get the artillery boys to do the job for them and the area would be subjected to an artillery concentration that exploded the mines by concussion. But not always. There'd certainly be one left behind and soon there'd be another engineer sitting on the scorched smoking earth, staring ashen-faced and shocked at the ragged stump, jetting bright blood, of what had once been his leg. Another life-long cripple had been created.

Slowly the engineers inched forward, building the new supply routes that General Cota needed so urgently and preparing the vital cart track through the Kall gorge to Schmidt, while the staffs toiled over their plans and tables.

3

At first light on Saturday, October 21st, 1944, two soldiers of the 'Big Red One,' Sergeant Ewart Padgett and PFC James Haswell – who had been captives of the last German defenders of the besieged city of Aachen – braved the fire of their own comrades to tell them that Colonel Wilck, Battle Commandant of Aachen, was at last ready to surrender. At midday negotiations were completed; after six weeks of combat all along the West Wall, the Americans had gained their first major prize.

It was the highpoint of a grim month. General Huebner of the 'Big Red One' attended Mass in the shattered city's great cathedral. Eisenhower came to visit and fell flat on his behind in the mud, much to the amusement of the troops whom he had intended to address. Correspondents and 'visiting firemen' flooded into the place to view the first German city to fall into Allied hands.

Robert Reid reported for the BBC on his visit to Charlemagne's cathedral. 'It was an eerie experience wandering through the historic old place,' he said. 'I walked through the cloisters. Three chickens fluttered in through the shattered windows and began pecking the dirt in search of food. Two American doughboys who'd just finished a meal of bread and cheese threw them some crumbs . . . I have seen many towns like this before. But this is Germany. Late this afternoon I watched a group of German prisoners being led through the wreckage. They were silent, bent and sick-looking. Maybe they saw more in that terrible scene than the wreckage of Aachen. They were taking with them into captivity a preview of the wreckage of Hitler's Germany.'[19]

A Czech correspondent attached to the First Army described the scene when one of the city's great bunkers was liberated. 'The doors opened and out came the drabbest, filthiest inhabitants of the underworld I have ever seen, as people came streaming out into the light, dazed, then catching a breath of fresh air and finally starting to jabber, push, scream and curse. Some precipitated themselves on me, brandishing their fists. "Where have you been so long?" they shouted. "Why didn't you deliver us sooner from those devils?"' 'It was the breakdown of a nation after having played for five years on the wrong cards,' he concluded. 'Maybe it was the rage of a gangster let down by his gangleader, but it was a hatred you only find in civil wars.'[20]

This belief that Aachen symbolized the 'breakdown of a nation' was shared by many *behind* the lines that day. A week before, Eisenhower had celebrated his fifty-fourth birthday at Bradley's new headquarters at the Hotel Alpha in the center of Luxembourg city. Naturally there was a cake complete with candles. But more serious matters were discussed that night too. It was decided that the US Army in conjunction with the British would launch a major offensive in the first week of November. It was also agreed that the newest army under Bradley's command, General Simpson's Ninth Army, would be withdrawn from the 80-mile-long 'Ghost Front' facing the West Wall in the Ardennes and moved to support Montgomery. Bradley had had a premonition since mid-October that 'Monty would wangle a US Army from our line-up to strengthen his British Army Group. Because Simpson's Army was still our greenest, I reasoned that it could be the most easily spared. Thus rather than leave First Army within Monty's reach, I inserted Ninth Army between them.'[21] To replace it along the 'Ghost Front,' Bradley placed a single corps of 80,000 men. But the thinness of his line didn't worry him – at the time. There was something almost pastoral and idyllic in the manner he described it then. 'Trout streams foamed through the steep hills in this quiet middle sector and wild boars roamed its forests.' The GIs even went hunting within the shadow of the West Wall, and as Bradley commented, 'Later the Luxembourg forest warden was to complain the GIs in their zest for barbecued pork were hunting the boar in low-flying cubs [single-winged spotter planes] with Thompson sub-machine guns. Inventive, I agreed, but a trifle rough on the game.'[22]

Now, with the battle for Aachen finally ended, and the roads to the rear relatively clear of urgent traffic, long convoys of trucks and tanks bearing no unit insignia were rumbling north behind Aachen to take up their positions facing the West Wall, next to the British. Soon they would join their comrades in the Huertgen Forest, waiting for the great November offensive that would spell the end for Hitler's Germany. Behind them they left the 'Ghost Front' manned by greenhorns and shattered veterans, a mere corps holding what once an army had held.

One day after Aachen had surrendered, with the convoys of the Ninth filling the roads to the rear while Cota's men prepared for their own 'D-Day,' Model's Chief-of-Staff General Krebs and von Rundstedt's General Westphal were ordered to report to the Führer's headquarters in East Prussia. Both of them thought that they had been summoned to give a routine briefing on the situation in the West. They were mistaken.

Immediately on arrival they were ordered to sign an undertaking, binding them to the utmost secrecy concerning a mysterious operation code-named 'Watch on the Rhine.' They were told bluntly that if any details of the plan were leaked by them, they would be shot forthwith.

Both of them swallowed this insult to their honor as soldiers and waited until the Führer deigned to see them.

At midday they were summoned to the presence and after routine business had been dealt with, everyone else was sent away except the two chiefs-of-staff and Colonel-General Jodl. Now Hitler got down to the real reason for the urgent summons to East Prussia.

It had all started nearly six weeks before. Hitler had been listening to a routine briefing by Jodl on the situation on the Western Front, sunk in his own unhappy thoughts, apparently uninterested. 'On the Western Front,' Jodl was saying, 'we're getting a real rest in the Ardennes – '

Hitler snapped out of his reverie abruptly. 'Stop!' he cried, raising his hand imperiously.

Jodl stopped.

Hitler took his time, while his generals tensed, then he said, 'I have made a momentous decision. I am taking the offensive. Here – out of the Ardennes!' He hit the map in front of him. 'Across the Meuse and on to Antwerp.'[23]

His generals stared at him as if he had suddenly gone mad.

The same thought occurred to Krebs and Westphal as Hitler now explained his plan. He wanted von Rundstedt and Model to prepare a striking force from his own strategic reserve of thirteen infantry divisions, two parachute divisions and six panzer which would drive through the Eifel splitting the Anglo-American armies, its objective being the key Allied supply port of Antwerp. The place he had picked for the massive 250,000 strike force, which would, he believed fervently, put the Allies out of the war for at least a year and bring Germany victory in the end, was that stretch of the American line opposite the West Wall between Monschau in the north and

Echternach in the south. It was that spot which Bradley was currently describing in such pastoral idyllic terms – his 'calculated risk' (as he called it later). By November 25, 1944, the two chiefs-of-staff would have to be ready to attack through the 'Ghost Front.'

November

'Then there was one other thing, I remember [about the Huertgen]. We had put an awful lot of white phosphorus on the town before we got in for good, or whatever you would call it. That was the first time I ever saw a Kraut dog eating a roasted German Kraut. Later on I saw a cat working on him too. You wouldn't think a good German cat would eat a good German soldier's ass which had been roasted by white phosphorus.'

Ernest Hemingway

1

Dawn, November 2, 1944. It was typical weather for this time of year in the 'Awful Eifel,' as the GIs were already beginning to call it: cold, damp and gray, with a thin mist curling itself in and out of the shattered dripping firs like a skinny Siamese cat.

At 8 o'clock precisely, the morning stillness erupted into an ear-splitting roar, as the 12,000-round artillery bombardment began. This was Western Front circa 1917 all over again. The enemy was being 'softened up' for the coming infantry attack. Now, just as their fathers had done in that war, the men in field-gray cowered at the bottom of their deep pits and in their vibrating bunkers and waited till the bombardment stopped; then they'd rush to their machine guns. The 'Amis,' it seemed, hadn't learnt much since World War One.

The artillery bombardment finally died away, leaving behind it the usual ringing echo that seemed to go on and on until it lost itself among the outermost ring of hills. The field-grays stood to, staring out at the smoking, transformed landscape with great new pits everywhere. But the 'Amis' did not come. Was this a new tactic, the puzzled Germans asked themselves. It wasn't. Playing safe this time, the Allied brass wanted the advance covered by TAC air force planes, but they wouldn't be able to operate until mid-afternoon. The infantry would have to go it alone.

The 28th Division's main effort started at noon. Under the command of Colonel Carl Petersen, a slender wiry man who had grown up in Pennsylvania among the miners, oilfield workers, and tradesmen who still made up the hard core of this National Guard outfit, the 112th Infantry set out through the woods to take the key village of Schmidt.

Everything seemed surprisingly easy. On the second day of the 'great push,' as some of the older officers were calling it, memories of the Argonne coming readily to mind as they surveyed that lunar landscape with its water-logged shell-holes, smashed trees and battle debris, Petersen's infantry forded the River Kall, climbed the steep slope on the other side, routed a bunch of second-rate German supply troops in Kommerscheidt, and reached Schmidt at midday. There for the first time since they had started their attack they met real opposition. But the jubilant infantry of the 28th Division were not to be stopped. Taking out the snipers, dismantling log barricades, blasting their way into the fortified village houses and turfing out their erstwhile occupants – by the time night was descending over the village like the shadow of a giant crow, Schmidt was in American hands.

Now the Americans began to set themselves up for the night in the houses around the four-road intersection at the center of the village, establishing outposts rather than a firm line because there weren't enough men for that. Tired and perhaps a little cocky after their triumph, they installed them in the houses and not in foxholes out in the open, as was standard operating procedure for the infantry.

It had been easy, all too easy.

During the night, without any particular sense of urgency because of the ease with which Schmidt had been captured, the engineers checked out the last of the Kall trail which up to now had been in German hands. They were followed by a company of medium tanks, grinding and groaning their way toward the village in the darkness, commanders sweating it out, drivers cursing and bitching, knowing that if they missed a gear at a crucial moment it could mean the end of one $20,000 vehicle.

But then the lead tank under Captain Hostrup ran into trouble. The left shoulder of the trail began to give way. In the darkness he couldn't risk going too far to the right shoulder; there was a 100-foot drop there. He cursed and ordered his driver to reverse. Gunning his engine the man did so until they reached the engineers. Hostrup told them he wasn't going any further until the trail was broadened and strengthened. Thus it was agreed that the tanks would resume the crossing along the key trail to Schmidt at dawn. In the meantime the engineers would get on with the job.

But still unaware of the need for haste, three platoons of engineers made only a start on the job. As corps and divisional commanders all along the Siegfried Line called to telephone their congratulations, so that Dutch Cota began to feel (in his own words) like 'a little Napoleon,' the 28th set a pattern for sloppy operations in the Huertgen which would lead to disgrace and disaster.

* * *

At dawn on November 4th, Captain Hostrup's tankers tried again. Bad luck struck them right from the start. Lieutenant Fleig's lead tank hit a mine almost immediately. A track was ripped off, partially blocking the trail. Cursing and blaspheming in the cold dawn, their breath fogging grayly in the freezing air, the tankers managed to winch four tanks past the stricken Sherman with the young Lieutenant taking over the new lead tank.

Up and up they went, fighting the gears and gunning their 425-HP engines frantically every time the tracks started to slide on the mud, inching their way around the tight bends, and losing one tank in the process. Now as light began to flood through the green gloom of the firs, three tanks were on their way to Schmidt. They were the only three that would do so that day. Behind them the Kall trail was buttoned up tight once more. Five disabled tanks blocked it now. Not even the little tracked Arctic Weasels could get by.

The German artillery sounded the first note of what was to come just as Fleig lost his second tank. The German gunners knew the terrain and they knew their weapons. Systematically they plastered the village of Schmidt. The US telephone lines went out one by one. Still sleepy radio operators failed to get on to their radios in time to call up counter-fire. By the time the first American concentrations started to fall (an hour and a quarter after the Germans had opened up), German infantry was streaming forward behind the cover of the tanks of the 116th Panzer Division.

There was no stopping them. They rolled contemptuously over the daisychains of anti-tank mines laid on the hard surfaces of the road. Bazooka-men tried to stop them, but to no avail. Their rockets bounced off the thickly armored and sloping glacis plates of the 116th's Panthers.

Thus began the series of disasters that would dog the 28th until they were finally withdrawn from the Forest. In the confusion of that attack – the Panthers opening up with their 75mms, blasting the first line of houses to bits, starting with the upper floors where the snipers and observers were and working down to the basements where any last-ditch stand might be made – frightened men started to tell each other that the order to withdraw had been given. The word spread from squad to squad, platoon to platoon, company to company. '*We're pulling back, guys. Pass the word – we're pulling back!*' The officers and non-coms were unable or unwilling to stop the men. Grabbing their rifles, the men of the 112th Infantry started to fall back, at first in some order and then in panic, racing for the shelter of the woods as the Panthers roared closer.

It was a rout pure and simple. Three hours later Schmidt was in German hands once more. The only Americans there now were the dead and dying.[1] The 28th Division had failed in its first attack in 'the Green Hell of the Huertgen.'

Now everything started to go wrong for Dutch Cota's unhappy men. Petersen's men, who had fled from Schmidt to battalion headquarters at Kommerscheidt, were tough to hold even there. Non-coms had to strike them and more than one officer threatened the terrified GIs with his .45. 'There was no holding them,' Staff Sergeant Frank Ripperdam reported later; 'they were pretty frantic and panicky.'[2] It took nearly two hours to gather together as few as 200 men from the whole battalion to bolster up the defenses of Kommerscheidt.

At Kommerscheidt, however, there was Lieutenant Fleig with his three Shermans. As the German tanks hove into sight, although he was out-gunned and out-armoured (a Panther could knock out a Sherman at 1,000 yards, while a Sherman needed to get as close as 300 yards to do the same thing, and even then there was little chance of penetrating the Panther's steep, armored glacis plate), Fleig moved out to tackle them. He knocked out three tanks in quick succession. A P-47 came howling in at 400mph from somewhere or other, its 20mm cannon chattering furiously. A Panther lurched to a stop, thick white smoke streaming from its stricken engine. A bazookaman struck lucky, and another tank was hit, a gleaming silver hole ripped in its turret, its crew fleeing for their lives followed by BAR fire. Suddenly the steam went out of the 116th Panzer's attack. They withdrew to the high ground opposite to regroup.

Cota ordered Petersen to retake Schmidt at once, to hit the Krauts on the rebound – apparently forgetting that the vital Kall trail to the rear of Kommerscheidt was still not open. All that night the engineers toiled to reopen it, while behind them Captain Hostrup edged his tanks up anxiously, inch by inch. By dawn on November 5th they'd made it. Nine self-propelled tank destroyers with their great 90mm guns plus Hostrup's six remaining Shermans rumbled into Kommerscheidt, welcomed by the miserable infantry of the 112th like the Seventh Cavalry itself coming to the rescue of some nineteenth-century prairie fort.

Now the Germans changed tactics. While Petersen prepared to assault Schmidt, they turned their attentions to the Kall trail.

That same evening a lone jeep bringing up ammunition to Kommerscheidt was suddenly confronted by German infantry filtering out of the dripping trees like gray timber wolves. At once the German patrol opened fire. Tracer zipped down the trail. 'Shoot, man! Shoot!' the lieutenant in charge of the jeep yelled frantically above the snarl of the German burp-guns.

'I can't, Lieutenant,' the man cried back, 'I'm dying right here!'[3]

Throughout the night reports flooded back to Divisional HQ that the Germans were infiltrating the Kall trail. Division Chief Engineer Colonel Daley commanded angrily, 'Get every man you have into the line fighting!'[4]

Cota had previously ordered Colonel Ripple of the 707th Tank Battalion to take a special task force of infantry and tanks and move up to Kommerscheidt to help Petersen retake Schmidt. Thus it was that they, not Daley's engineers, first ran into the Germans in strength.

Hardly had they entered the woods than they bumped into a reconnaissance outfit of the 116th Panzer. Ripple fought back. All that night he fought his way up the trail toward Kommerscheidt, but by the time he reached the beleaguered village, his task force was in such a state that a disheartened Colonel Petersen thought that there was little hope of recapturing Schmidt that day. He called the counter-attack off.

While this was going on, the Germans hit the neighboring regiment, Colonel Hatzfeld's 2nd Battalion. Dug in along the exposed Vossenack Ridge, they were already depressed and very nervous before the attack came. They reported to Regimental HQ that some of the men were crying like broken-hearted children, while others had had to be *ordered* to eat their cold K-rations. The battalion commander, for his part, was slumped in his cellar CP, apathetic and motionless, face buried in his hands.

When the attack came, the men broke. Panic spread from company to company, right back to the reserve company. 'It was the saddest sight I have ever seen,' Lieutenant Condon of Company E reported later. 'Down the road from the east came men from F, G, and E Companies pushing, shoving, throwing away equipment, trying to outrace the artillery and each other, all in a

frantic effort to escape. They were all scared and excited.
Some were terror-stricken. Some were helping the slightly
wounded to run, and many of the badly wounded, probably hit by the artillery, were lying in the road where they
fell, screaming for help. It was a heartbreaking, demor-
alizing scene.'[5]

No one had yet seen a single German of the 116th
Division, von Schwerin's old 'Greyhounds.' Yet it was no
use pointing this out to the panic-stricken fugitives. 'They
ran as fast as they could,' the Battalion Personnel Officer,
Captain James Nesbitt, remembered. 'Those we saw were
completely shattered . . . There was no sense fooling
ourselves about it; it was a disorderly retreat. The men
were going back pell-mell.'[6]

Officers of the battalion staff tried to hold the men.
They succeeded in forming a new line running through the
center of the village with some seventy men. But when the
officers' backs were turned, some of these melted away to
the rear, too.

At dawn on November 7th, with the rain pouring down,
the Germans finally made their appearance. From
Schmidt, fifteen tanks supported by a battalion of infantry started to attack toward Kommerscheidt. The TDs
thundered into action. One after another they knocked
out five Panthers. But they were taking losses themselves and were beginning to withdraw, not quickly, but
definitely. By noon the German tanks were in the outskirts of the village, shooting up the American foxholes,
pulling that old trick they had learnt in Russia of swirl-
ing around on a hole while the horror-struck infantryman crouched below, the earth pouring in to bury him
alive.

This time the men of the 28th Division did not break,
but their courage was ebbing away rapidly. A huge

German tank stuck its long, hooded cannon right through the door of the house which served as a command post for both battalions in Kommerscheidt. It was the last straw. As Sergeant Ripperdam of L Company remembers, 'There was a hellish amount of noise and confusion and everyone was pretty nervous. I was feeling pretty low. Then the first thing I knew one of the boys outside said there was a big tank right on top of the battalion CP. We took off to have a look. I saw the tank on the CP in a position to cover the entrance . . . There were American soldiers in front of it, and they had their hands raised in surrender. There was a white flag showing . . . With this scene in our minds, we saw A and B Company men streaming back to the rear, running, but most of them still had their weapons. We took off and joined them.'[7]

Colonel Petersen was shocked beyond measure, and very bitter. He had seen his regiment run in panic: men he had known since childhood. And he blamed General Cota, for it was he who had given them this impossible assignment. Casting all logic and reason to one side, Petersen handed what was left of his command to Colonel Ripple, telling him he was going to give Dutch Cota a piece of his mind; he would give him it straight, the true situation up in the Huertgen.

Making his way down the steep heights to the rear, Petersen was wounded once and then again by German shellfire. When the engineers working the trail found him he was babbling and incoherent. The medics took him to the divisional aid station where he demanded to see Dutch Cota. The General was appalled at Petersen's state, unshaven, ashen, red-eyed after four days of combat without sleep. Tired and alarmed himself, Cota could only think Petersen had abandoned his troops. Big tough

Dutch, the hero of the Normandy hedgerows, fainted clean away!

The next day, while the new commander of the 112th Infantry made his lonely way back beyond the Kall with orders to pull back everyone left over there on the night of November 8th, the brass came and went at Dutch's command post. Not only his corps commander and army commander made an appearance, but no less a personage than the Supreme Commander Eisenhower himself, with Army Group Commander Bradley in attendance.

None of them liked what they saw. But there was little they could do about the situation in which the 28th Infantry found itself. There was an air of postmortem about Cota's headquarters that day.

The second battle for the Kall trail and Schmidt had developed into one of the most costly divisional actions of World War Two, almost as bad as some of those fought by the Marines in the Pacific in the following year. Petersen's 112th Infantry alone had lost almost *two-thirds* of its strength, while the Division itself had a total of 6,184 casualties in those brief seven days, a staggering blood-letting. The 28th was a spent force.

While elements of the Division continued to fight on for another five days to fool German Intelligence, the mass of those demoralized National Guardsmen started to move out secretly, heading for Bradley's 'Ghost Front' where they had received their first bloody nose against the Great Wall of Germany back in September. There they would be able to rest in peace and regain the confidence they had lost in the Huertgen. Now it was the turn of another division which had been similarly surprised at the West Wall in September, General 'Tubby' Barton's 'Ivy League boys,' as Hemingway was wont to call the men of 'my favorite division.'

Stopped on the way to the offensive further north, the 4th Division was ordered to move into the Huertgen Forest at once, one regiment detailed to go first, the ill-fated 12th Infantry, to restore the crisis caused by the failure of the 28th. But in the end the whole division would be fated to go through the horror of the Huertgen.

2

In that first week of November while the 28th Division was being decimated in the Huertgen, further north the US Army's newest army commander in Europe, General Simpson – a paternal figure of rather unusual appearance who always kept a completely bald shaven head like an early 'Kojak' – invited his British neighbor Corps Commander Brian Horrocks to dinner to meet Ike.[8]

'Jorrocks,' as he was nicknamed, a skinny almost ascetic-looking commander who had seen more than enough of war – prisoner-of-war, badly wounded, in combat everywhere from Africa to Russia – accepted the Ninth Army Commander's invitation with alacrity. He liked 'Big Simp,' and was delighted to meet the Supreme Commander.

After the losses his Corps had suffered trying to relieve the trapped airborne troops at Arnhem Bridge, Horrocks had been warned by Montgomery not to involve himself in any further offensive action for the time being, but Montgomery and Horrocks had not reckoned with Ike's charm.

After an excellent dinner, Ike asked, 'Well, Jorrocks, are you going to take on Geilenkirchen for us?'

Horrocks replied that the spirit was willing but the flesh was weak. The only division he had available was the veteran 43rd Infantry, which had already taken tremendous casualties since D-Day (by the time the campaign ended, the Division would have a complete turnover in personnel, having had exactly 12,500 men killed, wounded or captured, its total strength). With that he couldn't be expected to take Geilenkirchen, one of the two strongest positions on the northern wing of the West Wall.

'Give him one of ours,' Eisenhower said to Simpson, who suggested the 84th Infantry, a completely green division, recently arrived from the States.

Horrocks protested that the task ahead was going to be very difficult; it didn't seem fair to launch a US outfit into its first battle under the command of a 'Limey' general.

Simpson and Eisenhower overrode his protests. As the after-dinner conversation continued, Eisenhower expressed anger over the behavior of the 82nd and 101st Airborne Divisions, who had caused a great deal of trouble back in France after being withdrawn from the Arnhem salient. There had been a lot of drunkenness, some rape and several score desertions. 'They are a disgrace to the American Army,' snorted Eisenhower, whereupon Horrocks sprang up angrily and said it was a pity that the whole US Army did not consist of such 'disgraces.'

His angry sally was met by a roar of laughter from Chief-of-Staff 'Beatle' Smith, who commented, 'Well, well, I never thought to hear a Britisher standing up for US troops against an American general!'

Thus it was that an Anglo-American formation was scheduled to attack the Great Wall of Germany. The die was cast.

In early November the two divisions, British and American, regrouped in order to be in the best position for their attacks on Geilenkirchen, the British from the north, the Americans from the south.

There was the usual good-natured badinage. The British called out, 'Where yer been since 1939, Yank?' The Americans answered, 'Waiting to get the order to come over here and save you from the Jerries!' For the British, the 'Yanks' were the soldiers whom they thought of as 'overfed, over-paid, over-sexed – and *over here.*' For the Americans, the 'Limeys' were a class-ridden bunch who downed tools and drank tea at the drop of a hat.

Yet the so-called class-conscious British with their formal 'Permission to speak, sir?' when addressing an officer, their insistence on spit-and-polish and drills which had gone out of fashion three hundred years before, did notice with alarm just how little American officers concerned themselves with the welfare of their men. There was no attempt to take care of the men's feet, for instance, whereas in the British Army an officer was compelled to examine the feet of each man after a long march, to check for blisters and foot disease. Later it did not surprise them to learn that the 'Rail-Splitters,' as the 84th was nicknamed, lost five hundred men – nearly three-quarters of a battalion – to trenchfoot, a preventable disease. Nor was there any great effort to supply them with a daily hot meal, as was the case in the British Army, even though it might only be 'M & V' (meat and vegetable stew out of a can) or corned-beef fritters. The GIs existed on cold K-rations.

The Americans' security was tremendously lax too. They had failed to evacuate the local German population who might well have betrayed them to their compatriots only a thousand yards away. The British had no such compunctions. They sent German civilians streaming back across the frontier into Holland with their pathetic bits and pieces laden on farmcarts, baby buggies, bicycles – anything that had wheels.

Worse was to come when the Americans had finally left. The British found that they had made no careful plan of the mines they had planted to their front through which the 43rd Division would have to advance. In the end the British sappers collected seven hundred of them. During the day the commander of the 43rd Division's 129 Brigade, Brigadier General Mole, was inspecting his line when the mines went off. There was an appalling explosion which blew a crater thirty feet wide and five feet deep. Brigadier General Mole and fourteen soldiers were killed. It was a bad start to the attack on Geilenkirchen.

In the late evening of November 15th, Bradley sat in General Hodges's war-room in the Hotel Britannique, where the rich of Europe had once gambled under the huge crystal chandeliers. Hodges's First Army was going to kick off its attack into the Reich, together with the new boys of Simpson's Ninth. Hodges and his Chief-of-Staff were chain-smoking, faces worried. The weather had been lousy for days now and they needed Air to batter their way through the West Wall. At one o'clock in the morning the weather report finally came in. The rain and fog might well disperse the following day. Hodges made his decision. 'Air or no air, we're going,' he snapped.

Next morning the brass woke up to find that the dark clouds were beginning to roll away, revealing the first pale yellow rays of a watery sun.

'Man, look at that ball of fire, just look at it!' Hodges exclaimed excitedly. Then, as Bradley and the rest pressed to the window, he added, 'But don't look at it too hard . . . You'll wear it out, or worse yet, maybe chase it away.'[9]

At 12:45, right on schedule, twelve hundred heavies of the US 8th Air Force flying in box-tight formation, plus a similar number of RAF bombers, guided by jeeps on the ground with vertical radio beams so they would know exactly where the First and Ninth Armies were, thundered across the West Wall. Friendly AA guns started to shoot colored flak. Barrage balloons ascended to 1,500 feet. Bradley was making doubly sure that they wouldn't drop their bombs on their own people (it had happened often enough before; indeed, the only American general to be killed in France, McNair, had been a victim of US bombing). The big offensive to crack the West Wall had commenced.

At Geilenkirchen the waiting British and Americans were cheered by the sight of the vast bomber fleet passing overhead. They prepared for their own little side-show with renewed hope, as the 1,000 guns of the 43rd British and General Bolling's US 84th Infantry Division poured shells at the enemy hidden in the deep bunkers of the West Wall. They wouldn't have been so happy if they had known that, in order to comply with Bradley's safety regulations, the bombers had dropped their lethal loads so far behind the enemy forward troops that only three percent of them seemed to have been hit.

The plan of attack was simple enough. They always were – on paper. The 84th would attack first, to take the high ground a mile and a half away, near a village called Prummen. With the right flank thus secure, the 43rd would start its attack to a depth of two and a half miles, completely encircling Geilenkirchen. Here the 84th Division would mop up. Thereafter, to complete the wiping out of the enemy-held Geilenkirchen salient, a further advance was contemplated on the small River Wurm to the four villages of Hoven, Wurm, Mullendorf and Beek. Everything had been timed to the last minute and everything depended upon the two divisions keeping to a strict timetable; if one didn't keep up, it would expose the flank of the other to a counter-attack. But on November 18th, everyone, American and British, was confident that they would keep up.

'Monty's Moonlight' – searchlights shining on the clouds, which reflected the light downward – illuminated the way at dawn that day as two troops of the 79th Armored Division[10] rumbled out into no man's land to begin clearing the mines by the simple expedient of whirling their chain flails two yards to their front and exploding them. It was a dangerous, unnerving business as anti-tank and anti-personnel mines erupted in furious showers of earth, stone and metal on all sides, but the men of the 79th Division were used to it by now. One hour later they had flogged two lanes through the minefield.

At this stage in the campaign, Montgomery had more artillerymen than infantry. Like Napoleon, the British Field Marshal loved and trusted artillery. By now, any one of his infantry brigadiers could give the command 'Victor!' and the British gunners, whose communications and discipline were much superior to those of both the Germans and the Americans, could bring down the fire of 300 guns *within sixty seconds* on any given point. Now they 'victored' and after five minutes' bombardment, two battalions of the 84th rose out of their holes to go into their first battle, supported by British tanks.

Things went well. Soon after midday Horrocks ordered the 43rd to attack. Again the British 'victored.' Two battalions of veteran British infantry began their advance too. Stocky farmboys for the most part from the West Country, the inevitable tea-mugs hanging from their packs, they plodded forward through the thick mud warily like the careful, slow country lads they had once been.

Their tanks started to lag behind. The mud was too thick. It was taking the American armaments industry a long time to learn that a tank needed broad tracks to surmount mud – a lesson the Germans had learnt long ago in Russia. The infantry marched doggedly on, leaving their American-built Shermans behind. Fighting-transport endeavoring to keep up with supplies became hopelessly bogged down too, right up to their axles in the clinging morass. The infantry kept going. A couple of German self-propelled guns rumbled out of the woods to the right. *They* had broad tracks; the mud didn't hamper them. They opened up at once, shooting the closest infantry platoon to ribbons. In a flash thirty-one men had fallen dead in the mud and the commanding officer of the nearest battalion was wounded and writhing in agony. Still the infantry pressed on.

All that long day and the next night, the British and Americans fought their way forward, capturing objective after objective on time until finally on the next day the West Wall strongpoint of Geilenkirchen was surrounded. 'Splendid,' the British senior officers chortled. 'Jolly splendid!' Both divisions had gained their objectives right on time.

But the battle had only just begun. That night the heavens opened, drenching the miserable freezing infantry and turning the fields into quagmires. To their front the guns of the West Wall opened up and for the first time the Americans learnt what it was to feel the weight of a heavy enemy artillery bombardment. At dawn they advanced across the sticky fields, ankle-deep in mud, to attack the concrete pillboxes of the Great Wall of Germany. They didn't get far. Tanks of the elite 15th Panzer Division rumbled into the attack. Watching them, Brigadier Essame of the 43rd Division thought, 'It was galling to see their tanks with their broad tracks maneuvering over muddy fields impassable to our own.'[11] The Americans were bogged down.

The veterans of the 43rd kept going until they reached

the River Wurm, but even they were feeling the strain. As the historian of the Duke of Cornwall's Light Infantry wrote after the war, 'Years after the event those who survived could recall the intensity of the enemy fire and the sloppy ground over which they had to move to reach their objective. What is difficult to describe is the physical agony of the infantryman . . . The November rain seemed piercingly cold. After exertion when the body warmed, the cold air and the wet seemed to penetrate the very marrow of every bone in the body so that the whole shook as with ague, and then after shaking would come a numbness of hand and leg and mind and a feeling of surrender to forces of nature far greater in strength than any enemy might impose.'[12]

It was a sensation that the men of the Huertgen knew well by now, and that, as the historian of the DCLI added, could only be conquered by 'the inherent claim of self-preservation and the determination to do one's duty.'

After four days of hard slogging and bitter combat, on November 22nd Horrocks ordered a final effort. Both divisions were now exhausted, particularly the green Americans. As Brigadier Essame wrote later, 'Only those with actual experience of such circumstances know the moral struggle over their own emotions which battalion and brigade commanders had to endure and overcome. It was not easy to order rain-soaked soldiers once more into action in the dripping woods.'[13]

Brigadier Essame was forced to overcome his emotions that day. He ordered the men of the Duke of Cornwall's Light Infantry, who had already lost one commanding officer killed in action and would lose another before the campaign was over, to capture the woods around the village of Hoven.

But General Harmel's 10th SS Panzer Division was

waiting for them. The *Grenadiere* met the British infantry with a hail of fire. They went down everywhere, the muddy fields littered with crumpled dead. Now the SS infiltrated to their rear. '*Stretcher-bearer!*' The pitiful cry went up on all sides as the medics struggled through the mud to find the wounded, plodding through the upturned rifles stuck bayonet-first into the ground to indicate that their former owners would never need medical attention again.

Taking casualties all the time, the DCLI somehow made it into the village of Hoven. A nightmare now began. Prisoners and the wounded had to be sent to the rear. But even as darkness fell, the slightest movement produced the bitter high-pitched whir of spandaus, emplaced everywhere in the ruins. Still the British fought on. They had done what they had been ordered to. Providing the Americans of the 84th on their flank managed to get forward before dawn, all would be well. If they failed, the survivors of the DCLI, now sharing the village of Hoven with the SS, would be cut off completely (to the rear, the 10th SS had broken through) and massacred.

But the Americans had been stalled by the West Wall at the village of Suggerath to the right flank. They simply couldn't get through the bunker line on the heights there, for the SS had been ordered to hold it at all costs.

What was Brigadier Essame to do? If he was going to pull his weary men out with any chance of success, he'd have to do it during the hours of darkness. It was then that Horrocks, the Corps Commander, muffled in a soaked raincoat, appeared out of the night. Essame explained the situation. His foremost troops had run into fresh German soldiers of the SS, the same SS which had stopped Horrocks's drive to link up at Arnhem the previous September. They were the best Germany had in the autumn of 1944, and at dawn they would undoubtedly launch a counter-attack on the positions of the DCLI cut off in Hoven, a mile to the front.

Horrocks, a firm believer in the Americans, told Essame that he thought the 'Yanks' would do it, but he left the decision in the Brigadier's hands. As Essame wrote later, 'If the Brigadier wished to withdraw the DCLI now while there was still time he could do so. If he chose to stay and gamble on the Americans resuming their attack at dawn, whatever happened, he would have Horrocks' backing.'[14]

It was a difficult decision for Essame, as he sat there in the gloomy farmhouse headquarters with the guns thundering outside and the rain beating furiously against the blacked out windows. Could he risk the lives of some six to eight hundred men for the inexperienced, unpredictable Americans? The DCLI had been fighting since June now and had had *one hundred percent casualties* in the rifle companies. As he wrote later, 'The DCLI had never since the early days in Normandy fought otherwise than to the bitter end.' But could he subject them yet again to such a terrible blood-letting?

As the rain pelted down outside, Horrocks waited patiently, watching Essame's face in the flickering yellow light of the petroleum lantern. The Brigadier made his decision. He nodded his head. He would hold Hoven.

Horrocks hedged his bets. He sped away into the night, his command car followed by enemy tracer, and reported to General Bolling's headquarters. He promised the American some of his 'Funnies' if they would attack at dawn, covering the one and a half miles that separated them from the cut-off battalion of British infantry. Bolling said his GIs would have a go.

Just before dawn, it happened. The SS rushed the company headquarters of the British troops nearest their own positions. The attack was beaten off but a 'potato masher' grenade smashed the company radio and a German tank split the telephone cable that the DCLI had laid down during the night. D Company was now isolated from the rest of the DCLI.

As the dawn arrived in Hoven, the SS came crawling up under cover of a hedgerow. The D company men sprang into action. For two and a half hours they held off the SS. A tank rumbled up in the street in the front of company headquarters. The company commander engaged it from a windowsill of the upper floor with a PIAT (a primitive, spring-loaded form of the bazooka). The heavy clumsy bomb howled off the Panther's thickly armored glacis plate like a ping-pong ball. The gunner fired his piece. As the long 75mm erupted flame and smoke, Company Commander Spencer reeled back severely wounded.

Another company of the DCLI was cut off. Severe house-to-house fighting developed. Now the cellars were full of moaning British and German wounded. A German doctor was captured. Truculently he told his captors, when asked why he fought, 'I'm fighting for my country the same as you.'[15] Now most of Hoven was aflame. The DCLI's ammunition ran out. The Tommies fought on with ammo and weapons taken from the SS dead, sprawled everywhere on the bloody cobbles in their camouflage uniforms. Both remaining infantry majors were wounded. And still the Americans were nowhere in sight.

Neither side, the SS nor the DCLI, relaxed their pressure. But now the SS were bringing up more and more tanks. The DCLI started to fall back. D Company was down to 15 men out of 120. A Company, attacked by two German self-propelled guns and infantry, counter-attacked and drove the enemy back fifty yards, but the cost was grievous.

In the end, refusing to surrender, the two wounded

majors brought out what was left, fighting their way out of
the burning village of Hoven. Little did they know that the
84th had finally broken through at Suggerath. But now it
was too late. Nor did the first and last joint Anglo-
American action at Geilenkirchen matter much any more.
The steam was going out of the whole of the huge
seventeen-division action. 'The last offensive necessary to
bring Germany to her knees,' as Hodges had called it
confidently at the start, had failed. As Essame wrote after
the war, Bradley had chosen to 'attack where the Germans were numerically stronger and where they had every
advantage in the form of concrete defenses and thick
forests – a military problem new to his troops and for
which they had not been trained . . . Condemned to a
battle of attrition, the infantry sustained such losses that
divisions quickly exhausted themselves in action.'[16]

Thus as the Ninth and First Armies began to dig in and
count their grievous losses, Bradley complained to Ike's
Chief-of-Staff Bedell Smith, 'If the other fellow would
only hit us now, I'd welcome a counter-attack. We could
kill many more Germans with a good deal less effort if
they would only climb out of their holes and come after us
for a change.'[17]

They were words he would live to regret. In less than a
month 'the other fellow,' as Bradley invariably called the
Germans, would be climbing out of his hole in the West
Wall in his thousands and hundreds of thousands. And
finally when they had been pushed back whence they had
come, at a cost of 80,000 US casualties, there would be
bitter recriminations, accusations and counter-accusations
among the top British and American brass. Thereafter
there would be no more Anglo-American attacks on the
Great Wall of Germany. The 'Limey-Yank' honeymoon
would be over.

3

Thus while the fighting died down everywhere and Model prepared for the great surprise-attack, husbanding his resources like a canny housewife, the only place in Germany where the Americans still attacked was in the Huertgen. The forest seemed to have got under the skin of the top brass; somehow their attitude to it was no longer based on cold military logic, with an eye to tactical and strategic advantage. Now the battle for the forest had become an almost personal obsession. Hodges, who should have known better – he had fought as a machine-gun company commander in the forest of the Argonne in 1918 – kept throwing in division after division, without getting to the root of the evil.

The fact was that the average American soldier was not trained for this kind of fighting, either by civilian life or by the military. As young men in civilian life before the war, the Americans had come to believe that the machine could solve every problem, whether it was an 'iron lung' to keep some polio victim alive or a Fordson plow that would cope with the toughest clod of earth. It had been no different in the service. The Army had certainly turned the one-time 'drugstore commandos' into soldiers, but it had not taken away their belief that the machine would do everything – in this case the tank, the heavy gun, the airplane.

But in the Huertgen, the machine was basically useless. The GI had to rely on himself and his personal weapon. Essentially it was an infantryman's war; on account of the terrain, the average GI had to do his thinking and his fighting without an officer or a senior non-com to command him. He had to withstand the freezing misery of the foxhole line, the lack of hot food or drink, the fear and worry, the constant depletion of the meager human resources he had brought with him from the States. Time and again, the values that American society, both civilian and military, had sent him to war with, were proved inadequate.

It was not that the average US soldier was unpatriotic. More often than not, he was thinking that his country was far superior to those inhabited by the 'Limeys,' 'Frogs,' 'Krauts' and all the rest of the 'natives' he came into contact with during his brief sojourn in Europe. Nor was he a coward. There were tales enough of heroism in the Battle of the Huertgen. All the same, the American soldier turned and ran too often during the fighting in the Huertgen. The 28th did. The 4th and 8th Divisions would; even the elite of the American Army, 'the Big Red One' did.

Society had failed him; the Army too. In the end, his allegiance was not to America, not to the Army, not even to his division or his regiment – but simply to his buddies, his battalion, even his company. And when, as now this grim November, those battalions and companies were beginning to fill up with raw replacements – men who, as General Bradley described it, 'went into the line at night and perished before the morning' or 'were evacuated as wounded even before they learned the names of their sergeants' – then there was trouble, serious trouble ahead . . .

Colonel James Luckett's 12th Infantry of the 4th Division were thrust into the line at the Huertgen without the slightest briefing. There was no time. The 28th had failed badly. The line had to be bolstered up, and quick.

Cold, wet, scared, plodding blindly through the wet

dripping trees, stumbling over the bodies of Petersen's ill-fated 109th, the doughs dropped into the strange muddy foxholes and waited apprehensively for what the dawn might bring.

It brought action, plenty of it. For three days the 12th tried to restore the 28th's lost positions. On the fourth day they were fighting for their very lives.

That day Colonel Siegfried von Waldenburg's 116th Panzer, von Schwerin's old 'Greyhounds,' came out of the woods firing. Two companies of Luckett's infantry were caught by surprise and surrounded. Desperately Luckett formed a final stop line to the rear. Another two companies were surrounded. Casualties were tremendous. By the end of the fourth day, the Regiment had already lost half of its effectives in battle or as a result of trenchfoot and that persistent malady which would plague the American command throughout the battle of the Great Wall of Germany: 'combat exhaustion.'

And the Germans were playing tough too. It was now that one of the most diabolical incidents of the whole three months' battle in the Huertgen took place. A soldier of Luckett's command was found wounded in the forest by three Germans. They robbed him of his cigarettes and watch. That was nothing unusual; American soldiers did the same with their prisoners. What they did next, however, was highly unusual. They rigged an explosive charge underneath his bleeding body. For the next seventy hours – *nearly three days* – he lay alone in the cold and rain, tortured by his wound to the point of delirium, hungry and parched with thirst (save for what he could lick from his hand in the way of raindrops), fighting desperately to stave off unconsciousness. For he was afraid that when American aid-men came to his rescue, as they eventually would, they would blow not only him but themselves to smithereens. He was found, warned his rescuers and lived to tell his terrible tale, truly a testimony to the courage and endurance of the human spirit.

By the fifth day of combat, the 12th had lost 1,600 men. High Command refused to understand the desperate position the Regiment found itself in. It was burnt out, there was no doubt of that. The men were hollow-eyed, drawn, trembling like ancient alcoholics with a bad case of the DTs, staggering about the forest on rubbery legs. But High Command flung them into the attack once more: they were to regain the ground that had been lost.

The 12th never came within sight of its objective. High Command believed that there were 'no bad soldiers, just bad officers,' as Napoleon had laid down. Colonel Luckett was obviously a bad officer. On November 16th, back where Petersen's men had jumped off exactly fourteen days before, the survivors of the 12th Infantry Regiment watched helplessly as Luckett was relieved of his command.

Watching the survivors limp back that day from the Huertgen, Courtney Hodges turned and muttered softly to his staff, 'I wish everybody could see them.' But Hodges in common with most of the top brass had no time for sentiment that November. They wanted results in the Huertgen, and it didn't matter how they were obtained.

Now the rest of the 4th Division, Colonel Lanham's 22nd and Colonel McKee's 8th Infantry Regiments, were ordered into the attack. McKee's 8th bit the bullet first. They had to break through a minefield, climb a steep ridge lined with barbed wire ten feet high and attack a position held by German machine-gunners. They were stopped immediately, of course. During the night engineers blasted a gap through the wire. At daylight on November 17th, the infantry attacked. The machine-gunners were waiting for them, and sang their old unholy song of death.

The attackers went down by the score. By midday the lead battalion had lost 200 men.

Men went crazy under such circumstances, although in the heat of battle their actions seemed sane enough at the time. A young infantry officer, First Lieutenant Bernard Ray, decided that the Germans couldn't cover two gaps at once with their machine guns. He volunteered to blow another hole in the wire. With slugs zipping just above his head, he crawled through the mud on his own, dragging a Bangalore torpedo behind him. He had just reached the wire when a mortar shell exploded close by. His prone body was riddled and ripped apart by shrapnel. Perhaps he thought he was dying, perhaps he just went crazy. No one ever found out. For now young Bernard Ray pulled a detonator cap from his pocket, attached it to the primer cord wrapped around his grievously wounded body and then fitted the primer cord to the Bangalore torpedo.

That done, Ray calmly set off the detonator.

A great gap appeared in the wire, as Ray's lifeless body flew high in the air like a rag doll. But still the 8th Infantry could not get past those machine guns.

On the afternoon of November 15th, 1944, Colonel Tom Kenan looked out of his CP, a deep hole in a small clearing in the Huertgen, to find a civilian staring down at him. His bulk, already large enough from the Battalion Commander's perspective, was accentuated by the white German combat jacket the bespectacled civilian was wearing. Under his arm was tucked a tommy-gun.

'Hemingway,' the newcomer introduced himself. 'Ernest Hemorrhoid,' he added with a grin, 'the poor man's Ernie Pyle.'[18] 'Papa' had reappeared in the lines of the 22nd Infantry.

That night, closeted in Colonel Lanham's trailer, which was equipped with a German helmet tastefully decorated with a flower design for use at night as a chamberpot, Hemingway and Lanham talked and drank into the early hours of the morning.[19]

Lanham was gloomy. He told Hemingway he'd had a premonition that he might not survive the Huertgen. Hemingway exploded. He was sick of 'all this shit' about premonitions. The 'Great Ernie Pyle,' a man he didn't like, was always having them. All the same Hemingway knocked on wood. The Huertgen, he told himself, was a place where a lot of people still would die.

Next morning Lanham went out to his 1st Battalion to inspect its positions. Hemingway tagged along and met the 'little gray sort of man' who was temporarily commanding the 1st. Later Lanham told Hemingway privately he wasn't too enthusiastic about the temporary battalion commander; in a few days he might have to relieve him, he feared.

Hemingway, very serious now, said, 'Buck, you won't ever have to relieve him.'

The little hot-tempered Colonel bristled. 'Why?' he demanded.

'He won't make it,' Hemingway replied. 'He stinks of death.'

Ten minutes later when their jeep reached the 22nd's command post, Colonel Ruggles, the executive officer, came running out. He saluted and said excitedly, 'Colonel, the major has just been killed! Who takes the 1st Battalion?'

Apparently a shell fragment had ripped through the logs of the 1st Battalion headquarters bunker. The major had been killed instantly. Hemingway strolled off and left Lanham to it. Later the Colonel asked, 'How the hell did you know that?'

Hemingway, drink in hand as always, shrugged and mumbled something about scenting the same curious smell of death that he had noted in Normandy three months earlier.

On November 20th, after a brief rest, the 22nd and 8th Infantry Regiments attacked again in the direction of the two hamlets of Kleinhau and Grosshau, unaware that a fresh German infantry division had been moving into the wooded heights to their front during the night.

The usual slog started, worsened by the fact that the Germans had hidden an artillery observer to the rear of Lanham's 22nd Regiment (he was never found). The lone and very brave officer directed the fire of the German guns all too accurately on the advancing doughs. Casualties were horrific. Now the new German infantry started to launch counter-attack after counter-attack at the Americans. By nightfall the 8th had advanced only a matter of a few hundred yards, and the Germans were so close in the forest that they were able to prevent the dog-tired infantry from cutting timber to cover the tops of their foxholes against tree bursts.

Just like their predecessors in the 9th and 28th Infantry Divisions, the 4th began to bleed to death in the Huertgen Forest. 'You can't see,' T-5 George Morgan of the 22nd told correspondents, 'you can't get fields of fire. Artillery slashes the trees like a scythe. Everything is tangled. You can scarcely walk. Everybody is cold and wet, and the mixture of cold rain and sleet keeps falling. Then we attack again and soon there is only a handful of the old men left.'[20]

The Germans suffered too. In a diary taken by men of the 4th from the dead body of a German soldier near Grosshau, they found these last two entries.

'It's Sunday. My God, today is Sunday! With dawn the edge of our forest received a barrage. The earth trembles. The

concusion takes our breath. Two wounded are brought to my
hole, one with both hands shot off. I am considering whether to
cut off the rest of the arm. I'll leave it on. How brave these two
are. I hope to God that all this is not in vain. To our left,
machine guns begin to clatter – and there comes Ami!

In broad waves you can see him across the field. Tanks all
around him are firing wildly. Now the American artillery ceases
and the tank guns are firing like mad. I can't stick my head out of
the hole – finally, here are three German assault guns. With a
few shots we can see several tanks burning once again. The
infantry take cover and the attack slows down. It's stopped. It's
unbelievable that with this handful of men we hold out against
such attacks.'

Two days later the German doctor, for that was what 4th
Division's Intelligence thought he must be, made his final
entry.

'Last night was pretty bad. We hardly got any sleep and in the
morning the artillery is worse than ever. I can hardly stand it,
and the planes are here again. Once more the quiet before the
storm. Then suddenly tanks and then hordes of Amis are
breaking out of the forest. Murderous fire meets him, but he
doesn't take cover any more. We shoot until the barrels sizzle
and finally he is stopped again.

We are glad to think that the worst is past when suddenly he
breaks through on our left. Hand grenades are bursting, but we
cannot hold them any longer. There are only five of us. We have
got to go back. Already we can see brown figures through the
trees. As they get to within seventy paces, I turn around and
walk away very calmly with my hands in my pockets. They are
not even shooting at me, perhaps on account of the red cross on
my back.

On the road to Grosshau we take up a new position. We can
hear tanks come closer, but Ami won't follow through his gains
anyway. He's too cowardly for that.'[21]

Hemingway was in his element, or so he said, but he
would be plagued by nightmares about the Huertgen
fighting for years to come. Once a German patrol attacked
Lanham's CP. The headquarters commandant Captain

Mitchell was killed at once, but Hemingway moved in fast with his tommy-gun and helped repulse the German attack.

But the future winner of the Nobel Prize usually confined his activities to bull sessions with Lanham's officers at the end of another weary day of bloody slogging, and occasional visits to the safer parts of the line.

He took pleasure in baiting the Divisional Chaplain about religion, especially about the oft-quoted remark that there are 'no atheists in foxholes.' He pulled the leg of the Divisional Psychiatrist, Major Maskin. Hemingway had always hated 'head shrinkers' intensely, and one night after the good doctor had been asking a lot of probing questions, Hemingway said, serious-faced, that he needed a bit of advice. Maskin jumped at the opportunity. Hemingway said he was troubled about his twenty or thirty cats back home at Key West. 'The little bastard was fascinated,' Hemingway recalled later. 'His eyes were bugging out.' Many people liked cats, said the doctor; that was no problem. 'With me it is,' Hemingway chortled. 'My problem is that I can't seem to stop having intercourse with them!'[22]

One day Lanham allowed Hemingway to go up front and visit the village of Grosshau which had been finally taken after terrible losses. Hemingway called it 'a potato village.' In fact, as Lanham explained later, 'It was part of the integrated defense of the Siegfried Line,' with bunkers that had walls of three to five feet in thickness.

On November 30th Hemingway set off through the mud and the slush, being forced to take cover from shellfire several times. Everywhere lay the dead, American and German. The 'butcher bill,' as Lanham called it, had been high. One American soldier lying in the road had been so flattened by the passing vehicles that he had been squashed to pulp, hardly recognizable as a human being.

A German had been half-roasted by white phosphorus and now a starving stray dog was feasting on his flesh.

These visions seared into Papa's memory. It was no wonder that they would form the substance of his nightmares and make of his only novel to come out of the war *Across the River and into the Trees* such a bitter, irrational, cynical book.

But Hemingway stayed until the end, playing his role of 'Ole Ernie Hemorrhoid, the Poor Man's Pyle,' fighting the war with two canteens attached to his German belt with its *Gott mit uns* buckle, one filled with gin, the other with dry vermouth. He was a little old for such play-acting, admittedly, but by this time, most of the 4th, young or old, were slightly crazy.

Lanham, normally rational, wrote later of the fight in the forest, 'At this time, my mental anguish was beyond description. My magnificent command had virtually ceased to exist . . . These men had accomplished miracles . . . My admiration and respect for them . . . was transcendental.'[23] Now as the 4th's attack started to peter out, Lanham began to count the cost. In the two weeks of the battle, the 22nd had lost 2,678 men, 500 of that total being non-battle casualties. The 22nd was virtually decimated.

4

Now it was the turn of the 8th Infantry Division, whose commander General Stroh was already a sorely troubled man. He had seen his only son shot down in a dive-bombing attack on a German-held fortress in Brittany the previous summer and burn to death in his blazing plane.

Colonel Jeter's 121st Infantry of the 8th Division bore the brunt of the Division's attack into the Huertgen that last week of November. By the fourth day of their fight, Thanksgiving Day, the regiment started to break. That day the 2nd Battalion ran into a German minefield. They got through it with casualties and swung around a road-block that had been holding up the tanks of the 5th Armored Division.

Captain Black, the commander of G Company, hurried up to assist. His company was caught by enfiladed machine-gun fire in a narrow gorge. The place was full of Bouncing Betties too. Men went down everywhere. Black withdrew, leaving a score of dead in the ditches on both sides of the trail. There to the rear, the veteran of months of fighting in France broke down and started to sob. His platoon leader did the same. 'They just went berserk,' a sergeant reported, 'crying and yelling.'[24]

The rot had begun. Jeter relieved the commander of the 2nd Battalion that day. It didn't help. Over the next four days Jeter relieved another three company commanders. In one company, *all* officers were either relieved of their commands or broke under the strain. A platoon leader who refused to go back into the line was placed under arrest. Next day a second battalion commander was relieved.

Hodges came down to see Stroh personally at his divisional CP and 'made it quite clear' that he 'expected better results.'[25] It was obvious to those in the know that General Stroh's days were numbered.

On November 26th, the 121st's luck picked up. The Germans started to withdraw. A wave of jubilation swept through the whole division, a mixture of relief and dis-belief. *The Krauts were pulling back!*

Colonel Cross, the new commander of the 121st Infan-try – for Jeter had gone the same way as all those officers he had relieved during the last few days – ordered his men to chase the Germans on the way to the village of

Huertgen that gave the forest its name.[26] The first company went racing in – and came out just as hurriedly with a bloody nose. The Germans were not withdrawing that quickly.

Cross ordered his 2nd Battalion to follow up the next morning. Neither of the commanders of the two lead companies was happy with the assignment he had just drawn; First Lieutenant Paul Boesch, a burly ex-wrestler, and Captain Cliett, a tall, heavy-set Southerner, both protested. They wanted a slight withdrawal before their own artillery started to soften the Germans for the attack. They were turned down. The 121st was having no more withdrawals; too many heads had rolled already.

Daylight was beginning to appear when the men of the two companies began to move out. The artillery beating up Huertgen had ceased. 'It was almost as if the silence itself had exploded,' Boesch wrote later. He and his men felt 'frightened, naked, alone.'[27]

Burp-gunners opened up to their front. Tracer zipped back and forth in a nervous lethal morse. As it grew lighter, the enemy fire increased and became more accurate. Some of Cliett's men took shelter in a house, got cut off and fought it out all day. Those who were alive at the end of the fighting surrendered. The rest of his company fell back into the woods.

Boesch and sixty men of his company made it as far as a trench near the first house. There the Germans kept them pinned down all morning. The trench started to fill up with wounded; for every time a soldier popped his head up above the log parapet, German machine-gunners ripped into action only a hundred yards away, chipping off wood and sending it flying in a frightening white rain.

'Lieutenant,' one of the wounded asked piteously, eyes full of longing, 'when are you gonna get us out of here?'[28]

Boesch, the tough, good-humored giant, had no answer for this overwhelming question.

That night Boesch managed to get the wounded out and food up. Next morning after a nerve-racking night out there at the point of the whole division, the strain-faced men heard the roar of tank motors – *and they were American!* Behind them came more and more infantry.

Boesch sprang into action. 'Get set to move!' he roared. 'Pass the word along. Get set to go with the tanks!'[29]

As the Shermans roared past them, churning up the mud with their flying tracks, the infantry rushed out of their holes. In minutes they were inside the first houses, encouraged by a bold officer, Colonel Ginder (on loan), who believed in being where the shooting was and who told one somewhat fearful officer, 'If you get wounded, you'll get a nice rest in hospital. If you get killed, you won't know anything more about it. If neither happens, you will have nothing to worry about. Let's get going!'[30] The officer's reaction was not recorded, but the GIs followed the bold Colonel with a will as they swept into the village, Boesch telling himself that he had never felt battle could be so incredibly impressive. And then it was over – the rattle of machine-guns, the sharp dry crack of the rifles, the screams of the wounded, the erupting clouds of dust and fire, as the mortar bombs struck home. All energy spent, the infantry collapsed. Huertgen, the obscure village which had given its name to this whole terrible killing ground, was American at last.

But the capture of Huertgen could not save General Stroh. By the end of November Donald Stroh was a tired man, bowed by the tragedy of his son and that of his Division. He was relieved and sent back to the States 'for rest and recuperation,' the way the top brass always phrased it when they wanted to save a commander from the stigma of a summary relief. In his place General

Hodges brought in an assistant division commander from Patton's Third.

The new man was very much in the Patton mold, brash, aggressive and blood-thirsty, and just like his former chief 'Ole Blood an' Guts,' he'd picked up a nickname somewhere or other. He called himself 'Wild Bill' Weaver. But he wouldn't be brash and aggressive for long. The Huertgen Forest would tame 'Wild Bill' as it had all the others before him.

5

'No mission too difficult! No sacrifice too great! Duty first!' This was the proud motto of the next outfit to brave the forest. The 1st Infantry Division had arrived on the scene. The 'Big Red One' was here!

The division had a noble history. It had been the first American outfit to land in France in World War One and on the morning of October 23, 1917, one of its artillery sergeants had fired the first American shot of the war (the empty case was sent home to President Wilson as a souvenir). In World War Two it had been the first US division to land in the United Kingdom, and thereafter it had taken part in three combat landings – in Africa, Sicily and Normandy – and again it had been the first outfit to fire a shot into Germany in September 1944.

But it was a temperamental outfit. In Sicily, for instance, Bradley, under whose corps command it was, thought it had 'become increasingly temperamental, disdainful of both regulations and senior commands. It thought itself exempted from the need for discipline by virtue of its months in the line. And it believed itself to be the only division carrying its fair share of the war.'[31]

Bradley decided to dismiss both the divisional commander, General Allen, and his assistant General Roosevelt. On their way to the fateful meeting with Bradley, the two were stopped in their jeep by an MP. The red-faced policeman told Allen, 'I'm sorry, General, but my orders are to ticket *anyone* riding without a helmet. My captain would give me hell if he saw you riding by.' Allen was without a helmet.

The Divisional General grinned, but Roosevelt objected and said, 'See here, my boy, don't you know that's General Allen of the 1st Division?'

'Yessir,' the MP replied, 'and you're General Roosevelt, sir. But I'm going to have to give you a ticket, too, sir, for wearing that stocking cap.'[32]

Both men received new commands in Europe later. Roosevelt, taking part in his fourth combat landing in Normandy at the age of 56, won the Medal of Honor and died of a heart attack a little later.

In Allen's place Bradley appointed tough, hollow-eyed General Clarence Huebner who had entered the Army as a private in 1910, been commissioned in World War One and had held every rank in the Division from private to colonel. He wasn't popular, especially on account of his emphasis on spit-and-polish and close-order drill. Indeed it took some of the veterans until after Normandy, those few who were left by then, to get to like and respect Huebner.

But by the time the 1st Infantry Division finally entered the Huertgen, they were their old selves again, a closed community, parochial and jealous of their reputation. Hemingway said of them: 'They believed their own publicity . . . the First Infantry Division of the Army of the United States, and they, and their calypso-singing PRO never let you forget it. He was a nice guy. And it was his job.'

Huebner had become infected too. He had become too defensive, thinking that the 'Big Red One' got all the rotten assignments, did all the work, while the rest of the US Army lazed. 'There's the Big Red One,' as his soldiers said contemptuously, 'and then the rest of the US Army.' General Collins, his corps commander, thought Huebner was overly protective, trying to avoid casualties by not pushing hard enough.

Thus it was that, after the 1st Division's first three days in the forest and only inconclusive gains, Collins went to see Huebner. He spared no words. He told Huebner he and his division weren't fighting hard enough.

There had just been a German counter-attack on the Division and with this in mind Huebner mentioned something about keeping the Krauts in check.

Lightning Joe pounced on the word. 'Holding the enemy in check?' he yelled. 'I knew you could do *that*. I want you to advance. *This is an offensive!*'[33]

Thus the men of the 'Big Red One' entered their first real engagement in the Huertgen Forest with General Huebner, chastened but still concerned about them, breathing down their necks.

They met elements of a whole German infantry division, whose commander Colonel Josef Kimbacher personally led a counter-attack until he was captured with 120 of his men. But help for the Germans was on the way from Holland, in the shape of the 3rd Parachute Division.

It was a parachute division in name only; just a few of its officers and NCOs were trained parachutists. But the sixteen- to nineteen-year-olds who made it up were imbued with the spirit of the long-gone men who had conquered Crete, Eben Emael, and had held out so long at Monte Cassino. Raw as they were, they stopped the 'Big Red One' at the village of Merode.

On November 29th, some of the 1st Division managed to break through to the village, but the tanks which were following them up shied off when the Germans opened up from the forest nearby. Now the infantry was cut off in the first houses of the little settlement, while the Shermans tried frantically to make it to them. To no avail.

That night the paras boxed in Merode with artillery fire, setting up a wall of lethal steel through which it was impossible to pass. Communications between the trapped men and the rear elements broke down under the bombardment. The staff officers hadn't the vaguest idea where their own men were dug in, so they could not even direct some counter-fire in an effort to protect them. General Huebner was desperate. One of his units was being slaughtered and there seemed to be nothing he could do about it.

At long last, after hours of waiting throughout that long November night, one radio message came through. It was barely audible, but brutal in its finality. 'There's a Tiger tank coming down the street now,' the unknown voice said, 'firing his gun at every house.' Then: 'He's three houses away now!' Silence, save for a metallic crackling. Then with sudden, electrifying alarm, making the staff officers in the poorly lit dugout sit up, the small hairs at the back of their heads erect: *Here he comes!*[34]

Thereafter the radio fell silent again. For good.

Out of the two companies in Merode, only one sergeant and twelve men escaped back to their own lines. Using these men as guides, another company tried to break through to the village, but the paras beat them back. And that was that. Colonel Seitz, commander of the leading regiment, declined to attack again. 'What is in town may be annihilated by now,' he said the following morning. 'Moreover, any attack on the town would have to be strictly an infantry attack. There is no road.'[35] The logic seemed weak for an infantryman, but no one objected.

It was an ignominious end to the 'Big Red One's' attack. It marked, too, the end of the 1st Infantry's fight in the forest. In their short time there they had taken 3,993 battle casualties and probably the same number in non-battle.

Three days after the débâcle at Merode, General Collins told Huebner that he would ask no more of the 'Big Red One.' All he wanted now from the Division was that it should straighten up its front and prepare its positions for the arrival of a fresh division. Soon the men of the 1st would depart the Huertgen, its reputation tarnished, tail between its legs, having suffered the same humiliating fate as all the other divisions that had gone before it.

'The division,' Hemingway wrote in his despatch for *Collier's* that week, 'had not advanced beyond its objective. It had reached its objective, the high ground we were now on, exactly when it should have. It had been doing this for day after day after day after week after month now. No one remembered the separate days any more, and history being made each day was never noticed but only merged into a great blur of tiredness and dust, of the smell of dead cattle, the smell of earth new-broken by TNT, the grinding sound of tanks and bulldozers, the sound of automatic rifle and machine-gun fire, the interceptive dry tattle of German machine-pistol fire, dry as a rattler rattling, and the quick spurting tap of the German light machine guns – and always waiting for others to come.

'History was now old K-ration boxes, empty foxholes, the drying leaves on the branches that were cut for camouflage. It was burned German vehicles, burned Sherman tanks, many burned German Panthers and some burned German Tigers, German dead along the roads, in the hedges and in the orchards, German equipment scattered everywhere. German horses roaming the fields and our own wounded and our dead passing back strapped two abreast on top of the evacuation jeeps. But mostly history was getting there when we were to get on time and waiting there for others to come up.'[36]

What division? Did it matter? In the Huertgen, whether they wore the Red One or the green sprig of the Ivy League or the triangle and five of the armored, it made no difference. They all came and died in their turn, thousands of those condemned young men in khaki, leaving the survivors to trail back through the dripping forests, shoulders bent in defeat, like old, old men . . .

December

'We're surrounded by the Germans. It's the Battle of the Bulge!
Hands up! Wait, I say. We just left Oklahoma. We're Americans! We're supposed to win.'

Mel Brooks, 1978

1

Dawn came slowly in the Huertgen Forest this icy December morning, as if God were reluctant to throw light on the war-torn lunar landscape below. Everywhere was destruction and carnage. The trees, stripped and shattered by weeks of gunfire, stood there like gaunt outsized toothpicks, stark against the morning light. Pillboxes, destroyed at last, lay everywhere in a mass of gray rubble linked by twisted steel wire and girders torn by TNT into grotesque shapes. Trucks, weasels, jeeps, tanks, ruined and rusting, squatted in the wrecked forest on all sides, together with discarded soldiers' equipment, gas-masks, helmet-liners, empty ration containers, blood-stained overcoats. And of course there were the bodies – there were always the bodies each new dawn in the Green Hell of the Huertgen.

Now the weary engineers came plodding back through the mud in their thigh boots, their shoulders sagging with the effort of that night. They had removed over 250 mines from the immediate front. The way ahead for the tanks of the 5th Armored Division, leading the drive for the embattled village of Brandenberg, was free of mines at least.

At eight o'clock precisely on that morning of December 3, 1944, Colonel Hamberg waved his arm. '*Roll 'em!*' he bellowed as the drivers started the engines of their Shermans with a thunderous roar and the glades and trails were filled with the blue smoke and stink of gasoline. One by one the 30-ton monsters, their decks loaded with sandbags and bits of extra track as additional protection against the German *panzerfausts*, began to waddle forward through the mud.

Minutes later, as the weather began to pick up, the fat-bellied, radial-engined Thunderbolts came zooming in low, adding their din to the infernal racket of yet another attack in the Huertgen.

The tankers didn't mind the ear-splitting noise as the fighter bombers came hurtling along at tree-top height, skimming the green peaks of the pines, tearing great evil black shadows behind them. The Thunderbolts provided just the kind of protection they needed in the forest. 'Keep the buzz boys up,' a delighted tank commander radioed as his Sherman raced across the dip toward Brandenberg, keeping well between the white tapes that indicated the area cleared of mines, 'they're doing a good job!'[1]

Now the first tanks were nosing their way into the first shattered half-timbered and white stucco houses that made up Brandenberg, long barreled 75mms swinging from left to right like the snouts of primeval monsters seeking out their prey. Even here the tankers didn't want to lose the 'buzz boys.'

'Keep the buzz boys up,' the leading tank commander radioed again. 'We're at the critical stage now!'[2]

Obediently the silver planes howled and snarled above the village, cutting white vapor trails in the freezing gray air above the houses, vigilant for the first sign of enemy reaction, cannon chattering, machine guns rippling the length of their stubby wings with electric purple fire.

Five minutes later the Shermans were inside the village, roaring up and down the muddy cobbled streets, their machine guns ripping the upper floors and windows of the little houses to pieces.

Now the armored infantry began to roll in after them in their clattering half-tracks, while the cowed, beaten enemy scuttled out of their cellars and holes to surrender in their droves.

Carried away by the heady excitement of it all, young Lieutenant George Kleinsteiber, platoon commander of a force of three tanks, charged right through the village and on another half mile into the next hamlet of Bergstein. A white blob which was an armor-piercing shell came hurrying his way. It missed – and the German anti-tank gun crew didn't get a second chance. Kleinsteiber's 75mm roared. The gun crew was sent reeling, limbs flailing the air wildly, like a bunch of crazy skittles. Another anti-tank gun opened up. It, too, was knocked out. To the jubilant Kleinsteiber it seemed that the whole village was his for the taking.

But Colonel Hamberg called him back. He didn't think he had enough infantry to defend both Brandenberg and Bergstein against the inevitable German counter-attack. Reluctantly Kleinsteiber and his mud-splattered Shermans started to trail back the way they had come, suddenly despondent and deflated.

Infantry was now in very short supply, and what there was, was of little use in most cases. In that first week of December, one of General 'Wild Bill' Weaver's regimental officers laid it on the line. This is how he described the condition of the men of the 8th Infantry Division: 'The men of this battalion are physically exhausted. The spirit and the will to fight are there; the physical ability to continue is gone . . . These men are shivering with cold and their hands are so numb that they have to help one another on with their equipment. I firmly believe every man up there should be evacuated through medical channels.'[3]

While the attackers regrouped, Robert Barr of the BBC went up to Grosshau to see how they were getting on and vividly recorded the conditions under which the riflemen lived that first week of December.

'An infantry platoon was approaching the village . . . crouching watchfully in the ditches, then moving forward to the next turn in the road and crouching again. Three riflemen lay flat in the thick mud on the road itself, rifles to their shoulders, watching the wrecked village for snipers . . . A German with his leg swathed in bandages came limping out with his hands well up. Three of his comrades lay dead and mud-splashed behind a garden wall. Behind the garden wall the debris had been pushed aside to clear a coal chute which led down to the cellar. One of the soldiers pulled back from his peep-hole and pointing his thumb at the coal chute said, "Go down there and mind your feet." '[4]

Barr went down and in the poor light could make out 'some forty soldiers lying in groups of threes and fours around fires made from the grease-soaked cardboard of their ration boxes. Over the flames they were heating water to make coffee. One Joe began to fidget with an over-heated pan of pork loaf . . . An officer was crouched over a table, talking into a field telephone. He was covered in mud, his cheeks were gray and hollowed and his eyes sunken and red-rimmed. Somebody said, "They're mortaring the road again." '[5]

On the night of December 5th, trying to hold what few gains they had made in the last forty-eight hours, the infantry's misery was made even worse by a sleet storm.

When they groped their way out of their foxholes at
daylight the next morning, they found the trees, the fields,
themselves covered with a blanket of ice. Men started to
refuse to go into action once more and left the line without
orders. The 8th began to order court-martials and reliefs
just as the 28th had done in the previous month.

It was like the worst trench fighting of World War One.
Greatcoats soaked with sleet and freezing mud became
too heavy for the men to wear. Soldiers broke down,
sobbing helplessly in the mud, not from combat but from
the sheer physical strain of moving themselves and their
supplies forward. Again it became every man for himself,
with no radio contact, no artillery support, the enemy so
close that hand grenades were often the only weapons that
could be used effectively.

The Germans suffered too, though the hard-pressed
doughboys of the 8th Division on the verge of collapse did
not think so. They thought the unseen Germans lurking in
that Green Hell were immune to the mud, the misery, the
mayhem. Later a German officer would recall that his
command suffered great losses from frostbite that first
week of December. 'In some cases, soldiers were found
dead in their foxholes from sheer exhaustion.'[6]

Captain Paul Boesch, plodding forward to the attack
with his company of the 121st Infantry, recalled later how,
in the darkness, they stumbled upon a 'ghastly column' of
dead Germans and their horses obviously surprised by
American planes or gunfire. 'The stench was overwhelming,' the hard-bitten veteran reported. 'Bloated men and
horses, some of which had burst, lay full in our path. We
had to step high to shake the entrails off our boots.'[7]

But if the infantry's spirit was waning in the 8th Division,
that of its anti-aircraft gunners was not. Fully aware of the
danger presented by the Americans' occupation of Bran-

denberg, Model managed to persuade 'Fat Hermann' (as Air Marshal Goering of the Luftwaffe was called behind his back) to 'lend' him sixty of his precious Me 109s being carefully hoarded for that great surprise attack so soon to come.

At the crucial moment when the Thunderbolts had disappeared to refuel at their landing strips in Belgium, the yellow-nosed Messerschmitts came roaring in, machine guns chattering, engines howling, wings heavy with 100lb bombs. For the American anti-aircraft gunners they were a sight for sore eyes. Ever since the 8th had first gone into action in Brittany the previous August, they had been toting their cannon back and forth across Western Europe praying for targets like this. They went to work with a will.

The gunners put up a tremendous barrage, filling the gray afternoon sky with ugly puff balls of brown smoke, as the sixty planes bombed and strafed the American positions for about an hour. Within that time the sweating ecstatic gunners shot down nineteen of the fighter-bombers and claimed a further ten unconfirmed. Even the weary infantrymen managed to get up enough energy to share their jubilation, and one excited officer radioed from beleaguered Brandenberg, 'Send up more .50 caliber ammo . . . We've knocked down three Me 109s – and there are still plenty more to shoot at!' That afternoon the Messerschmitts flew back to their fields around Cologne, their ranks sorely depleted. For once a German counter-attack had been beaten off by the Americans. Not one man in the whole of V Corps had been killed; not even one had been wounded.

But the Germans did not give up so easily. On the morning of December 6, 1944, with the great offensive only ten days off now and with the ground sugared by a little sprinkling of snow, five German tanks rumbled into the start line of the grenadiers of the 272nd *Volksgrenadier* Division, who were going to counter-attack the village of Bergstein which now was in American hands. It was a race against time for the Germans, because the grenadiers would be needed for the coming offensive. As for the American defenders, they were stretched to the limit; even the 8th Division's engineer battalion was in the line.

The Germans came with first light. They used their usual attack formation, *die Traube* ('the grape'), a platoon of infantry crouched to the rear of each tank. The fact that its tracks churned up mud and showered them with dirt and pebbles didn't matter. The tank was armored and provided them with the protection they needed. Soon they were in the village. Now the tanks swung to one side and the deadly business of house-to-house fighting commenced.

A grenade through an upper window. A blast of burp gun fire at the door. A kick and it reeled back broken on its hinges. More grenades. More bursts of high-pitched hysterical fire from the Schmeisser machine pistols and then the confused angry back-and-forth of close combat. No quarter was given or expected. When a man went down, American or German, he stayed down. Carried away by the frenzy of close combat, men hacked, chopped, gouged until their opponents were dead.

Then American Shermans started to rumble into the western edge of the village. The German infantry started to withdraw under the cover of their tanks, leaving the village streets filled with their own and American dead. The snap and crackle of small arms fire gave way to an occasional single shot and burst of machine-gun fire. For the time being the young grenadiers had had enough, while the weary defenders just slumped where they were.

All that long day the German artillery and self-propelled guns continued to attack the village from their position
on the prominent *Burgberg* ('Castle-hill') at the eastern
end of Bergstein. By the time night began to fall once
more on the Huertgen, the combat command of the 5th
Armored Division was down to seven tanks, just over a
platoon. If they could not hold the place, General 'Wild
Bill' Weaver knew, his infantry would turn and run.
Something had to be done about Castle Hill. Weaver
appealed to his corps commander for speedy action. The
Corps Commander appealed, in his turn, to General
Hodges, who now after the débâcle of the 28th Infantry,
was taking a personal interest in the Battle of the Huert-
gen Forest. The First Army Commander agreed to release
one of his finest units to Weaver in order to take Castle
Hill on the following morning; he was to receive the 2nd
Ranger Battalion.

Colonel Rudder's 2nd Rangers had gone ashore at Omaha
Beach on D-Day One. Their task had been to scale a high
cliff on which was located a powerful coastal battery which
could, according to Intelligence, threaten both Omaha
and Utah beaches. With just over two hundred men,
Rudder had assaulted the cliff. Again and again they shot
up their grapnels towing ropes behind them while the
Germans raked the beaches and their own shells plastered
the cliff top, deluging them with great clods of earth. Here
and there lone German soldiers lobbed 'potato masher'
grenades or ripped off a burst of burp gunfire at them. But
somehow the Rangers had made it, only to find that the
casemates were wrecked and the guns had gone!
  Now the survivors of that same elite battalion tackled
Castle Hill. They did it in their own style, in the dark,
silently and swiftly. Before the German defenders had
become aware of the fact, the Rangers were among them,

dashing through the trees on the crest of the hill, sweeping all before them. It was the quickest and easiest victory of all the long weary Battle of the Huertgen Forest.

But everyone who entered that Green Hell had to pay his toll, and as always it was in blood. The Rangers were forced to hold Castle Hill for forty-eight long hours until General Weaver could relieve them with a battalion from his 8th Infantry. By that time, the Rangers had lost three-quarters of their strength. The Huertgen had claimed yet another victim; and the killing was not over yet.

Now, however, as yet two further divisions, the 2nd and 83rd Infantry, started to trudge up to continue the drive beyond the forest, one-eighth of which was still in German hands, the generals made an interim report. In the previous three months of battle, five US infantry divisions, the 1st, 4th, 8th, 9th and 28th, plus the 5th Armored Division, had fought full-scale engagements in the Huertgen. Together with support troops and the 2nd Rangers, they represented a force of 120,000 American soldiers. Of that number 24,000 were killed, wounded, reported missing or captured. Another 9,000 fell victim to the diseases of the forest – pneumonia, trenchfoot and 'combat fatigue.' The total was an appalling 33,000, a loss of more than a quarter of the divisions' effectives – even more terrible when one considers that many of that original 120,000 never actually saw the frontline as did the infantry, tankers and combat engineers. In terms of fighting men the percentage might well have been as high as fifty percent.

Was it worth it, one might ask. To British General H. Essame, who fought throughout the campaign himself from D-Day onward as an infantry brigadier, it was an enigma 'why Bradley chose to make his main effort in the shambles of the Huertgen Forest instead of over the easier going on the Ninth Army's front . . . Better still, he could have attacked through the Ardennes to the immediate south where the Germans were known to be in no great strength.'[8] It was a conclusion shared by Infantry Captain and future historian Charles MacDonald, whose 2nd Infantry Division would soon take part in the last battle for the Huertgen: 'Those in the Huertgen Forest fought a misconceived and basically fruitless battle that could have, and should have, been avoided. This is the real tragedy of the battle of the Huertgen Forest.'[9]

2

On December 3, 1944, the same day that the 8th Infantry commenced their last battle in the Huertgen Forest before their relief, far to the south the 1st Battalion of the US 95th Division edged its way to the two bunkers which barred the exit from the Saarlautern Bridge. They had captured it the day before after a brief but exciting skirmish. In the half-light of December 2/3, the infantry had crept along the bridge, half-fearing it was going to go up under them at any moment, any noise they made drowned by the thunder of their own guns. A German tank loomed up out of the gloom. The German radio operator woke up to the impending danger. He started to work his radio furiously. Too late. A GI knifed him. Another German spotted the advancing Americans. He pelted to the demolition switch. Colonel Philbin, the infantry battalion commander, shot him 'on the wing.' He hit the wet cobbles – hard.

Now the American engineers raced forward. Four guards tried to oppose them. They were mown down. The engineers wasted no time. They slashed the demolition cables. Tanks and infantry started to cross. But the

German defenders, knowing just how vital this bridge across the River Saar was, pulled a daredevil trick on the Americans. They ran in tanks loaded with explosives. It was a suicide mission, 'an Ascension Day commando' – i.e. a one-way trip to heaven – the German commander told his volunteers.

It certainly was. The lead tank got as close as two hundred yards to the bridge when a lucky shot struck it. The TNT-laden Mark IV disintegrated, simply disappeared. The German tank commander gave in.

That same morning, the infantry of the 1st Battalion, 379th Infantry, 95th Division, weary from three months of the long campaign in the French district of Lorraine, pushed forward to capture those two gray concrete bunkers. Fortunately for them the German defenders were as weary as they were. Although Field Marshal von Rundstedt personally had been informed the bridge had been lost and had ordered immediately that it should be destroyed and the 'Saar held at all costs,' they surrendered after not too much of a fight. Unknown to the dog-tired victors, they were the first men of General George S. Patton's Third Army to hit the West Wall. Soon another hard slog against that Great Wall of Germany would commence.

After his brilliant lightning armored campaign the previous summer in Brittany, General Patton's luck had run out. His Third Army had been bogged down around the Lorraine city of Metz. Since late September he had slogged it out there with the Germans and still not all of the city had surrendered. More than once Patton had been forced to threaten to relieve not only divisional commanders, but also corps commanders, if they didn't get a move on. 'Ole Blood an' Guts' as he was called ('yeah,' his troops wisecracked, '*our* blood and *his* guts') was in a hurry to get to Germany and win the kudos of being the first to cross the River Rhine.

Now Patton had at last reached the Reich, exactly at the spot where the Germans themselves thought the West Wall was at its toughest. Back in 1939 General von Brauchitsch, then Commander-in-Chief, had estimated that the French would attack Germany just here between Saarlautern and Merzig in order to reach the Rhine. They hadn't, but all the same this section of the West Wall had been strengthened, not only in 1939, but also in 1943 and the early months of 1944. Thus while Hodges in the north attacked an unprepared West Wall back in September, now in December Patton was faced with a fortification command which had had three months to prepare for his coming.

The forces the Germans had to hold the line here were not great, but Hitler personally intervened and insisted that *every* bunker and pillbox should be held, even if only by a single short-trousered Hitler Youth or toothless ancient of the *Volkssturm*. Yet whatever their physical condition, the defenders were in a position to make a stubborn fight. Besides, this was the 1,000 Year Reich's last ditch. The worn-out infantry, the boys and the old men were fighting on 'Germany's sacred soil.' It was going to be a hard nut to crack even for General Patton.

The 95th Division hit the West Wall on December 6th. In the fortifications grouped around Saarlautern-Roden, Fraulautern and Ensdorf, the defenders contested every yard of ground, every house and every street. The Germans filtered behind the American attackers every time the GIs pushed on, and reoccupied their lost bunkers. As a result the infantry had to return and fight for each bunker again and again. The men of Patton's Third had not yet learned what Hodges's First had learned long ago:

once a bunker was taken, its door had to be sealed up by the engineers so that it could not be reoccupied.

That morning the Americans were shelled by an estimated 1,500 rounds in a matter of three hours. They refused to let themselves be demoralized, although they had never before experienced such severe shelling, and they battled on. But by nightfall the steam started to go out of their attack and their commander was not inclined to tackle the bunkers and pillboxes in the darkness. He ordered his men to rest for that day.

Their neighbor the 90th Division had also had a hard day of it. They had made a successful surprise assault on the River Saar near the industrial city of Dillingen under cover of smoke. But once the leading infantry had emerged from the smoke the guns of the West Wall on the heights beyond had opened up with savage fury. In spite of the tremendous US counterfire, which amounted to 8,000 shells in one small area in forty-five minutes, the German guns swept the terrain ahead of the 90th Division GIs. They went to ground, scooping up shallow pits in the clay of the river bank, widely dispersed and disorganized, harassed all the time by wild little charges from the nearby pillboxes. As their commander radioed back across the Saar, which the engineers were now frantically trying to bridge under heavy fire, the situation was 'fluid.' It was not very encouraging.

But still here and there individual soldiers got up and fought back. Sergeant Joe Williams of the 315th Engineer Combat Battalion volunteered to 'crack' a pillbox. He rushed it with an explosive charge in his hands. He was hit. He staggered, but did not fall, while the men crouching in the foxholes to his rear watched with bated breath. Bleeding hard, he staggered to the concrete monster and fired his charge. Black-faced terrified prisoners came streaming out, their hands in the air, waving dirty white undershirts in token of surrender. Williams pushed on. He was hit again. But he seemed carried away with that wild unthinking courage that sometimes inspires men under fire. The Germans saw hi... coming. They threw in the towel. That night when Williams finally allowed himself to be evacuated, he took back with him sixteen prisoners. Later he was awarded the Distinguished Service Cross.

Private Ernie Johnson of the infantry was similarly honored. He was with a patrol that was stopped by fire from a bunker. While the rest went to ground, Ernie found a plank, laid it from the top of the nearby house onto the roof of the bunker. Then, while his comrades watched awe-stricken, the lone soldier crawled along the plank right onto the roof of the unsuspecting bunker. With a cheeky grin, he dropped two grenades right down the ventilator shaft. From inside there came a thick muffled crump, followed by screams of agony. A thick mushroom of black smoke erupted from the shaft. A minute later the blackened, wounded survivors came blundering out to surrender.

But individual bravery was not enough. By nightfall on December 6th, Patton did indeed have two divisions across the River Saar, but for the most part they were either groveling in the mud of the river bank, or bogged down in the ruins along the river. The West Wall was still intact and waiting for them to come again on the morrow.

All the same von Rundstedt was alarmed. He warned that the Americans might well break out of the Saarlautern-Dillingen bridgehead and roll up the flanks of his command; the West Wall had to be held at all costs, and he ordered immediate punitive measures against any officer involved in the loss of a West Wall position – 'the strongest defense of the Reich,' as he phrased it. That night reinforcements were rushed to the bridgehead area and staffs and headquarters combed ruthlessly to ensure that there was one officer for each bunker. Now even the 'rear echelon stallions,' as the German front-swine called the canteen commandos contemptuously, were being thrown into the line. Patton had a fight on his hands.

All day long on December 7th, the Germans threw in counter-attacks which the defenders beat off with ever-growing losses to themselves, while behind them engineers worked in the mud and rain under the cover of a smoke-screen to build a bridge in the 90th Division area. But in spite of the smoke-screen, the German artillery on the heights in the West Wall bunkers was as accurate as ever. Time and time again, a shell would erupt in a mad spurt of boiling white water near the hard-pressed engineers and yet another man would be hit, staining the water with his own blood as he disappeared beneath its surface.

The infantry were taking severe casualties too. Standing in water-logged foxholes up to their knees in freezing rainwater, the troops of the 90th Infantry were taking high casualties, not only from bullets but also from the dreaded trenchfoot. By the evening of the second day of the Third Army's attack on the West Wall, battalion commanders such as Colonel Mason of the 357th Infantry were radioing back that the situation was 'critical'; and in the end the harassed regimental commander ordered that the over-extended battalions on the eastern bank of the River Saar should be withdrawn to a shortened line.

But if the 90th Division was being held up, the 95th, attacking the strongest sector of the West Wall, was growing lucky. They were advancing through a tremendous variety of bunkers and pillboxes built into the suburbs of Saarlautern-Roden, Fraulautern and Ensdorf.

Some had walls and roofs ten feet thick, impervious to the shells of the tank destroyers' 90mm gun. Others were mere pillboxes, manned by a couple of men, but cunningly camouflaged as the manure heaps – 'honey-dew piles,' as the infantry called them – which rested in front of every house in the rural suburbs. In happier times in the Saar, the size of the manure heap resting in front of the kitchen window was a sign of just how prosperous the occupant was; the bigger the heap the more cows the farmer had. This was truly the day when the 'shit hit the fan,' as the GIs wisecracked.

Not only were the fortifications of the West Wall seemingly everywhere, but the enemy had also turned ordinary houses, shops, even factories into defended positions, held at first by poor quality *Volkssturm* companies, but later by regular infantry.

The 95th battled it out with the Germans. Bazookas were employed at a range of one hundred yards and proved very effective at blasting holes in the concrete pillboxes. Engineers rushed them with satchel charges and Bangalore torpedoes. Sticky grenades and hollow charges were used. Every and any weapon was employed against the loathsome gray-concrete monsters that barred the 90th's advance into open ground; for now the GIs had developed an unmitigated hatred of the bunkers and pillboxes. Every new one captured or destroyed was an occasion for rejoicing. Unit journals and records of that time are full of entries such as that of 377th Infantry: 'took another pillbox today,' repeated over and over again.

Finally, on December 10th, resistance to the 90th Division in Fraulautern began to crack. That day the relatively fresh 377th Infantry fought a day-long battle with the Germans in a large hotel. The Americans and the Germans fought from room to room, ending up with a hand-to-hand struggle in the hotel's ballroom. A weary grinning squad-leader commented wryly afterward, 'There was plenty of dancing in that ballroom today. But it sure wasn't a slow fox trot!'

That day the triumphant Americans employed a Luxembourger known as the 'old Kraut,' who spoke the fluent if strange German of his native country, to convince the Germans holding five strong pillboxes to surrender if they didn't want to 'be blown to hell.'

But not everything was that easy. Men of the 357th Infantry captured a strong German bunker by conventional assault tactics. They buttoned up the defenders by a hail of fire, then blasted the steel door down with demolition charges. But the American platoon assaulting the bunker forgot to post riflemen to guard the side of the smoking bunker. They lived to regret the oversight. As they stormed into the bunker, the Germans crept out, sealed in the Americans and forced them to surrender. Thirty-one Americans went 'into the bag.'

And in other parts of the bridgehead across the Saar, the ranks of the attacking infantry were so thin and the situation so desperate, with the Germans counter-attacking time after time, that officers even had to order men suffering from trenchfoot into the line. Their comrades carried them piggy-back into the forward foxholes that day.

On December 10th, the Germans counter-attacked in divisional strength. Time was running out fast. There were only six days to go for Model and von Rundstedt and they wanted that 'damned Dillingen bridgehead' eradicated once and for all. That morning two German divisions started piecemeal attacks all along the line of the ill-fated 90th Infantry Division.

Covered by a barrage of 110 guns, the *Volksgrenadiere* rushed the surprised GIs through a snow blizzard. Here and there panic set in. Private Leslie Atwell, who had just been made an infantry battalion medic because he was over thirty-five and thought too old for the hard life of a rifleman, was busy attending the wounded when the first of the non-wounded came streaming back. 'We're licked,' one of them said hoarsely. 'I tell you it's suicide,' another small private was shouting. 'There's not ten men left in the whole of A Company. They're all wiped out!'[10]

One of the wounded lying on the ground said something to the small private in a voice so low that Atwell, busy with the bandages and wound pills, couldn't hear what was said.

'All right!' the small private cried. '*Call* it desertion. Call it any goddamn thing you want. I'm not going back there. They can line me up tomorrow morning and *shoot* me – I'm not going back to be killed! Don't you see? Don't you see what's happened? They led us into a trap! They don't know what they're doing. They'll all be killed and so will we. What's the sense in that? We'll all be killed if we go back. It's crazy, I tell you. You can't do any good by going back. You can't *win* anything!'[11]

Five minutes after that cry from the heart, the small private, shoulders slumped in resignation started to stumble back into the line.

The 90th Infantry held. Now General Patton determined he was going to break out of the bridgehead on the Saar. He would lead off with a tremendous air blitz, using more planes for one raid than had ever been used before, 3,000 of them to be exact. On December 19th, the bombers would blast a tremendous hole in the German defenses right along the West Wall. The 90th and 95th Divisions would attack out of their bridgeheads at Dillingen and Saarlautern. They would be followed by the 10th Armored Division and the race for the River Rhine could commence.

But that wasn't to be. On December 19th Patton would find himself not supervising the great dash for the Rhine, but locked in Fort Maginot at far away Verdun, facing up to the greatest crisis of the whole Allied campaign in Western Europe in 1944/45 . . .

3

Strange things were happening on the 'Ghost Front' immediately facing the West Wall in that second week of December 1944. While running along the 'Sky Line Drive' in Luxembourg with the West Wall positions eight hundred yards away on the other side of the River Our, an American tank disappeared, crew and all.

Not many miles away, in the area where the battered 28th Infantry Division were resting and refitting after their experiences in the Huertgen, German soldiers mysteriously appeared every night on the *American* side and took their pleasure with willing farm wenches in the nearest Luxembourg farms. They told the girls they were from the West Wall positions opposite, but didn't tell them how they had crossed the River Our without being detected: they had discovered culverts across the Our (when the great attack came, one of them was used to slip the 5th Para Division across). Further north in the East Cantons of Belgium, soldierly-looking men in civilian clothes who did not speak the German patois of the area appeared in the most unlikely places asking questions about the 'Amis,' their positions, their habits. Some of the simple farmers took them for 'Amis' who had deserted – there were plenty of them about – and wanted to know what was going on in order to avoid being captured.

Others, not so simple, thought it wiser to keep their thoughts to themselves. In the half-abandoned villages of the Ardennes, in front of the crackling pot-belly stoves where the locals gathered after curfew, there was much talk of 'green letters'[12] and 'front-runners' – mysterious figures only half glimpsed in the early morning when the call of nature forced the farmers out into the freezing dawn to their outside privies. Who they were and what their errand was, as they melted away among the gray trees, the farmers thought it best not to ask.

One such front-runner blundered into the arms of an American patrol that second week of December. He told them he was a forced laborer, recruited in Luxembourg and made to work in a German labor camp near the border, together with many other Belgians and Luxembourgers recruited in the same manner. Fortunately the engineer in charge was a Communist and a sympathizer with the Allied cause. He had let this man escape to bring a message to the Americans; the details were written on a piece of paper secreted in his tobacco pouch. The Luxembourger escapee was rushed to Intelligence. One day later Radio Luxembourg, now in American hands and being used as a propaganda station, broadcast the cryptic message to its German audience across the nearby border: 'Regards to Otto from Saxony.'

It meant nothing to ninety-nine point nine percent of the German listeners. But one man, a middle-aged Major of the German *Abwehr* (the wartime German Secret Service) stationed at Dersdorf near Bonn, smiled sardonically when he heard the message. His plan was working. He could push ahead now.

Giskes, the *Abwehr*'s counter-intelligence ace, had played a tremendously successful role in this field since 1939. He had helped to wind up the whole Continental network of the British SIS in 1939/40. During 1942/43, he had run Operation North Pole which had bagged 42 Dutch SOE operatives of the network run by a certain Major Blunt, later Sir Anthony Blunt, who was to be revealed in 1980 as a double agent. In 1944 he had succeeded in planting an agent code-named 'Freddie' on no less a person than French Jacqueline de Broglio, scion of the American Singer sewing machine family and hence related to Churchill himself. In due course, Churchill had his new relative (for 'Freddie' married Jacqueline, who was working with the Resistance) brought to England in the uniform of a British captain before he disappeared for good.[13]

In November 1944, Giskes had been summoned to the headquarters of no less a person than Field Marshal Model. Model's Chief-of-Intelligence asked Giskes if he could think up a scheme to fool the Allies about the Model Group's strategic intentions. Giskes said he might be able to do so, but first could he know what the Field Marshal intended. He was told firmly 'no.' All the Chief-of-Intelligence would say was that a big operation was on its way which would shake the Allies out of their overweening complacency.

The result of that puzzling meeting was Operation Heinrich. Giskes recruited the services of a German engineer working in a labor camp who got on well with his foreign charges. He told the engineer that he wanted him to help some of his charges to escape. The engineer was horrified, but Giskes reassured him that it was all for the good of the Fatherland. In the end the engineer agreed. He approached selected Luxembourgers and Belgians from the border area and told them he was a secret Communist, with vital information about the West Wall defenses, German intentions in the West etc., etc., which he wanted them to hand to the Americans.

In the end Giskes managed to smuggle ten 'escapees'

safely through the German lines – he couldn't inform the troops of the West Wall what was going on, so the escapees genuinely risked their lives to deliver his faked messages – each carrying a piece of the jigsaw which added up to the whole. Which was: the Germans intended to launch a spoiling attack on the American-held city of Aachen.[14]

The information from the German Communist 'Otto from Saxony' fitted in well with Colonel 'Monk' Dickson's own conclusions that second week of December. On December 10th, Hodges's scholarly-looking Chief-of-Intelligence (hence the nickname) summarized his opinion of Hitler's future intentions on the Western Front thus: 'Make good the Siegfried Line, recapture the forts lost in the Aix-la-Chapelle [Aachen] area, accepting defeats in the south rather than compromise his hope of a decisive success in the north.'[15]

The Colonel couldn't have been more wrong. In just over a week, he and the rest of Hodges's staff would be making a very hasty and undignified flight from the palatial surroundings of the Hôtel Britannique in Spa, abandoning their fine food to the delighted doughboys left behind to stave off the advance of *Obersturmbannführer* Peiper's panzers rushing toward them, apparently unstoppably.

4

But while German spies and soldiers slipped out of the West Wall to the south, the slogging match to the north still went on. As Giskes's escapees sneaked through the bunker line to fool the Americans, other Americans were sneaking through the positions of the green US 99th

Infantry Division holding the left flank of the 'Ghost Front,' their objective to launch a surprise attack on one of the most strongly defended spots in the Great Wall of Germany. The site picked for the initial breakthrough was a heavily defended crossroads deep in the Huertgen near Monschau which could only be approached from the twin Belgian villages of Rocherath and Krinkelt on the edge of the forest. It would go down in the history of that bloody struggle for the German frontier as 'Heartbreak Cross-roads.'

The weather was miserable as the men of the 2nd Infantry started their attack. Captain MacDonald, going into action for the very first time, recalled, 'We finally reached our destination, a giant fir forest three miles west of Elsenborn, at nine o'clock, half-frozen from a five-hour nightmare of cold snow and hazardous blackout driving. The men half jumped and half fell from the open trucks to the ice-covered road, cursing the misfortune which had subjected them to such an ordeal. We had plowed along snow-covered roads at break-neck speed, the drivers endeavoring to keep the tail light of the preceding vehicle in view, only to experience a period of freezing waiting while the convoy was held up. The snow had grown steadily deeper as we went further north until there was a foot of frozen whiteness covering the ground.'[16]

Now the lead regiment, the 9th, began to enter the uncanny stillness of the Monschau Forest. The road was known to be mined, so the doughs had to wade through the snowy underbrush on both sides. In places the snow was so deep that it oozed over the tops of their black felt overshoes. At 12:40, however, they reached the clearing near the crossroads and their commanding officer Colonel Hirschfelder reported, 'Both battalions have dropped packs . . . contact imminent.'[17]

Not a mile away, unknown to the freezing weary

Americans, another regiment was doing exactly the same, the only difference being that this one was clad in field-gray. They were the men of a *Volksgrenadier* Division, whose mission was to smash a hole in the 'Ami' line in order to open a gap for the giant Tigers and Panthers of the SS Armored Corps.

Now both groups hovered around the crossroads, neither as yet aware of each other, while Colonel Hirschfelder surveyed the position his men were going to attack.

It didn't look good. Indeed, to his experienced eye it looked like a damned small fortress. Grouped around the crossroads, there were four pillboxes, six concrete bunkers and two strengthened buildings, a forester's lodge and a customs house, all covered by anti-personnel mines which were hidden by the falling snow. If that wasn't bad enough, there were ten lines of rusting barbed wire and the ravines around the place formed a kind of moat. There was no way of springing a surprise on the place.

Now the Germans began to fire on the resting infantrymen. Hirschfelder reluctantly gave the order for the men of his 1st Battalion to start clearing the mines to the immediate front so that the rest of the battalion could pass. Whistles blew. Officers and NCOs bellowed orders above the roar of the German mortars and 88s. Miserably the first eight men of the 1st Battalion began to move out with the mine detectors. Not one of them would survive and by the time the attack on the crossroads was called off three days later, another 737 men would have suffered the same fate at that corner. The battle for Heartbreak Crossroads had commenced.

While the 2nd Infantry fought what was to turn out to be the last battle of the first campaign against the West Wall, further north the men of Simpson's Ninth Army were just finishing theirs.

For a whole month now the Ninth had been battling through the twin strongpoints of the Wall at Geilenkirchen and Wurselen heading for the River Roer. It had been a bitter, heart-breaking thirty days. As London *Sunday Times* correspondent R. W. Thompson described it in late November, 'Against a determined enemy, even without the very strong defenses in depth of the Siegfried Line, this hilly country mazed with its towns, villages, tall chimneys, slag-heaps and furnaces would be a nightmare.'

'It was not a matter of taking a township or a village and then pushing on,' Robert Barr of the BBC explained it to his listeners on December 3, 1944. 'It's a question of taking a village and digging in under fire until the villages on either side of you are taken – or until the whole line has been taken and then getting up from your waterlogged foxhole or from your cellar and crouching forward to the next line of villages with new names and with more cellars and more machine guns, and more snipers who are prepared to stay and die for the Fatherland.'[18]

For thirty days the men of the 29th, 30th and 104th Infantry Divisions plus gravel-voiced Ernest Harmon's 2nd Armored Division had been doing just what the BBC commentator described. Now the weary men of the 29th Infantry faced the last strongpoints that December: a hamlet of fortified farm buildings named Gut Hasenfeld and the local swimming pool alongside the River Roer facing the town of Juelich. These unlikely-looking mini-forts turned out, just like the ones at Heartbreak Crossroads, to be man-traps.

The Americans attacked at night across open country littered with anti-personnel mines. Second-Lieutenant Sears of the 116th Infantry, recalling that night, said, 'A man would hit a trip wire and there would be a click, then the mine would spring out of the ground and explode five or six feet in the air, spraying metal splinters.'[19] At the first sound of these exploding 'Bouncing Betties,' as they were called by the infantry, the enemy would open up with machine guns, mortars and heavy artillery. In an instant, night would be transformed into day as white, red and green tracer zipped back and forth and signal flares flushed the sky, a fiery shower of sparks and thick mushrooms of smoke erupting every time the ground was struck. It was no use attempting to drop. The soldier doing so ran the fearful risk of exploding another Bouncing Betty. Scared out of their wits, men would remain perfectly erect under intense shellfire rather than drop on the mines. As Colonel Reagor of the 116th related afterwards, 'Nothing was more feared than mines. They were insidious treacherous things hiding in the deep grass and in the earth.'[20]

For two days the men of the 29th tried to take Gut Hasenfeld, sometimes coming within a hundred yards of its walls before being driven back. Once the GIs thought they were going to be lucky as they advanced through a path cleared in the minefield. All was silent, the night inky black, the enemy obviously quite unaware of their presence. But not for long. Suddenly the moon scudded from behind the clouds to illuminate the battleground a bright, cruel silver. The German machine guns opened up at once and the GIs fled the way they had come, chased by tracer hissing after them like a flight of angry hornets.

By the morning of December 7th, a week later, Colonel Bingham commanding the 116th Infantry reported to General Gerhardt, the divisional commander, that his men were too exhausted to continue with any real hope of success. In six days, the Regiment had lost 250 men and it had already been understrength at the outset of the attack. Reluctantly General Gerhardt withdrew the battered 116th and replaced it with the 115th.

At last the Americans struck lucky. The staff of the 115th had examined the fire patterns of the defenders, and their analysis revealed that there was a blind spot to the northwest of Gut Hasenfeld where no enemy artillery fire had yet fallen. The 115th's Commander took a calculated risk. He sent in a company under the cover of a thick smokescreen. And the scheme paid off. They got through with hardly a casualty. Now exactly eighteen men went on alone. They found a hole in the high wall which surrounded the farm. Fearful but impelled to go on, the adventurous little group of GIs crawled through the hole to find the defenders cowering in their deep cellars while American artillery softened them up for the main attack. The eighteen didn't wait for the attack. They cried, 'All right, you sons of bitches, come on out!'

They re-emerged from their hole with eighty-five surprised German prisoners and with the knowledge that they had broken the back of the defense at Gut Hasenfeld.

The swimming pool strongpoint was next. By some strange stroke of fortune, a whole company got through the minefields without a casualty. Two sergeants took on a group of Germans with rifle grenades: the Germans surrendered. Then two giant 105mm howitzers rumbled up, daring German small-arms fire. Before them lay the swimming pool like a 'giant concrete foxhole.' The big guns started to pound the German position, chipping off huge chunks of concrete every time their shells struck home, setting the whole structure vibrating.

By late afternoon its surface was pocked by shellholes like the symptom of some loathsome skin disease. Now the infantry judged it was time to go in. Under the command of Staff Sergeant Daniel Menkovitz a platoon rushed the place through the thick acrid choking gunsmoke – and the swimming pool 'foxhole' surrendered docilely. It was all over at last.

Before the offensive had been launched, back in November Corps Commander General McLain had told General Gerhardt to get plenty of rest because 'when you go again it will be a long drive. Right into Berlin!'[21]

Now, thirty-odd days later, the Ninth Army had penetrated the West Wall to a depth of six to ten miles at a cost of 1,133 killed, 6,864 wounded and 2,059 missing, not to mention the thousands of non-battle casualties, victims of the pneumonia, the trenchfoot, the 'combat exhaustion,' always endemic, it seemed, in the battles along the Great Wall of Germany. And Berlin was still a good three hundred miles away.

5

Dawn on December 14th came slowly. A thin mist hung over the wet ground near the Wahlerscheid crossroads which men were already beginning to call Heartbreak Crossroads. Here and there men rose out of their foxholes, glad of the protection of the mist, to stretch their legs after another long night of cramp and cold. Others stayed in their holes heating K-ration cans with the cardboard boxes they came in. Some just squatted there apathetically, eyes glazed and unseeing. They were the ones who would soon start to scream and weep and break down. They were on the verge of that madness which the GIs euphemistically called 'section eight' and the Army head-shrinkers equally euphemistically entitled 'combat exhaustion.'

Back in the forest to the rear, as miserable and cold as

his men, Colonel Hirschfelder waited. The previous day had brought failure after failure. Now he hoped this new day would bring success. His poor men certainly needed it after a terrible night, drenched to the skin, their uniforms frozen to their trembling bodies.

From behind them came the first heavy rumble. The waiting staff officers could feel the forest floor tremble under their feet. The barrage had started. 'Incoming mail!' some optimist gave the customary cry, as the first US shells ripped the gray sky above their heads apart and came screaming down on the positions around Heartbreak Crossroads.

Whistles shrilled. Orders were bellowed. Like sleep-walkers, the weary men of the 2nd Division came out of their holes and started that slow heavy plod through the mud to their appointment with destiny, each wrapped in his personal cocoon of worries, fears, hopes, tensing his soft flesh for the first hard death-dealing blow of red-hot steel.

The machine guns in the pillboxes and the bunkers, somewhere in the mist ahead of them, rattled into action at once. As they stumbled into a run, some of the men were hit, sinking to the soaked grass. Their comrades did not look down. They never did. It would have been too much to have looked at that cruelly torn flesh, the wounds that bled like the dark-red juice of a squashed ripe fig, the entrails that crept from ripped open stomachs like obscene gray pulsating snakes, the severed arteries that jetted blood high into the air.

Now they were running all out. Fewer and fewer of them. To their front through the mist the machine guns screeched like a German MG 42 as they scythed the front with tracer, a thousand rounds per minute. And then abruptly, as if someone had closed a door, their courage went. In an instant, those who had survived were dropping to the ground already littered with the bodies of their comrades, furiously digging themselves into the earth – or running wildly for the rear, jostling and clawing at their buddies in their panic to escape that killing fire, their eyes wide with unreasoning, overwhelming fear.

All that long December day, Colonel Hirschfelder's men continued their attacks to the front, to the left flank, to the right flank, but the Germans holding the crossroads were not giving up easily. In forty-eight hours, their officers knew, the great counter-offensive would start which would transform the whole situation on the Western Front to Germany's advantage. They couldn't let their country down *now*.

By nightfall, a bitterly disappointed Hirschfelder called off his attack. It didn't make him any happier to receive a directive from his commander General Robertson that same night which stated bluntly, 'Base future operations on thorough reconnaissance, infiltration and finesse. Get deliberate picture, then act.'[22]

Squatting there in the dripping forest, eating hash out of a can with the rest of his officers, Hirschfelder didn't need a crystal ball to know that the directive was a reprimand. General Robertson was obviously not pleased with the way he had conducted his operations that day. He knew, too, something that Robertson didn't. There was no way up at the crossroads that he could employ 'infiltration and finesse.' The Krauts had everything sewed up tight. The next day, December 15th, would bring another slogging match, he knew that in his heart of hearts; there was no alternative.

But Colonel Hirschfelder was wrong.

On the afternoon of December 14th, an infantry squad had slipped under the German wire up at the crossroads. Behind them another squad had cut four narrow paths in it. None of this got back to their company; indeed, their company commander had just been wounded and evacuated by that time. In the end, the news that there was a breach in the wire only reached their battalion commander Lieutenant Colonel Higgins when the squads finally straggled back to their outfit twenty-four hours later.

By now, like every other senior officer in the 9th Infantry, Higgins was clutching at straws. He decided he'd use the four-foot-wide gap if he could. Soon after dark on December 15th, Higgins sent off an eleven-man patrol armed with a sound-powered phone to crawl through the gap and report on the enemy's strength and state of alertness.

The patrol was joined by one of the men who had cut the wire the previous day. He showed them the way and then at half-past nine that night, the power phone crackled to life and a tense expectant Higgins was electrified by the statement that the little patrol had *surrounded a German pillbox*! The Germans were not even aware that the Americans were there outside in the freezing darkness.

Higgins did not need a second invitation. Within minutes, two of his companies were making their way in single file through the gap, Higgins bringing up the second company personally. By midnight his battalion held a substantial bridgehead within the fortifications of Heartbreak Crossroads.

Another battalion silently followed them, again in single file, nearly 800 men moving through the freezing darkness like gray ghosts, tense and expectant, wondering how this impossible adventure would end.

Now the two battalions went into action. One moved northwest, the other northeast. Swiftly the men of the 2nd Infantry Division began to roll up the enemy positions which had frustrated them so long. Germans were taken still fast asleep. The customs house was captured with

The Great Wall of Germany is built. Here Hitler (in light-coloured coat) inspects a bunker in 1939. Note first Volkswagens in background

The troops move in 1939

Allied supply trucks at a beach in the Siegfried Line, September 1944

"Fat Hermann" Reichsmarschall Hermann Goering views Luxembourg from the bridge at Echternach, 1940. Five years later this would be the exact spot where Patton would attack the West Wall first in February 1945

American infantrymen pass a camouflaged pillbox

Five years late, but finally the washing was hung

An infantry attack on the Siegfried Line

Canadian troops watch a German woman heading for safety

The worst winter in Europe in living memory stops the advance

Still the Germans won't give in. "The Führer lives!" "Germany lives!" the painted slogans proclaim

February 1945. Now the Americans are over on the River Saver and are attacking the line everywhere, in strength. Patton displays his "War Face No. 2"

Last attacks on the West Wall in the Saar

Aerial view of Siegfried positions (the V's)

seventy-seven sleep-drunk prisoners. Pillbox after pillbox was successfully taken, the infantry employing all the new tools they had learnt to use at the West Wall – the Bangalore torpedo, the hollow charge, the beehive charge, the bazooka, the flame-thrower.

Two hours after dawn on December 16th, the job was over. Heartbreak Crossroads had been taken at last at a cost of one man killed, one missing and seventeen wounded; and the 38th Infantry Regiment was already beginning to move through the tired but happy infantry of the 9th on their way to their next assignment.

But that was not to be. For on the horizon to the south, strange pink flickers had begun to be observed and by dint of turning their heads into the icy wind which blew over the battle-littered crossroads, the doughs could hear the faint rumble of heavy artillery coming from that direction. Something was going on, something big. But what was it?

Captain MacDonald of the 2nd Infantry Division's 23rd Infantry Regiment, located to the rear of the green 99th Division through which his own was attacking, first knew that something very serious had happened on the morning of December 16th, when the 99th began to filter through the wooded heights to his front. There were perhaps two hundred of them and they weren't stopping. All they knew was that they had been hit hard by the Krauts that morning and had taken severe losses. Only two volunteered to stay with MacDonald's company and wait for the enemy to come across those somber brooding heights.

Nervous and apprehensive, for this might well be his first action, 22-year-old MacDonald called for covering fire. Now all along the 23rd's front frantic infantry commanders were calling for support and covering fire. Then it happened. 'Wave after wave of fanatically screaming German infantry stormed the slight tree-covered rise held by the three platoons. A continuous hail of fire exuded from their weapons, answered by volley after volley from the defenders. Germans fell right and left. The few rounds of artillery we did succeed in bringing down caught the attackers in the draw to our front, and we could hear their screams of pain when the small arms fire slackened. But they still came on!'[23]

Ammunition began to give out. MacDonald informed Battalion. He was told to 'hold at all costs.' MacDonald wondered if they knew what those words meant up at Battalion. 'We must hold until every last man was killed or captured. Company I's last stand! And what is to be gained? Nothing but time. Time born of the bodies of dead men. Time.'[24]

All about MacDonald's embattled positions 88mm shells started to explode as Tiger tanks, great white-painted monsters weighing over sixty tons, began to appear through the firs, knocking them over like skittles.

'For God's sake, Cap'n,' one of his platoon commanders sobbed over the phone, 'get those tanks down here. Do something for God's sake! These bastards are sitting seventy-five yards away pumping 88s into our foxholes like we were sitting ducks. *For God's sake!*'

But the supporting Shermans had already turned tail at the sight of the Tigers and scuttled to the rear.

'*Hold*, Long!' was all the encouragement MacDonald could offer the sobbing officer. 'For God's sake, hold. We've got to hold!'

But the time for holding was about over. Now men started to drift back with 'vague blank expressions' on their faces. MacDonald jumped from his hole, ignoring the bullets slapping into the trees all around him, and angrily waved them back to their positions. But he couldn't stop them. They wandered off to the rear, dazed and zombie-like.

Half an hour later the whole company was running for its life. 'Over the noise of Lopez's machine gun, I could hear Captain Wilson shouting to withdraw,' MacDonald recalled later. 'I wanted to obey, but I was caught in the cross-fire of the heavy machine gun and the attackers. I gritted my teeth and waiting for a lull in the fighting. None came. I jumped from the hole and ran blindly toward the rear. Bullets snipped at my heels. The tank saw we were running again and opened with renewed vigor, the big shells snapping the tops from the trees around us as if they were matchsticks, but I saw no one fall.'[25]

Dusk was approaching and MacDonald and his survivors knew they could not make Rocherath. They plunged blindly into the trees. 'I slipped and fell face down in the snow,' MacDonald remembered. 'I cursed my slick overshoes. I rose and fell again. I found myself not caring if the Germans did fire. My feet were soaked. My clothes were drenched. Perspiration covered my body, and my mouth was dry. I wanted a cigarette. I felt like we were helpless little bugs scurrying blindly about now that some man monster had lifted the log under which we had been hiding. I wondered if it would not be better to be killed and perhaps that would be an end to everything.'[26]

A lot of American soldiers felt like 'helpless little bugs' as the Germans emerged from the West Wall all along the 'Ghost Front' that Saturday. The green divisions, the 99th and 106th Infantry, were hit and broke, just as did the veterans of the 28th. Colonel Mark Devine of the 14th Cavalry Group departed his command with most of his staff, leaving his 1,600 men to fend for themselves up at the Losheim Gap through which the SS armor would soon be rolling. Later he was relieved of his command as were most of his staff officers. The men of the 106th, the newest Allied division in the line, went to ground and simply let it

The First Attack
December 16, 1944

GERMAN ATTACKS
FORTIFIED HEDGEHOGS
Lanzerath Krewinkel Roth Merlscheid
Berterath and Kobscheid

to Monschau
to Büllingen
and Liège

Losheim
Allmuthen
Lanzerath   Afst   3rd PARA
14th Cavalry
Manderfeld
Devine

BELGIUM

Herresbach
Andler
Auw   18th Volksgrenadier
Roth

GERMANY
N

to St Vith
Schoenberg
422 Infantry Regt   Schlausenbach
Descheneaux

Lascheid

miles
kms

423 Infantry Regt
Bleialf   to Prum
18th Volksgrenadier

happen. Tragedy was in the making.[27] Its supply troops and the canteen commandos did even less. They turned and fled. As Colonel Dupuy, historian of the ill-fated division, wrote later: 'Let's get down to hard facts. Panic, sheer unreasoning panic, flamed that road all day and into the night. Everyone, it seemed, who had any excuse, and many who had none, was going west that day – west from Schoenberg, west from St Vith, too. Jeeps, trucks, tanks, guns and great limbering Corps Artillery vehicles which took three-quarters of the road – some of them double-banking. Now and again vehicles were weaving into a third line, now and again crashing into ditches. All this on a two-line highway. And this was what the 7th Armored Division [ordered up from Holland to St Vith] was bucking as it drove – practically the only eastbound element to get from Vielsalm to St Vith.'

The feelings of the average civilian soldier, caught up in the enormous war machine which had dumped him in this remote frontier country just in time for the surprise blood-letting, might best be expressed in the words of Mel Brooks, the Jewish comic, actor and movie-maker, who described his own brief experience of the fighting. 'Then one day they put us all in trucks, drove us to the railroad station, put us in a locked train with the windows blacked out. We get off the train, we get on a boat. We get off the boat, we get into trucks. We get out of the trucks, we start walking. Suddenly all around us, *Waauhwaahwaauh*! Sirens! Tiger Tanks! We're surrounded by the Germans. It's the Battle of the Bulge! Hands up! "Wait," I say. "We just left Oklahoma! We're Americans! We're supposed to win!" *Very* scary, but we escaped . . . And then *they* started shooting. "Incoming mail!" Bullshit! Only Burt Lancaster says that. We said, "Oh God, Oh Christ!" Who knows, he might help. He was Jewish, too. "MOTHER!"'[28]

* * *

As dusk descended on the Western Front that day, far away at Supreme Headquarters in Versailles General Eisenhower was discussing the all-important problem of replacements for the infantry with General Bradley and the staff.

That Saturday had been an easy one for Eisenhower. Montgomery had written to ask for Christmas leave in England. Ever since his boy's mother had died just before the war, the boy had been attending boarding schools, spending his holidays with a friend (a retired major) and his wife. Now as the whole front was dead, Montgomery wanted Ike's permission to pass Christmas with the child. He also reminded Ike he had wagered him that the war would be over by Christmas. Could he have his 'fiver' now, he asked.

Eisenhower had remarked jokingly to his PR man Lieutenant Commander Butcher, a former radio executive, 'I'll pay, but not before Christmas. He can let me have these nine days.'

Later that morning Eisenhower had gone to the wedding of his servant Mickey, a former bell-boy, at the chapel of the Château of Versailles. Mickey, who wrote a personal letter each week to Mrs Eisenhower to tell her how her husband was getting on (though naturally he did not tell her everything), harbored the private ambition to become a saloon-keeper after the war. During the ceremony he wondered what his new bride, Pearlie, a former history teacher and now a WAC corporal, would say if he told her. So far he had not yet dared to tell even his boss.

After the wedding Eisenhower had given a reception for the happy young couple. There had been champagne, a cake and Eisenhower had kissed the bride. Then at two o'clock the vital replacement conference commenced, after Bradley had congratulated Ike on being the first US general since 'Black Jack' Pershing in the old war to receive a fifth star, which had been granted him the previous day by Congress.

Bradley explained that his Army Group lacked 19,000 riflemen. Most divisions were going into action with only three-quarters of their allotment of frontline infantry. In the First Army alone there had been 60,000-odd casualties in the firing line of only twelve miles in length. The situation was urgent. They had to find 'new bodies' from somewhere.

About four o'clock on the gray winter afternoon with the sky taking on the leaden hue that indicated snow after dark, Brigadier General Betts appeared at the door and asked in a whisper if he could speak to his boss, Ike's Chief-of-Intelligence, Brigadier Ken Strong, a tall, very dark Scot who spoke German fluently and was an expert on the country (before the war he had been tempted to marry a German girl, but nothing had come of it).

Betts, 'normally a calm, phlegmatic man,' looked shaken. He had reason to. He brought bad news from the 'Ghost Front.' He whispered the little he knew to Strong, who nodded his understanding and returned swiftly. 'Gentlemen,' Strong announced solemnly, 'this morning the enemy counter-attacked at five separate points across the First Army sector.'[29]

The cozy little world of Versailles fell apart that afternoon. Ike's Chief-of-Staff, hot-tempered, red-haired General Bedell Smith, reacted angrily, telling Bradley he had been warned about this thinness of his troop concentrations on the 'Ghost Front'; hadn't Strong gone personally to warn him only the other week, and been laughed at for his fears?

Bradley blustered a little, saying, 'The other fellow knows that he must lighten the pressure Patton has built up against him [he meant the Third Army attack against the West Wall in the Saar]. If by coming through the

Ardennes he can force us to pull Patton's troops out of the Saar and throw them against his counter-offensive, he'll get what he's after. And that's just a little more time.'

Eisenhower wasn't impressed by Bradley's words. 'This is no local attack, Brad,' he snapped. 'It's not logical for the Germans to launch a local attack at our weakest point.'

'If it's not a local attack,' Bradley persisted, 'what kind of an attack is it?'

Ike shrugged. 'That remains to be seen. But I don't think we can afford to sit on our hands until we've found out.'

'What do you think we should do then?' Bradley asked, obviously realizing that he was no longer so popular at Supreme Headquarters; he had got the big brass into trouble and just before Christmas too.

'Send Middleton[30] some help,' Eisenhower answered. 'About two armored divisions.'

'I suppose that would be safer,' Bradley mused thoughtfully. 'Of course, you know one of those divisions will have to come from Patton?'

'So?' Eisenhower demanded, his face like thunder.

'So – Georgie won't like losing a division a few days before his big attack on the Saar,' Bradley answered, not reading the storm warning correctly.

'You tell him,' Eisenhower snapped angrily, 'that Ike is running this damned war!'[31]

Thus the conference broke up on a note of rancor and recrimination which would be typical of the next six weeks, the top brass leveling accusations and counter-accusations at each other, trying to allot the blame for the fiasco in the far-off Ardennes where riflemen were now dying in their thousands in the shadow of that Great Wall of Germany.

* * *

The German counter-attack in the Ardennes, soon to be named 'the Battle of the Bulge' by Winston Churchill, marked the end of the first campaign against the West Wall. Since September 13th, it had taken nearly one million fighting men to penetrate it at half a dozen spots from Geilenkirchen up north opposite Holland in the British sector, around Aachen in the American sector and then further south in the Saar opposite France.

At the most they had not gone deeper than twenty miles, near Juelich, and had conquered a length of it not much more than thirty miles between the *Huertgenwald* and Aachen, still not wide enough for a really powerful thrust to the Rhine. And the cost in human life and misery had been prohibitive.

During this first campaign, the US First Army lost 7,024 men killed, 35,155 wounded and missing and some 4,860 captured. The Ninth Army's battle losses were 1,133 killed, 6,864 wounded and missing and another 2,059 captured. To this must be added another 11,000 American casualties suffered by outfits serving under the British and Canadians, bringing the total US losses in Germany to some 68,000 men. In addition there were another 50,867 non-battle casualties in the First Army and 20,787 in the Ninth. In the Saar and West Wall fighting Patton's Third Army lost 64,956 men, both battle and non-battle casualties. A grand total for the three and a bit months' fighting was therefore two hundred thousand men, the population of a medium-sized city.

Basically the Germans had dominated the battle the whole way through, just as they had brought it to an end. Though Model had never held the initiative and had been on the defensive until December 16th, he had determined its outcome, defending the West Wall with meager and second-rate forces while he had built up the forces for the attack into the Ardennes. The first campaign against the

West Wall had inflicted grievous losses on Model's armies too.[32] Yet it was the German soldier who had come out fighting after ninety-six days of siege, and it was the American soldier who had fallen back on Saturday, December 16th, 1944.

Whose victory?

That December the men in field-gray and olive drab slogging it out in the woods of the Ardennes did not care. They had other things on their mind, such as survival. And on the heights now covered with thick snow, the Great Wall of Germany rested for a while, the fight taking place elsewhere now, rested and waited. For the young men in khaki would come again. Of that, there was no doubt.

Book Two: 1945

'Gentlemen, let us all urinate on the great West Wall of Germany!'

Winston Churchill, March 3, 1945

January

1

All that night and early into the morning of Tuesday, January 16, 1945, the men of the two American armies had been fighting their way to the little Belgian border town of Houffalize, the funnel through which ran the last German escape route out of the Ardennes.

Now the men of Hodges's First Army and Patton's Third fought to make the link-up and have done with the bloody Battle of the Bulge for good. For thirty-one long days they had waged war in the worst conditions Europe had known for a quarter of a century. The weather had been consistently bleak, the ground covered by a thick blanket of coarse snow. In the constant sub-zero temperatures the infantry plodded forward, their faces like leather, tanned a brick-red by the howling wind filled with razor-sharp particles of frozen snow. As for the tanks, they slid and skidded on the roads, freed of snow by the bulldozers only to be turned into sheets of solid ice.

Now Houffalize was being pounded by Britain's latest secret weapon: the proximity fuse, a radar-directed shell with unprecedented accuracy and deadly effect.

Desperately Model struggled to hold the little town.

After fighting hard with Hitler for permission to withdraw his armor east of the Ardennes, he finally had it, and in the last five days he had made the 'Amis' pay a heavy price for their attempts to take Houffalize. They were advancing, admittedly, but at a rate of only one mile a day.

British war correspondent and former army captain R. W. Thompson, following up the advance, noted the beauty of the snow-covered Ardennes hill, but he also noted that 'with every mile forward this loveliness becomes a menace and a horror to fight with all the energy each man can muster . . . Up every hill the troops are manhandling the heavy trucks trying to gain a wheel grip even with chains. Here and there the tracked vehicles slither hopelessly to subside deep into the ditches . . . But all the time bulldozers are working, clearing and breaking up the snow and ice to powder, and civilians are smashing away with picks and shovels while every man with a spade digs down to the earthy roadside banks beneath the snow to shovel soil for the wheels that must grip . . . their ears blasted by the constant shock as the heavy guns roar and splash this white world with bursts of flame.'[1]

But now it was almost over at Houffalize. The Germans knew they could not hold out any longer. They set to, destroying or disabling what armor they couldn't take with them, draining the engine oil and running the engines, throwing sugar in the petrol tanks of the trucks, or running lines of petrol-soaked lavatory paper into the open tanks – a match, a *whoosh* and the truck was burning merrily. They pulled the firing pins out of the breech blocks of abandoned cannon and smashed them; they sowed booby traps under easy chairs, in the doors of pantries, behind family portraits. Then one by one they slunk back the way they had come so triumphantly that December 16th, back into the hills and the waiting West Wall.

Now Captain Herbert Foye's men of the 41st Cavalry Squadron of the 11th Armored Division, which belonged to Patton's Third Army, and Colonel Hinds's 41st Armored Infantry Regiment, of the division which before the war Patton himself had commanded, the 2nd 'Hell on Wheels' Division from Hodges's First Army, started to steal cautiously into Houffalize.

Watching from above on the heights, Thompson described the scene thus. 'This morning infantry patrols edging forward from Mabompre entered the town in a silence that was truly of the grave. There was that kind of vacuum that seems to grip a place in the first moments: the enemy have gone; all that remains is dead; and there is this terrible silence that is as eerie as any sensation I know.'[2]

Thompson followed the troops down the steep road into the newly captured town, noting 'the ice deep in the gorge, the shattered trunks of the trees, the icicles veiling the outcropping rocks, the awful carcasses of homes shattered beyond all hope', to stop at the sight of the first human being.

Between the rubble which formed the street came an old man leaning on a stick, 'the saddest, most utterly hopeless sight I can remember,' wrote Thompson. 'My daughter lived here,' the old man said, indicating the wrecked house, its rubble covered with snow, the upper floor ripped open in all its pathetic domesticity. Then his eyes moved away and he plodded 'slowly on from this emptiness to an even greater emptiness of life.'

The First and Third US Armies had linked up. The line was whole again. Officially the Battle of the Bulge was over.

That afternoon Patton and his driver Sergeant Mims set off along the icy roads from his headquarters in

Luxembourg to view the newly liberated township on the border. Thirty-one days before, he and Mims had been setting off for the Ardennes to fight a battle where the whole front had crumbled and the Germans had seemed unstoppable. Now Patton was the general who had restored the front in the south. *He* had fought the battle, not Bradley, who many thought privately had been responsible for the débâcle in the Ardennes. Occasionally, brooding over the events of that first week of the battle in his tactical headquarters, Bradley tried to intervene in the running of the Third, the sole army left to him (he had lost his First and Ninth to Montgomery who ran the front in the north). But Patton was having none of it. Twice Patton turned down his chief's suggestions because they indicated the 'inadvisability of commanding from too far back.' Ironically, their positions had been reversed. In Sicily, after he had slapped a shell-shocked soldier, the resultant scandal had cost Patton his army command and the chance to lead the US armies in Europe. But now he was the boss again and Bradley little better than the subordinate he had once been.

The drive to Houffalize, which turned out to be 'extremely well liberated,' as Patton phrased it later, developed into more than just a sightseeing tour. At one point he ordered Mims to stop to pick up a German machine-gunner apparently wanting to surrender, his arms outstretched. When Mims spoke to the man, he didn't respond. Mims touched him and he fell over. He had been frozen stiff immediately he had been hit by the American slug, his outstretched hands still holding a belt of cartridges for the MG 42.

A little after this unnerving experience, Patton ordered his driver to halt again so that they could investigate what appeared to be a line of black twigs sticking up above the surface of the snow. They turned out to be the toes of soldiers whose boots had been removed after they had been hit. It was 'a nasty sight,' Patton, as hard-boiled as he made himself out to be, recalled to his staff later. The last action of the Battle of the Bulge had been fought in a giant refrigerator, it seemed, which turned the dead the color of old claret.

That afternoon, however, after congratulating his men, Patton did not indulge in the sentimentalities of Bradley who wrote of Houffalize: 'Simple, poor and unpretentious, the village had offended no one. Yet it was destroyed simply because it sat astride an undistinguished road junction. This road junction had made it more a strategic objective than cities fifty times its size.'[3] For Patton the capture of Houffalize and the end of the Battle of the Bulge signified the completion of a tremendous phase in his military career in Europe.

At midnight on December 19th, alarmed by the progress of the German drive into the Ardennes, Eisenhower, in a surprise move, had placed the First and Ninth US Armies under the command of Field Marshal Montgomery, who took over the First as if he were 'Christ come to cleanse the temple,' as one irreverent young officer put it.

On that same day, however, in Verdun, Eisenhower had ordered Patton to break off his attack against the West Wall in the Saar and turn about to bolster up the southern flank of the US Army. He had done so brilliantly and had gained tremendous publicity back in the States through his relief of the beleaguered Belgian city of Bastogne.

But what was to happen now? The Battle of the Bulge was over. Would Patton be relegated again to some sideshow while Montgomery, his rival, got an opportunity to win newspaper headlines?

In spite of his profanity and his apparent coarseness,

General Patton was a man with a great sense of history and his own place in it. He was a glory-hunter, the stuff that military heroes are made of, and he wanted to be remembered as a great American warrior for all time to come. He paid none of the conventional lip-service to the theory touted by other generals that war was a terrible thing which they were reluctantly forced by circumstances to take part in. Patton reveled in it.

Once, traveling through war-torn Brittany with his aide, Colonel Codman, Patton ordered the latter to stop. Together they had surveyed 'the rubbled farms and bordering fields scarred with grass fires, smoldering ruins and the swollen carcasses of stiff-legged cattle.' 'Just look at that, Codman,' Patton shouted. 'Could anything be more magnificent?' A battery of heavy guns opened up nearby and cupping his hands around his mouth, Patton roared, 'Compared to war all other forms of human endeavor shrink to insignificance.' His voice shook with emotion. '*God, how I love it!*'[4]

Viewing the sights that icy afternoon in ruined Houffalize, stopping here and there to praise the frozen GIs who had achieved the historic link-up as the last of the field-grays, ragged, starving and beaten, staggered back to the safety of the West Wall, Patton must have been asking himself the question, '*What now?*'

Patton was not the only general who was considering his personal future that day. Relegated to the role of a spectator by the events of December 19th, in his Hotel Alpha headquarters in Luxembourg, Bradley was in reflective mood. Since then he had, it seemed, received one body-blow after another. Patton was no longer taking orders from him. Eisenhower had decorated him over Christmas and recommended him for promotion to Washington as a face-saving operation. But he knew that all of them – General Strong, Bedell Smith, Montgomery, Patton, perhaps even Hodges and Simpson – thought him responsible for the fiasco on the 'Ghost Front.'

Then, at the beginning of January, *Time* magazine had betrayed the secret that Montgomery was in real command in the Ardennes, that the British Field Marshal was controlling more American troops than any American general. US public opinion wanted to know why. On January 7th, Montgomery had taken it upon himself to reveal to SHAEF press correspondents, who would then transmit his words back to the States, what had happened since December 19th.

It was an unfortunate decision, for the way Montgomery's words were interpreted by Bradley and his fellow American generals would confuse and embitter Anglo-American military relations to the end of the campaign in Europe and ensure that the whole direction of the battle for the West Wall to come would change – with disastrous results for Central Europe.

The skinny little Britisher, with his rather prissy voice and typical upper-class difficulty in pronouncing the letter 'r,' tending to make it sound like a 'w,' commenced his talk to the correspondents in that apparently innocent manner of his which was always so offensive to his American critics. 'The battle has been most interesting; I think possibly one of the most interesting and tricky battles I have ever handled, with great issues at stake. The first thing to be done was to head the enemy from the tender spots and vital places. Having done that successfully, the next thing was to seal him off, i.e. rope him in and make quite certain that he could not get the places he wanted.'[5]

Thereafter he went on to praise the American soldier, laud Anglo-American staffwork and pledge his renewed support for General Eisenhower. Then the interview was over. Monty had had his little triumph. He'd got his name in the headlines again, shown what a fine fellow he was and indirectly rubbed the American generals' noses lightly in the dirt. The correspondents hurried away to file their interview.

One of those correspondents was Chester Wilmot, a stocky Australian who later would become one of Montgomery's greatest defenders. Wilmot's report of the talk, broadcast on the BBC, was picked up by the German-run Radio Arnhem. Hurriedly doctored and slightly rewritten and broadcast at once, it was *this* report of Montgomery's celebrated talk which was received at Bradley's headquarters. Unfortunately, the staff officers who heard it took the doctored version for the original BBC broadcast. The result was immediate and drastic.

Colonel Hansen, Colonel Ingersoll, a former newspaper editor himself, and Major Munson burst into Bradley's office. 'You've got to get something on record,' Hansen said excitedly to the Commanding General, 'that tells the whole story of this changeover in command. Until you do so the American people will have nothing to go on except Montgomery's statement . . . They do not realize that you had the situation pretty well in hand when the change came three days later' (i.e. when Montgomery took control of the First and Ninth Armies).[6]

Hansen then handed Bradley a copy of the *Washington Post*, then as now a crusading paper. In its editorial it asked for the truth about the Ardennes reversal, maintaining that the 'American people need an authoritative interpretation of what the Rundstedt offensive is all about.'

That did it. Bradley decided to issue a statement himself. However, as he says in his own memoirs, he was worried about putting 'Ike on the spot' by not asking for Eisenhower's permission to make it.

'But you have a precedent,' Ingersoll insisted. 'After all, Montgomery spoke to the press yesterday.'

'Yes, but – ' Bradley began.

Ingersoll cut him short. 'Do you think that Montgomery cleared his interview with Eisenhower?'

'You know darned well he didn't,' Bradley agreed firmly.

One day later, therefore, Bradley issued his own statement in which he maintained that the handing over of command to Montgomery was only 'a temporary measure.' He confidently asserted that 'when the lines are rejoined, 12th Army Group will resume command of all American troops in this area.'[7]

Now the fat was in the fire. What was Eisenhower to do? After his triumph in the Ardennes, when he had helped to save the US front, Montgomery was now pressing for a single decisive thrust in the north through the West Wall and into the heart of the Reich. But Montgomery had only fifteen divisions. To achieve the desired result he'd need the sizable portion of troops from Bradley's Army Group presently under his command. But if he supported Montgomery, Eisenhower knew he'd face a bad press back home and since wars were always in public thanks to the media, generals, especially American ones, had a great deal of respect for the press. There was the question of Bradley, too. Might he not be regarded as a scapegoat, a sign that US leadership had failed?

A day or two later Bradley and Eisenhower met to discuss the problem. When Bradley raised the issue directly, Eisenhower tried to fob him off with 'a reassuring reply.'

Bradley wasn't buying it. As he told Eisenhower, 'After what has happened I cannot serve under Montgomery. If he is to be put in command of all ground forces, you must send me home, for if Montgomery goes in over me, I will have lost the confidence of my command.'

Ike flushed, stiffening in his chair. 'Well, I thought you were the one person I could count on for doing anything I asked you to do,' he said.

'You can, Ike,' Bradley replied. 'I've enjoyed every bit of my service with you. But this is the one thing I cannot take.'[8]

Several days before, Bradley had sounded Patton out on the question of what his reaction would be if Montgomery came in as supreme commander of all ground forces. Patton had clasped him by the arm and had said emotionally, 'If you quit, Brad, then *I'll* be quitting with you!'

Assured now that if Montgomery came in, there would be one devil of a scandal, with Eisenhower right in the middle of it, playing the 'best general the British had' (as Patton maintained cynically) and favoring a British commander to the detriment of not only one but *two* senior American generals, Bradley left Eisenhower to make the decisions. They were: where would the main attack on the West Wall go through, and who would lead that main attack?

So it was that as Patton ordered Mims to drive him on further to the rear to decorate two American commanders for bravery, the decisions were being made in far-off Versailles which would ensure that he achieved his immortal glory – *and that the fate of Central Europe would be settled for the rest of the twentieth century!*

Earlier on, that January 16th, Montgomery had launched the first attack of the second campaign against the West Wall. He had picked as his place of attack a triangular section of Germany, roughly twenty miles long on each side, called the Heinsberg salient, defended by the three main lines of defense as off-shoots of the West Wall. The first comprised a continuous line of trenches and weapon pits with trip wires and mines in front and some reserve positions about half a mile to the rear. The second lay two miles behind the first. The third extended from the West Wall to the small town of Heinsberg and a short distance beyond. The whole formidable system was held by two infantry divisions, supported by 156 guns and 18 assault guns.

It would not be an easy position to crack, although Montgomery had one armored division, two infantry divisions and a commando brigade at his disposal. But the Field Marshal was confident. His armored division and the 43rd Infantry Division were veterans which had fought since D-Day, and although his 52nd Lowland Division and the 1st Commando Brigade were fighting their first action in Germany, they were tough, reliable troops.

The 'Jocks,' as they liked to call themselves, of the 52nd Lowland Division had spent most of the war in Scotland training for mountain warfare. The Invasion came and went and they were still training. General Hakewill-Smith appealed to Montgomery for a role for his division. He didn't receive one. It was rumored that once Montgomery had learned Hakewill-Smith had not been one of his students in the thirties when Montgomery had been an instructor at staff college, he had no longer been interested in the General and his 'mountain men.' Arnhem came. Hakewill-Smith volunteered to fly in his 52nd to support the hard-pressed paratroopers. Again he was turned down. Then in October, after four years of waiting, the 52nd Division went into action – not in the mountains of Norway as they had anticipated but at the lowest point of Europe, *the Dutch coast*!

The Jocks' casualties had been heavy, but the 52nd, in

comparison with Montgomery's other divisions, still had a large number of its original members within its ranks; and they were tough. They did not subscribe to the nice 'fair play' tradition of Montgomery's home county divisions from the south of England. These 'ladies from hell,' as the Germans had called them in World War One on account of their kilts, were small men, products of the Depression in the industrial cities of central Scotland and the north of England, who had survived the years 'on the dole' with threepenny bags of fish and chips and 'penny ducks'[9] and peas. The Army and the exceedingly hard winter training in the remote glens and mountains of northern Scotland had filled them out, given them brawn and muscle; but the Army had not been able to break the vicious, trigger-sharp temper of these Celts, many of whom could have been taken for Frenchmen on account of their stature and dark looks.

Once, for instance, when Colonel Lindsay of the Gordon Highlanders was going for a walk in the woods behind the line that January, he came across Sergeant B, lighting a wood fire underneath a dead and frozen Hun strung up to the branch of a tree. He was trying to thaw him out, in order to take off his boots. 'Personally,' Colonel Lindsay commented, 'I have found the Army boots quite adequate, but most people seem to think that the type which goes up to the knee is warmer.'

If a prisoner didn't surrender quick enough to the Jocks, he did not get a second chance. Then the official report to Battalion would read, 'no prisoners taken.' When they were drunk on looted schnapps, they were almost impossible to restrain. Once a drunken squad of the 52nd Reconnaissance Regiment were viewed playing soccer in a minefield, so carried away by the alcohol that they forgot all danger.

The other new boys facing the West Wall that January

had last gone into action in that same flat stretch of Holland where they had taken fifty percent casualties, and they were equally tough. The men of the 1st Commando Brigade had been in action since 1940, unlike the 52nd, raiding the coast of Europe from the Arctic Circle in the north right down to the Gironne in the south of France. Unlike the 52nd, too, they had learnt to control their tempers in the process, training themselves to deliver their attacks at the most unexpected moment. Their commanding officer's maxim was: 'React quickly on first contact with the enemy and hold your fire until you can be certain to kill.' These then were the two outfits which would bear the brunt of the first battle of the second campaign against the Great Wall of Germany.

The attack went in through thick milky-white fog at seven thirty that morning, the Jocks clad in their camouflage smocks, bayonets fixed, wading through it in silent waves, waiting for the first high-pitched hysterical screech of the Spandau machine gun.

It came soon enough, with the same old startling effect that made even the veterans jump. Now as the Jocks of the 4/5th Royal Scots Fusiliers began to cross the first stream and scramble up the high bank on the other side, protected by barbed wire and mines, German MGs opened up from the houses to their front. The Jocks were galvanized into violent action. They doubled forward, great gaps appearing in their white-clad lines.

Fusilier Dennis Donnini, the nineteen-year-old son of an Italian ice-cream merchant from northern England who had never been naturalized and had already lost one son in battle, was hit in the head and fell to the frozen ground. But the young Fusilier, who had been in the Army only seven months, regained consciousness a few moments later. He struggled to his feet, staggered down the road for thirty yards, pouring with blood, and lobbed an egg-grenade through the shattered window of the nearest house. It exploded with a muffled crump, thick black smoke pouring from the window. The survivors fled in panic deeper into the pillbox line.

Donnini and the few survivors of his decimated platoon ran on. They crossed a field under intense machine-gun fire. Leathern-lunged and panting frantically, they flung themselves into a barn less than a hundred feet from the Germans' main trenches. While the others collapsed in the cover, Donnini, weakening visibly, ducked out and brought in a wounded Jock. Still he wasn't done. He seized a Bren light machine gun and charged the trenches, firing from the hip. He was hit again and dropped to one knee, still firing. Somehow, with the last of his strength, he got to his feet again and went on firing until finally a German stick grenade, flung when he was only ten yards from the trenches, exploded immediately in front of him. He went down, Bren gun dropping from his nerveless fingers, legs collapsing like those of a newly born foal, the front of his young body ripped to pieces by the grenade. He was later awarded Britain's highest honor, the Victoria Cross. Posthumously.

Donnini wasn't the only soldier to earn the Victoria Cross during that first battle of the West Wall in 1945. After crossing a stream and attacking the first fortified positions on the other side, the Commandos were pinned down by intense enemy fire at the village of St Joostburg. They lay in the snow, hardly able to move as their ranks were swept by machine-gun fire, their wounded lying with them.

Lance-Corporal Harden of the Royal Army Medical Corps volunteered to bring in the wounded. Running across 120 yards of fire-swept open ground, he bandaged the wounds of two Commandos and an officer. Then he proceeded to drag the most seriously wounded soldier back with the slugs ripping up the snow all around him. He was hit in the side, but carried on until finally he reached safety.

One of the sweating medical officers, already working frantically to cope with the wounded, ordered him not to expose himself again. Harden refused the order. He took volunteer parties of stretcher-bearers to bring in the wounded twice, weakening noticeably all the time. On his third trip, carrying back a wounded officer, he was hit in the head and went down for good. He, too, was posthumously awarded the Victoria Cross.

The advance went on. The first line of defenses was taken. Then the second. The Commandos fighting their way through the massed, confused positions, found themselves completely lost. The only prisoner they had was of no use. He revealed nothing of his comrades' positions. Repeating it like a litany, all he would say was, '*I wish to die for the Führer . . . I wish to die for the Führer . . .*' Whether his wish was fulfilled is not recorded in the Commandos' history. They blundered on through the gunsmoke and fog, tracer zig-zagging confusingly everywhere like flights of angry hornets in the shattered houses.

Medical Officer Captain Moore found his way into a tiny cellar, where in the guttering flame of a stump of candle he could see a filthy confusion of 'old and withered people huddled together under ragged sheets and blankets.' Some were German, some were Dutch brought over the border to work in the fields – and one was well advanced in pregnancy. Indeed, the young Dutch worker was about to give birth. Forgetting the battle raging all around him, Captain Moore set to work to deliver a 'tiny Dutch boy,' while mortar bombs landed all around and his orderlies handed over their greatcoats to 'keep the poor girl warm.'[10]

The Germans were everywhere in the chaos. Commando

Wheeler, left behind in a cellar to hold the newly captured strongpoint while the rest of his comrades were out on patrol, was suddenly confronted with half a dozen shadowy figures. In the dim light he could just make out they were wearing coal-scuttle helmets, not the Commandos' green beret. Wheeler reasoned immediately that his pals were trying to play a joke on him. 'You can't frighten me, yer silly buggers!' he called out.

'Can't we?' a voice called back in German-accented English.

One moment later Wheeler was a prisoner-of-war.

Further up the line, a jeep containing three Commandos ran into the German positions in the dark and was brought to a sudden and frightening halt by a steel wire stretched across the narrow road. Corporal Selby, the driver, reacted in true Commando fashion, swinging the jeep around before the Germans could react. He was unlucky. A mine exploded right beneath the jeep. Its rear axle shattered. Selby was flung out, his leg fractured, one shoulder badly injured.

Commando Connolly fled into the darkness, chased by German machine-gun fire. Later that night, half exhausted, he reached his own lines and asked for Selby. But Selby had not turned up. Neither did he turn up on the following day. He was posted 'missing, believed dead.'

Two and a half days later, a sentry reported 'a figure crawling on the road half-way between the two front lines.'[11]

It was Selby, blood-stained and terribly emaciated, an improvised tourniquet wrapped around his injured leg. He had spent over sixty hours out in that sub-zero weather, without food, water or shelter, and during that time he had been severely wounded. All the same he had observed the enemy positions as he had crawled back to his own lines, and he insisted on reporting them to

Intelligence before finally he received the blessing of a morphia shot and the boon of oblivion.

Now the 1st Commando Brigade was facing the strongly fortified switch running east and west just north of the village of Linne, and forming part of the West Wall defenses around the town of Roermond.

The attack on the position was carefully planned, as it always was with the Commandos. A detachment of the Inter-Allied Commando, the unit's 'Foreign Legion' as the British members called it humorously, would attack over the River Meuse in assault boats and make for 'Bell Island,' so named because of its shape. They would drag their boats across the island on sledges through the snow and continue to the other side. While all this was going on, the main party would make their assault, hopefully without being detected.

Under the command of Captain Griffiths, a German-born Jew,[12] a man 'who was without fear . . . and revelled in danger,' the Inter-Allied Commando set off moving through a landscape white and sparkling under the brilliant moon.

The river was running at six and a half knots, due to the winter rains, but Griffiths' 'Foreign Legion' crossed successfully. But they were spotted on Bell Island. A violent fire-fight erupted. Casualties were high. Griffiths abandoned the action and fighting his way back to the boats managed to get his survivors back to his own lines, some of the Commandos swimming through the icy torrent or hanging onto the side of the boats, with the tracer zipping everywhere. As cool as ever, Griffiths brought back with him a map of the German positions. He had taken it from the dead body of a German officer, while under intense fire. It would help the Commandos in their next attack.

* * *

Meanwhile the Jocks were closing steadily on their final objective: Heinsberg. On January 24th they were in the open fields outside the village, after thirty hours of solid shelling and mortaring from the West Wall positions. B Company of the King's Own Scottish Borderers in the lead were caught by heavy shellfire west of the town. Major Hogg, the Company Commander, was badly wounded. Before he passed out he asked for a smokescreen to conceal his trapped men, who were completely in the open. The gunners asked for instructions, but by then B Company's communications were beginning to break down. The Company Sergeant-Major was badly hit. He was followed by the second-in-command who was killed by a mortar bomb. Communications collapsed altogether.

Then suddenly a clear, calm Scottish voice cut through the static of the gunners' radio. Lance-Corporal Alexander Leitch, the sole surviving NCO at company headquarters and quite alone in the smoking ruins of the bunker, was calling for covering fire. His request granted, the survivors were able to withdraw from the trap.

Finally help arrived at Leitch's bunker in the shape of stretcher-bearers who were going to evacuate the wounded. Just as they were preparing to leave, Leitch asked whether they would be coming back again.

The medics asked why.

As calm as ever, Leitch said, 'I think I have been wounded in both legs.'

In fact, just before he had radioed the gunners for covering fire, Leitch had been hit by shell fragments in both legs, one being nearly severed, the other badly mangled.

Half an hour later the King's Own Scottish Borderers followed the Royal Scots into Heinsberg.

For once an attack by an Allied force on the Great Wall

of Germany had ended successfully, without a tremendous blood-letting, the Jocks losing eleven hundred men, a mere nothing in comparison with the slaughter of the previous campaign.

The British were jubilant. Brigadier Essame of the 43rd Division, which had also played a part in the attack, wrote later, 'By the end of January, the Army whose spirits had sagged somewhat in October at the prospects of a long winter war, had attained a standard of offensive eagerness as high as at any time in World War Two and higher than in 1917 and the last months of World War One.'[13]

Montgomery's infantry had by now reached a peak of efficiency. The dead wood had long since been weeded out by action or by dismissal. Virtually every battalion commander was in his late twenties and battle-wise. Their soldiers mostly were in that best age group for assault infantry, between eighteen and twenty-two, when they are physically fit, with all the recklessness of young men and none of the ties of married men. American infantry were supposed to 'wear out' after 200–240 days in combat. Thereafter, according to the head-shrinkers, 'combat exhaustion,' that bugbear of US commanders, would set in. The British Army expected its young infantrymen to last 400 days – that is, if they survived, which was rare in view of the high casualties incurred.

But then the British were better prepared for the battlefield than their American counterparts. Each division had a divisional battle-school through which every replacement went, unless there was a sudden emergency, where he was taught the latest techniques by battle-experienced officers under realistic conditions. In the 43rd Division, for instance, to show just how effective the divisional artillery was, replacements were handed shovels and told to dig themselves in. As soon as they had done so, the artillery opened up and placed a barrage down within yards of their foxholes. In the 52nd, replacements advanced against a mock enemy while picked marksmen would box them in to right and left, flank and rear, with live tracer to teach them to advance as close as possible to the barrage which usually preceded infantry into battle and was only of any use if the soldiers kept as close as humanly feasible to it. As the battle-school instructors used to crack, 'Death'll come as a happy release to you, lads, after this.'

Their personal war aims were clear too. They were not fighting for abstractions such as the 'balance of power' in Europe or to purge the Continent of the 'curse of fascism.' They were fighting to avenge those of their families who had died in battle before them or in the great raids on the cities back home; and in England innocent civilians were *still* dying by their thousands as the German secret weapons, the V-1s and V-2s, continued to plaster southern England (it would be March, with the Allies already crossing the Rhine, before the last one exploded in Britain). They were fighting for themselves and their families and, if necessary, they were prepared to die for them.

Their allies, the Yanks, amazed and amused them. Two miles behind the American front, huge notices warned that anyone not wearing his steel helmet would automatically be fined 50 dollars. Many British units went into action without helmets. Patton's Third Army was even worse. There men were expected to go into combat wearing *neckties*!

The British infantryman cared little about dress, unlike his Commander-in-Chief. This winter Montgomery's attire was a civilian sweater, corduroy trousers, suede boots and a paratrooper's smock with khaki scarf. American generals always wore full uniform, complete with helmet-liner, even miles behind the front. For representatives of a great democratic nation, they seemed to the British to be great sticklers for military courtesies: the whole traditional business of salutes, turning out the guard, flag-hoisting and all the rest of the 'bull' which the British soldier had long left behind him in his regimental depot.

Yet in the American line, all the 'bull' seemed to depart. In British units, instant and unquestioning compliance with orders was expected, men had to shave if humanly possible and amateur barbers cut everybody's hair short, even if it were by dint of placing a pudding bowl on the unfortunate victim's head and cutting around it. The cheap rations that the infantry received – corned beef, sardines and 'soya-links,' sausages made of soybeans, and naturally tea (here a dried mixture of milk, sugar and tea called 'compo tea') – were heated up whenever possible. Trenchfoot and 'combat exhaustion' (the Tommies still called it 'shell-shock,' the name used in the Old War) were rarities. In the Yank outfits, orders were 'discussed.' The men didn't shave, indeed seemed to take pride in being unshaven and unwashed. Their food often consisted of cold K-rations (lemonade powder in the height of winter was not the average Tommy's idea of 'good grub or drink'). It didn't surprise the Tommies that the Yanks suffered so much from trenchfoot and 'combat exhaustion' and that their infantry wore out so soon. Once the Americans were in the line, they seemed to be regarded as cannonfodder, highly expendable, therefore not worth wasting too much care upon. Discipline went, efficiency went, and in the end morale went, too, in the opinion of the British viewing their American counterparts that winter.

But soon, the critical British would see, things would begin to change in the state of mind and purpose of the

average GI. He had taken a nasty bloody nose in the
Ardennes. From now onward there would be no more
running away on the long desolate frontier with Germany.
When they attacked the Great Wall of Germany again,
the GI was going in to win – and win, he would.

2

That day General Eisenhower made his decision. For the
coming breakthrough at the West Wall and the drive for
the Rhine, he intended to develop his operations in three
phases.

First, Montgomery was to seize the west bank of the
Rhine after clearing the Lower Rhineland by means of
converging attacks, using the First Canadian Army and
the Ninth US Army to do so. During this phase of the
great attack, Bradley's forces in the Ardennes were to
maintain an aggressive defense.

Secondly, while Montgomery prepared for a set-piece
assault across the Lower Rhine, Bradley's First Army and
his Third were to clear up the Rhineland from Düsseldorf
to Koblenz.

Thirdly, while Montgomery crossed the Rhine, the
Third and Seventh Armies (the Seventh was still in
France) were to clean out the triangle formed by the
Rivers Moselle, Saar, and Rhine.

As always in his career, Eisenhower had not been able
to make a clear-cut decision on where to make the main
thrust, although by this time his relations with the 'insuf-
ferable Monty,' as Churchill once called his Field Marshal, were at the breaking point stage. Indeed, as
Eisenhower revealed many years after the war in a

conversation with the writer Cornelius Ryan, 'He [Montgomery] got so damn personal to make sure that the Americans and me, in particular, had no credit, had nothing to do with the war, that I eventually just stopped communicating with him . . . I was not interested in keeping up communications with a man that just can't tell the truth.'[14]

His American generals didn't like it. That afternoon Simpson, the Commander of the US Ninth Army, rang Bradley up from his headquarters in the Dutch town of Maastricht. 'Hey, Brad,' he laughed over the phone, 'what can you do to save us? If this goes on much longer, they'll begin to think that we were given to them along with a shipment of lend-lease.'

Bradley was not in a joking mood. 'There's nothing we can do,' he answered sourly. 'Ike's already committed himself. You'd better polish up your British accent. You may be needing it for some time.'[15] Naturally Bradley was not pleased with the plan. It meant, as he saw it, that Montgomery would make the running, aided by Ninth Army and six divisions transferred to it from his First and Third Armies, while he sat on his thumbs in a purely defensive role in the Ardennes-Eifel.

Although Bradley well knew from the bitter, bloody struggles of the previous autumn that the strongest positions of the West Wall were to his front, he 'wanted to break straight on through without a change in pace, force the Siegfried Line, plunge through the Eifel behind it and break a path through to Bonn on the Rhine.' As he wrote after the war, by doing this he could 'avert the loss in the time it would take to reorganize an Allied offensive elsewhere . . . This route through the Eifel would carry us south of the Roer dams and thus enable us to reach the Rhine without being entangled in another dam campaign. We already carried the wounds of two previous assaults against those dam sites; I had no wish to add the wounds of a third.'[16]

In short, Bradley wanted a complete reversal of the Eisenhower plan, with Montgomery marking time in the north while *he* attacked the Wall in the south. His attitude was understandable. His troops had taken a drubbing in the Ardennes; he wished them to have a chance to avenge the reverse they had suffered there during the Battle of the Bulge. He personally had been maligned and insulted, so he believed, by Montgomery, and his capabilities as a commander severely criticized.

He was so angry that he told one of Eisenhower's staff, who had just informed him that Patton would have to surrender some of his divisions earmarked for the Eifel attack to Montgomery in the north, if SHAEF wanted 'to destroy the whole operation' they could do so and be damned and that 'much more than a tactical operation was involved, in that the prestige of the American Army was at stake.'[17]

That wet foggy January 16th, Bradley worried needlessly. Patton personally would ensure that Montgomery would not make the running in the north. Soon the whole strategic picture would change and the 'prestige of the American Army' would be saved.

They weren't great men, these generals who won World War Two in the West for the Allies: Eisenhower, Montgomery, Bradley, Hodges, Simpson and Patton, though of all of them 'Ole Blood an' Guts' at least had the makings of a great general.

They were too conscious of their position, their rights, their public image. After all, they were the first commanders to fight a war against the background of 'instant communication,' surrounded by skilled, critical, sometimes cynical journalists and radio reporters, men-of-the-world who were not as impressed by the top brass as were the ordinary soldiers. They had to be treated accordingly. As a result all the senior commanders were highly publicity-conscious and very much concerned that the general public back home should think highly of them and their actions.

They had all made amazing careers in late middle-age, being suddenly propelled into the limelight from out of the obscurity of barracks life in peacetime America or England. In the whole of the US Army there was only one single limousine available in 1939 (reserved for the Chief-of-Staff), while in the UK judges sentencing lightly convicted men would say routinely 'either six months' hard labor – *or the Army*.' Overnight these obscure colonels and brigadier generals had become household names, their faces known throughout the whole of the western world thanks to newspapers and newsreels. In 1940, after being photographed during an exercise, Eisenhower saw his picture in a local paper captioned as 'Lieut-Colonel DD Ersenbeing.' Two years later, after having been promoted to 'Supremo' over the heads of 366 other generals all senior to him, he could tell his wife Mamie over the phone, 'Looks like I'm going to London next week to be in command there.' 'In command of what?' Mamie had asked. '*Of the whole shebang!*' Eisenhower had roared back triumphantly.[18]

These same officers who in 1939 had been thinking in terms of retirement, carpet-slippers and golf were now commanding the most awesome military machine the world had ever seen, in charge of corps as big as the whole of the peacetime British or American armies. Within four short years they had all made careers like some twentieth-century Grant, save that the power Grant had possessed back in the Civil War had been multiplied a thousand times, and the decisions they made weren't taken in some obscure place in the backwoods of the Republic, but before the eyes of the world in Africa, Sicily, Italy, England, France, and Germany.

Understandably they had become touchy, often blinded to reality by this comet-like change in their fortunes, vain, self-opinionated and almost hysterically concerned with protecting and furthering their reputation – their 'image' as we would call it today.

Although Bradley presented the image of being modest and plain-talking (Ernie Pyle, after visiting with Bradley for three days, presented him to his readers as the 'GIs' General,' an image that stuck), he was as touchy and as concerned about his reputation as all the rest of them. Bradley had none of Montgomery's authority, Patton's ability or Eisenhower's charm. Chester Wilmot, the Australian correspondent who spent the whole campaign closely observing the top brass, thought that 'Bradley was forever conscious that Patton was not only his senior in rank, but also his superior in tactical skill and experience.'

Now Bradley needed Patton badly if he were going to retain control of an *active* army, which would gain some of the laurels in the coming battles with the weakened Germans and thus restore his damaged reputation. Thus, as January 1945 neared its close and a great Russian army rolled ever closer to the German frontier, advancing at an average of fourteen miles a day, Patton and Bradley put their heads together and plotted.

'I don't really care where we attack,' Patton had snorted on January 12th, 'because if we don't, Brad, the Germans certainly will.'[19]

On the 23rd, Bradley gave Patton the green light to attack the Wall once again. Soon Eisenhower's 'aggressive defense' would become in the hands of 'Ole Blood an' Guts' nothing short of a full-scale campaign.

*   *   *

By the last week of January, Patton had the thirteen divisions of his Third Army abreast of the three frontier rivers, from north to south, the Our, Sauer and Moselle, ready to crack the West Wall between St Vith down to Saarlautern; and now he was going to use them to do more than provide Eisenhower's 'aggressive defense.' Before Bradley had given him the go-ahead, Patton had told him that 'I was the oldest leader in age and combat experience in the United States Army in Europe and that if I had to go on the defensive, I wanted to be relieved.'[20]

Bradley had now given him his approval to conduct his 'defense' any way he saw it and Patton was not slow to seize the opportunity. He would conduct an 'armored reconnaissance' of the West Wall, with the Eifel township Bitburg and then the old Roman city of Trier as its objective, using his famed 'rock-soup' method.

Patton had explained this tactic to his amused staff back in 1944. 'A tramp once went to a house and asked for some boiling water to make "rock soup." The lady was interested and gave him the water in which he placed two polished white stones. He then asked if he might have some potatoes and carrots to flavor it a little, and finally ended up with some meat.'

'In other words,' Patton went on, 'in order to attack, we'll have to pretend to reconnoiter, then reinforce the reconnaissance, and finally put on the attack.'[21] He had beamed at them, obviously pleased with his ingenuity and ability to cock a snoot at the top brass.

Thus in the last days of January, starting on the 29th, he would allow one battalion of the 4th Infantry Division to cross the River Our almost where it had been crossed the previous September. The rest of the division would follow and thereafter Middleton's VIII Corps, to which it belonged. To the south, its neighbor the III Corps would then jump off across the River Sauer, followed by the XII

Corps on February 6th or 7th and Patton's last corps the XX on February 19th. Within three weeks Patton hoped to have his whole army committed to the 'armored reconnaissance' by this rock-soup method, then he would see what Eisenhower would do about it. With luck, Patton told himself, he would discover that the Third Army was so deeply committed in the West Wall and Eifel beyond that there would be nothing he could do.

The plan was brash and bold, worthy of Patton, but typical of these wartime generals who had lost contact with reality, each of them 'running the war' as if it were a private matter, independent of overall strategy and political considerations. For if Patton's ruse – it was little better than that – worked, he would drag the whole Allied battlefront further south than intended. Once that had been achieved, the mass of the Allied armies in Europe under General Bradley's command might well end up fighting for the scenery of rural Bavaria, while the Red Army would capture the glittering prizes of Prague, Vienna and Berlin. What was being planned that week in the rundown Hotel Alpha, in the shabby, provincial, Ruritanian atmosphere of the Grand Duchy of Luxembourg, could well decide the fate of Central Europe.[22]

And now the young men on both sides of the West Wall waited for what had inevitably to come. Some of Germany's best soldiers still manned the defenses, the paratroopers of General Schlemm's First Parachute Army facing Montgomery in the north, for instance.

Schlemm, small and dark with a great beak of a nose that made him look more like a Turk than a German, had fought everywhere. He had been appointed to his present command in November 1944 and had been told by Marshal von Rundstedt, 'You're in a defensive sector. You must hold the front between the juncture of the Meuse and the Rhine to Roermond in the south. There are only four divisions under your command. And you mustn't yield an inch of ground without my authorization.'[23]

Schlemm worked hard with his men, paratroopers who had never jumped from an airplane but who possessed the fanatical courage of their predecessors in these once-elite formations. They learnt that 'You are the elite of the German Army. You are to seek out combat and to be ready to endure hardship. Your greatest ambition should be to do battle.' The Colonel of the 6th Parachute Battalion told his new recruits entering the line, 'From the moment a man volunteers for the airborne troops and joins my regiment, he enters into a new order of humanity. He is ruled by one law only, that of our unit. He must give up personal weaknesses and ambitions and realize that our battle is for the existence of the whole German nation and that no end to the war other than a German victory is conceivable. He must believe in this victory even when reason tells him it cannot be.'[24]

They were tough and rightly respected by the English who would soon fight them to the death in the *Reichswald* – for Schlemm had been correct when he told von Rundstedt in late January, 'The attack will come through the Reichswald forest – that's the ideal place for an attack.'[25]

R. M. Wingfield recalled after the war that he and most of his fellow soldiers 'felt quite a professional affection for these paratroops. They were infantry like us, trained to use their own initiative. They had the same system of "trench-mates." They fought cleanly and treated prisoners, wounded and dead, with the same respect they expected from us. If our uniforms had been the same, we would have welcomed them as kindred spirits.

'On one occasion the paratroops acquitted themselves

as honorable gentlemen . . . It was the first time many of us had ever seen them. We never forgot them. We had attacked a wood and been thrown out. The platoon was being "stonked" in a ditch. Two of our stretcher-bearers went out to collect a casualty hit in the leg by a splinter. As soon as the Medics appeared small-arms fire stopped as if turned off at the main. Unfortunately, the German mortars could not see the target and sent over one more bomb before the "cease-fire" reached them. That bomb hit one of the stretcher-bearers in the leg. One stretcher-bearer was left in no-man's-land with two casualties and one stretcher.

'Immediately two paras burst out of the woods, holding up their hands to show they were not armed. They ran to the group in the field. They loaded the two casualties on the stretcher in sitting positions and, under the direction of the surviving medic, they carried the men to safety in our lines. Waving farewell they doubled back to the wood. We cheered them all the way back. A twelve-hour truce followed. No one had the heart to spoil the gesture by firing. So, temporarily the war stopped. Next morning they were gone.'[26]

Soon, when the great last battle for the West Wall commenced, there would be no more truces, whatever individual infantrymen thought of their opponents.

The GIs harbored less friendly feelings for these paratroopers, it seemed. In the last days of January, the 2nd Infantry Division of Hodges's First Army was still fighting the German rearguard, composed of the 3rd German Parachute Division, as they struggled back to the cover of the West Wall.

During the course of that action, Captain MacDonald's company captured one of the paratroops. The prisoner asked in careful English, 'Would you be so kind as to give me a cigarette?' One of the infantrymen kicked the young soldier and snarled: 'Why, you Nazi sonofabitch – of all the goddamned nerve! If it wasn't for you and all your — kind, all of us would be smoking now!'

MacDonald intervened quickly and ordered his men to take the prisoner to the rear. The men returned from headquarters surprisingly speedily and a curious Mac-Donald asked, 'Did you get him back OK?'

'Yessir,' they answered and turned quickly to their platoons.

'Wait a minute,' MacDonald ordered. 'Did you find A Company? What did Lieutenant Smith say?'

The men hesitated, then one of them spoke out suddenly. 'To tell you the truth, Cap'n, we didn't get to A Company. The sonofabitch tried to make a run for it. Know what I mean?'

'Oh, I see,' MacDonald said slowly, nodding his head. 'I see.'[27]

One day later MacDonald was wounded in the leg and that was the end of his days fighting the Great Wall of Germany.

But there were others coming back into the line to resume the struggle. Staff Sergeant Giles, returning from hospital after a two-month absence, rejoined his combat engineer battalion near St Vith the day before Patton launched his 'armored reconnaissance' over the River Our a couple of miles away. He thought that his comrades who had survived the Battle of the Bulge while he had been away looked 'ten years older and ten years dirtier and ten years tireder . . . Riding down here yesterday gave me some idea of what it's been like. The whole countryside is frozen, drifts two and three feet deep, but burned out tanks, halftracks, jeeps, every kind of vehicle are everywhere and most of the villages are nothing but rubble.' Then Giles concluded: 'One thing – this offensive has been expensive to us, but I hope it has been the ruin of the Krauts.'[28]

Many of the tense young men who had been through the Bulge hoped the same, as the day set for the new battle came ever closer. Medic Leslie Atwell noted that last week of January, 'A wave of self-inflicted wounds broke out. Time after time, men were carried into the aid station from nearby houses wincing with pain, shot through the foot. Each swore it had been an accident. "I was cleaning my rifle," sometimes the wounded man would say, pointing to a friend, "He can tell you. He was in the room with me." And often on the face of the friend there would be a look of duplicity as he backed up the story.'[29]

But there were genuine casualties too that terrible freezing last week of January. A friend of Atwell's came in one morning, grinning all over his face and saying good-bye.

'Where are you going?' Atwell asked him.

'Home, I hope,' the friend answered. 'I have a pair of winners here. Two frozen feet.' He asked if he could go in to see the medical officer. Twenty minutes later he was out, an evacuation ticket tied to his overcoat.

'He's a lucky bastard,' the men of C Company commented. One of them moaned: 'And there I was, leavin' my feet out, stickin' them in ice water, trying everything. They wouldn't freeze!'[30]

Now as it began to snow yet once again in that remote border countryside with the stark black tree boughs heavy with white, the young men of the attack force along the Rivers Our and Sauer crowded the cobbled roads and half wrecked villages of the frontline area: a confusion of Sherman tanks, White halftracks, great 8-inch howitzers and 105mm cannon – the infantry called them 'Long

Toms' – deuce-and-a-half trucks, bridging equipment, a great mass of olive-painted machinery clogging every track, every field, every little farmyard, and all pointing one way: *toward Germany!*

Now the GIs waited and prepared for what was to come. There weren't many veterans left in the 87th and 4th Divisions, who were going to jump off first. The autumn and winter fighting had taken its toll; their ranks were filled with men culled from the military police, Army Air Corps, supply units, and the eighteen-year-old draftees from the States. Soon black faces would appear among them, too, volunteers for the combat infantry, who had given up their stripes in order to get a chance of some fighting on equal terms with the whites in an Army which was still strictly segregated.

They froze in the poorly heated ruins, sitting cross-legged on the floor near the glowing pot-bellied stoves, stripping their weapons methodically, checking that every third cartridge was tracer; bathing and changing their underwear in spite of the difficulties, for they knew that gas gangrene might result if they were hit and cloth forced into the wound; tucking metal shaving mirrors into their breast pockets, for they had all heard of a GI who had been saved thus from a 'Kraut slug with his number on it'; and praying. For behind them the clumsy boxlike ambulances were already stationed, that ominous little sign in position in their windshields: '*Priority One – Carrying Casualties.*'

On the morning of January 29th the guns commenced their old song of death yet again. Over the frozen Our, the sky lit up a startling orange as the barrage descended upon the German positions in the snow-covered heights beyond, where, in what seemed another age, the men of the 4th Infantry had attacked for the first time in the previous September. A fantastic pattern of a myriad stabs and flashes of orange flame took shape and died. Tracer zipped back and forth in an urgent lethal morse. Rockets hissed into the sky like man-made forked lightning. Here and there a maverick shell exploded and tossed up a ball of fire like a Roman candle. Awed and gaping like village yokels, the waiting infantry watched and waited.

The whistles shrilled. Non-coms bellowed orders. Officers rose to their feet. '*Let's go!*' they cried above the thunder of the barrage. Like old and weary men, the infantry rose from their holes along the western bank of the River Our and followed them onto the ice. They began to cross. Now the killing would start once again.

Two days later the first German settlement to fall into American hands since before the Battle of the Bulge, the village of Elcherrath, was captured by the 4th Infantry Division. By the end of that day, a whole series of hamlets and villages from which the ill-fated 14th Cavalry Group and the 106th Infantry Division had been driven on December 16th were back in US control.

This time the few remaining German civilians who had avoided forcible removal under the terms of the mass evacuation of the 'Red Zone,' as the Eifel frontier area was called, or who had been allowed to stay behind to look after the animals, met a different type of American from the one they first had gotten to know back in September. This time there were no Hershey bars and chewing gum for the kids, no coffee and canned rations for the women, no Camels for the old men. This time there were blows and kicks and threats with rifles leveled. Everywhere the civilians were flung out into the snow, while the 'Amis' took over their humble homes that stank of boiled cabbage and animal droppings. In the village of Winterspelt, the 180 remaining villagers, including those who were seriously ill, were crowded together in two small houses for five weeks. In Auw, which had been the headquarters of the 18th *Volksgrenadier* Division, the GIs forced the terrified German civilians to cover them as they winkled out the last of the German defenders, and more than one civilian was killed in the process.

Everywhere the soldiers threw out of the windows the things they could use, until the village streets were littered with the civilians' pathetic possessions. They then set fire to the hand-carved peasant cupboards and sideboards that had been in families for generations, smashing the pictures, tearing down the curtains, seemingly taking a malicious pleasure in destroying them in front of their horrified owners.

Later the villagers would reason that these were different troops from the friendly GIs who had first occupied their villages in September. But they weren't; they were still the men of General Barton's 4th Infantry Division. Yet the hard fighting of the last months had taken its toll. The men had become hard and brutalized; it was one of the prices of war that young men, who face the prospect of being killed violently every new dawn, must pay.

Young Johannes Nobuesch, who was among those present at Elcherrath, wrote later, 'Perhaps it was the destruction and carnage they, the Americans, had seen in North Belgium and Luxembourg, which caused them to do these things. Perhaps too, Goebbels's propaganda, which declared every German house should become a fortress, played a role. At all events the results of their actions on the border were catastrophic, but in contrast to the Russians now advancing through East Prussia, one must certify that the Americans rarely attacked women or attempted to kill male civilians . . . It took the Americans a long time to realize that the German propaganda picture of the will to resist on the part of the civilian population was wrong. How tired and weary of the war the people really were! They longed for peace! Now one thing and one thing only occupied the civilians' every thought. *When in God's name would this terrible war be over?*'[31]

Now Patton had the hot water and the two white stones for his 'rock soup.' But would the General, who thought of himself as the Lazarus of the Allied attack in the West, picking up merely crumbs of a sumptuous feast like that Biblical beggar, get the carrots and vegetables to ensure his thick rich soup?

He had his doubts. SHAEF and Bradley were strangely silent. Apparently there had been no reaction to his 'armored reconnaissance' into the Eifel, to the tune of a whole corps of three divisions. What was going on back there at Versailles? Were they turning a blind eye to his activities? Patton didn't know, but he worried.

The portly General Eddy, Commander of XII Corps, due to kick off the attack across the River Sauer, with Bitburg as its objective, planned to start his river assault on February 6th.

'Make it the 4th,' Patton told him.

Eddy, who suffered from high blood pressure which he managed to conceal from Patton until he finally had to be evacuated to the States, exploded. 'Goddammit, General, you never give me time to get ready! . . . The trouble is you have no appreciation of the time and space factor in this war!'

Patton was in no mood for arguments. He snapped back at the crimson-faced corps commander, whom he had already threatened to fire more than once. 'Is that so?' he countered hotly. 'If I had any appreciation of it, we'd still be sitting on the Seine!'[32]

Eddy gave in, as he always had to with Patton; 'Ole Blood an' Guts' rarely brooked any opposition to his imperious will. February 4th it would be.

Now Patton decided to take a calculated risk. He called Bradley's headquarters at Namur to clear the deadline with him. Bradley wasn't there. Apparently he was at Versailles for a conference with Eisenhower. Patton breathed a sigh of relief: at least Bradley was out of the way. General Lev Allen, Bradley's Chief-of-Staff, who took the call and who was one of the 'hawks' favoring action by US troops regardless of Montgomery's grandiose plans, said he saw no objections to the plan or the date.

Patton could go ahead; he was going to get his carrots and vegetables after all. But his relief was short-lived.

Exactly one hour later Allen rang Patton back. In a small voice he said, 'No dice, George. You are to commit nothing – pending further orders.'

Patton was stunned. He returned to a waiting Eddy, his jaw set, eyes angry, and told him to suspend all operations for the time being. A little later he called a conference. 'This doesn't sound good to me,' he told his staff. 'I'm afraid we're going to be halted again in the middle of a going attack in order to start another one, you know where, that has little promise of success. I have the sneaking suspicion that SHAEF is out as usual to exalt the Field Marshal.'[33]

To try to shake off the apprehension, Patton set out on one of his whirlwind tours of his front-line troops, this time the men of the XX Corps, which according to the original plan would be the last corps of the Third Army to go into action on the River Moselle.

He conferred at one spot with General Maloney, commander of the 94th Division, which had done less well in the Saar. There he went into a blind rage when he learnt from Maloney that the Division's ratio of combat to non- combat casualties was the worst in the whole of the Third Army. 'If you don't do something to improve this situation,' he thundered, 'you'll be a non-combat casualty yourself – and pretty soon!' Then Patton relented a little and patted Maloney on the back, 'You're doing fine otherwise – but Goddammit, do something about those slackers.'

When Patton returned to his CP, a call from Bradley was waiting. 'Monty did it again, George,' Bradley said without preamble. 'You and Hodges will go on the defensive, while Montgomery will resume the offensive in the north.' Then, anticipating Patton's usual explosive reaction, Bradley added hastily: 'It wasn't Ike this time. Orders from the Combined Chiefs. Brooke [British Chief-of-Staff] even got General Marshall [American Chief-of-Staff] to go along with him. I don't know what made him agree. Probably he's anxious to get those fourteen British divisions sitting on their butts in Belgium back into action.'

'What are they hoping to accomplish?' Patton asked.

'Montgomery wants to secure a wide stretch of the Rhine as quickly as possible, so that we would have a quick entry if Germany collapsed suddenly.'

'Horseshit!' Patton snorted. 'I'm convinced that we have a much better chance to get to the Rhine first with our present attack. When are the British supposed to jump off?'

'Probably on the 10th,' Bradley answered.

'I doubt if Monty will be ready by the 10th,' Patton affirmed. 'But what are *we* supposed to be doing in the meantime?'

'You can continue your attack until February 10th,' Bradley answered, 'and maybe after that even, provided your casualties aren't excessive and you have enough ammunition left.'[34]

It wasn't much but, after the events of the last twenty-four hours, Patton was glad of any crumb of hope. He still had ten more days before he would be halted on the orders of America's most senior soldier, General Marshall, who, now that President Roosevelt was going into his final decline, was running America's war. In the old war Patton had served on Marshall's staff; he knew the Chief-of-Staff couldn't be bucked. But still he had ten more precious days. The Third Army attack on the West Wall could continue.

February

1

On February 2nd, accompanied by Colonel Harkins and Colonel Codman, General Patton drove to Spa to confer at Hodges's headquarters in the Hôtel Britannique. It was freezingly cold in the open jeeps and Codman wrote to his wife, 'Thank God for those long drawers. I have on two pairs, two undershirts, fleece-lined boots, fleece-lined leather coat, your wool caterpillar helmet under the regulation helmet, yet long before the end of the day, the cold has permeated every aching bone in one's body. How the boys in the line, who have no warm place to come back to, take it, day after day, and week after week, is beyond my comprehension.'[1]

Patton did not seem to notice the cold, apart from a blanket he'd spread over his knees, although he was nearly sixty. He was too concerned that nothing should stop his campaign at the last moment. As Codman commented, 'The General's every waking hour is concentrated on our next forward move to the Rhine,' for Patton was convinced (Codman thought) 'that the Germans have finally shot their bolt and that it is folly to slow down now. The difficulty, as heretofore, is to get the green light from Topside.'[2]

The brass met in Hodges's big office from whose windows they could see the lake around which the Kaiser had walked impatiently while he had waited for Field Marshal Hindenburg, the Imperial warlord, to decide whether or not the war against the Entente Powers should be continued.

Patton must have felt a fellow feeling for the Kaiser that cold February day, as he waited to hear what Eisenhower had dreamed up for his Army. Nothing had changed much since the end of January. Montgomery was going to make the really important attack; until he was ready to start on the 10th, the Third Army could continue its 'armored reconnaissance,' and, as what Patton thought to be a sop to his pride, the Third would be allowed to attack in the direction of the old Roman city of Trier, a prize on which he had set his eyes since the previous September.

Back at his own headquarters, Patton called an immediate conference of his four corps commanders to tell them what had transpired at Spa. He started the meeting in a frivolous mood, obviously pleased with the prospect of capturing Trier (for he had private plans of his own on that score, unknown to Ike), regaling his audience with one of his contemptuous Montgomery stories.

'The Field Marshal was outlining his plans to Eisenhower,' Patton started impishly, 'and concluded as follows: "I shall dispose several divisions on my flank and lie in wait for the Hun. Then at the proper moment, I shall leap on him . . ."' Patton paused to give his illustrious audience the full impact of the punchline, '"*like a savage rabbit!*"'

Then Patton was serious again. 'Gentlemen,' he said, 'I participated in a Group conference with Generals Bradley, Hodges and Simpson. General Bradley informed us that General Eisenhower had been ordered by the Combined Chiefs-of-Staff to make the main effort in the north, under Field Marshal Montgomery. For this offensive the Field Marshal is to get nine United States infantry and several armored divisions . . . Third Army will be required to transfer several divisions to Ninth Army. We will get the bad news later. Whatever it is, we will comply promptly and without argument. However it is very obvious now who is running this war over here and how it is being run.'

Now Patton revealed to his generals that he was going to have his own way even if it meant disobeying the Combined Chiefs-of-Staff. 'Personally,' he said slowly and carefully, 'I think that it would be a foolish and ignoble way for the Americans to end the war by sitting on our butts. And gentlemen, we are not going to do anything foolish or ignoble.'[3]

For a while they discussed how they would continue their fight against the West Wall. Then Patton closed the meeting with an urgent warning that they should all maintain the strictest secrecy. 'Let the gentlemen up north learn what we are doing,' he declared, 'when they see it on their maps.'

The conference broke up with the corps commanders hurrying back to their outfits, ready to set the wheels in motion again with renewed energy. 'Ole Blood an' Guts' had eight short days to go before Montgomery launched his tremendous set-piece attack against the West Wall in the north. By then they wanted to have covered a lot of German territory. Then let Monty and Ike see if they could stop them and the glorious Third Army!

Attack!

Exactly ninety days before, the greenhorns of the US 76th Infantry Division had still been training against a simulated foe in the peaceful hills of Wisconsin. Now, with the veteran 5th Infantry Division, the men of the 76th

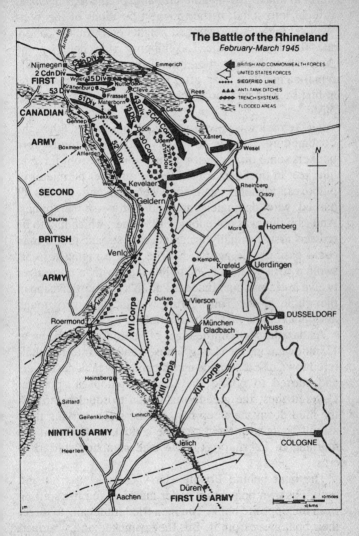

The Battle of the Rhineland
February–March 1945

BRITISH AND COMMONWEALTH FORCES
UNITED STATES FORCES
SIEGFRIED LINE
ANTI-TANK DITCHES
TRENCH SYSTEMS
FLOODED AREAS

to Arnhem

Nijmegen
2 Cdn Div
FIRST
53 Div

Emmerich

Wyler 15 Div

Kranenburg

Rütterden

CANADIAN

Frasselt

Cleve

Rees

51 Div

Materborn

Calcar

Hekkens

2 Cdn Corps

43 Div

ARMY

Gennep

Goch

Xanten

Boxmeer

Udem

Wesel

Afferden

52 Div

30 Corps

SECOND

Well

Kevelaer

Rheinberg
Orsoy

Geldern

BRITISH

Deurne

Mors

Homberg

ARMY

Venlo

Kempen

Krefeld

Uerdingen

Roermond

Dülken

Vierson

DUSSELDORF

XVI Corps

München
Gladbach

Neuss

Heinsberg

XIII Corps

XIX Corps

Sittard

Geilenkirchen

Linnich

NINTH US ARMY

Jülich

COLOGNE

Heerlen

Düren

FIRST US ARMY

Aachen

2 4 6 8 10 miles
10 kms

N

were to make an assault crossing of the River Sauer straight into some of the toughest positions of the West Wall set high on the wooded heights of Germany, opposite the bank on the Luxembourg side held by the Americans. 'So help me,' one of the green troops would remark a few days later, after the killing was over, 'the job at first seemed just too much for human beings to accomplish!'[4]

The remark was not surprising. Opposite the 76th at the Luxembourg frontier town of Echternach there were bunkers some three stories deep, with walls from three to nine feet in thickness, protected by an outer perimeter of pillboxes, foxholes, gun emplacements and a mass of barbed wire entanglements and anti-personnel mines. And as if that was not enough, the Sauer, which had to be crossed first, normally a meandering stream that a man could easily wade across, had become a raging torrent, swollen to a width of 90 to 180 feet, with a current of twelve miles an hour. Indeed, Patton's greenest division in the whole of the Third Army was facing a very tough assignment in its first taste of combat.

As darkness fell on the night of February 6th, the great 155mm cannon, the 'Long Toms,' rumbled into the shattered town of Echternach accompanied by tank destroyers and started to pound the German pillboxes opposite. Covered thus, the greenhorns began to squelch through the mud down the steep bank of the river carrying their assault boats with them. At one o'clock precisely on the morning of February 7th, the lead company started to cross.

The boat behind Private Harry Goedde was hit and sank. His own boat came under machine-gun fire spitting from the opposite bank. The men tried frantically to direct their boat away from it. But they panicked and swamped the flimsy craft. Goedde went overboard. Most of his companions who did the same were swept away by the fierce current, but Goedde was a strong swimmer. A medic screamed for help. Goedde took him in tow and managed to get him to the opposite bank. Frozen and trembling in the reeds, both without weapons, Goedde and the medic watched, by the light of the fires that German shells had started on the opposite bank, the slaughter of the boats. By the time the two lead companies finally made the German side they had lost exactly fifty percent of their effectives, with only five officers left.

But the survivors went into the attack. Under withering machine-gun fire they started up the hill toward the West Wall. Sergeant Bliss and Private Meyer got cut off from their platoon. They went to ground, only to discover that the 'cave' they had found was 'on top of what later turned out to be a seven-room pillbox full of Jerries'!

Private Ulrich's platoon was wiped out just after they had left the boats. Ulrich, his rifle torn from his grasp, dazed and temporarily blinded by the flash of the shells, wandered into the woods. The German machine-gunners spotted him. Lead winged its way angrily toward him and he dropped to the ground terrified. Later he reported, 'I couldn't see anyone else from my outfit. I felt all alone . . . It seemed to me that I was the only Yank in Germany and the whole *Wehrmacht* was zeroing in on me!'[5]

The senior non-com in a heavy weapons platoon, Sergeant John Shepherd took over command when his superior was wounded. He was scared and he knew the men were too. But they all accepted the challenge of their first battle. 'We've got to protect the battalion's left flank!' Shepherd shouted above the mad snap-and-crackle of small-arms fire.

A GI wisecracked, 'Hell, Sarge, you mean right up there with those mean old Krauts?'

But up they went and later a proud Shepherd could

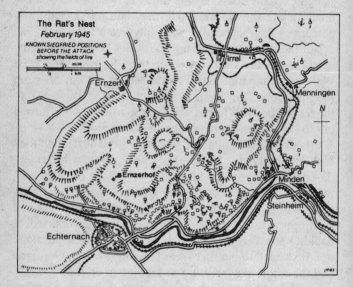

The Rat's Nest
February 1945
KNOWN SIEGFRIED POSITIONS
BEFORE THE ATTACK
showing the fields of fire

report to his commanding officer: 'The men held their own against Jerry counter-attacks and protected the battalion's left flank for five days.'[6]

That morning the Germans counter-attacked what was left of the lead companies with three tanks and infantry. Sergeant Charles Smith watched aghast as the first tank came rumbling within twenty yards of his foxhole line. Back in Wisconsin he had heard what German tankers did to dug-in infantry. They positioned themselves over the foxholes and revved their engines to choke the terrified men below with exhaust gas, or rumbled around and around until the earth walls fell in and their racing tracks could crush the infantry to death. Smith need not have worried. The sole remaining bazooka-man, Private Lyle Corcoran, sprang to his feet in full view of the tank. As it turned broadside-on to commence its deadly work, the lone David tackling the metal Goliath let it have two blasts. The tank shuddered to a stop and started to burn fiercely.

Some of the 76th Infantry greenhorns were not so lucky. Sergeant Guida Fenice watched the second tank 'run over one of our men in a foxhole. There were about seven German soldiers riding on the outside and I saw a buddy of mine running alongside the tank firing at them with a pistol. They shot him down so I grabbed his gun and continued to fire.'[7] Then the tank got bogged down in the mud.

The Americans were not slow to take advantage of the new situation. One sergeant and a private dashed forward and lobbed grenades into the open turret of the trapped monster. It went up in flames. That was the end of the German attack. The infantry fled back into the safety of their pillboxes and the third tank scuttled into the cover of the woods. For the time being the greenhorns were safe.

* * *

All that night the engineers worked frantically to recover what was left of the assault boats for the follow-up troops, while others worked under fire to construct a bridge across the Sauer, fighting both the enemy shelling and the fierce current which twice tore away their pontoons. Meanwhile the men of the divisional signals attempted to get a phone wire across to the survivors of the first assault on the German side of the river. Two volunteers swam it across, but couldn't advance any further because of mines. Another attempt was made to shoot the wire across with a bazooka. But German fire blew it out. More volunteers swam another line across, weighting it so that it would sink to the bottom of the Sauer. This time a smokescreen covered them from the watching Germans on the heights above. They made it, just as the Germans further up the river started to float mines down, an old trick of theirs, in an attempt to knock out any bridge being built. One exploded exactly above the cable but, sunk fifteen feet below the surface, the line held, and now the doughs on both sides of the river were linked at last.

Messages started to fly back and forth. Food, ammunition and oil for cleaning river-soaked weapons were all needed urgently. The divisional commander General Schmidt ordered all available artillery spotter planes into action. He had a novel use for the Piper Cubs. As the bridge was not yet completed and there were so few boats available, they would carry over the desperately needed supplies.

As soon as it was light, the planes came winging in low over the river, ignoring the deadly tracer of the German machine guns, the pilots dropping the supplies out of their doors like fliers of World War One vintage. 'We were getting pretty short of ammunition and food when Piper Cubs started dropping stuff to us,' Sergeant Williams recalled later. 'The first bundles landed out in open fields under snipers' fire, but later they hit the edge of the woods where we were.'[8] Lieutenant Robert Seiter was one soldier who was glad to see the spotter planes that first morning of battle, for his men were down to half a K-ration per meal. The water situation was even worse. 'Here's some water in my canteen,' he told relief parties a few days later, 'that drained through the blanket over my foxhole. Tastes a little like dye, but it's not bad. Our Halazone tablets purified it.'[9]

Some of the trapped men, however, would be without food for thirty-six hours, despite the efforts of men like Private Lowell, who risked his life by rushing into no man's land under heavy machine-gun fire to pull in a bundle of food and ammo which had landed there; or like Captain Dean, who was decorated that day on the field of battle by Corps Commander General Eddy for having flown three missions in the face of intense enemy fire to take ammunition and food across the Sauer.

Eddy wasn't the only high-ranking general to visit the greenhorn division that day. Patton did too. Later he told his nephew Fred Ayres – to whom he had cabled earlier that month: 'GET OFF YOUR DEAD BUTT AND COME UP. WE ARE ABOUT TO HAVE A DAMNED FINE WAR' – 'You know, Freddy, the psychology of the fighting man is a strange thing. Early, well before dawn, I watched men of an almost green division [the 76th], soaking wet and cold, cross a swollen river in the face of steep hills packed deep with concrete gun emplacements, machine guns, mines, and barbed wire. They crossed without hesitation and walked right through that concentration of fire. They never hesitated.'[10]

High praise indeed for the greenhorns! But sitting in his headquarters that night with Ayres over a bottle of bourbon, Patton was not so complimentary about some elements of Irwin's 5th Division. As he told his nephew,

'Later in the day I came across another outfit stalled along an open road. Do you know what was holding them up? A length of yellow string tied across their path between trees. No one dared touch it. I guess it is the unknown a man is scared to face.'[11]

Patton was probably right. In March he would decorate Private Harold Garman of that same 5th Division with the Medal of Honor in recognition of his part in the Sauer River crossing that February 7th. Garman had been in an assault boat with three walking wounded and one GI so badly hurt that he had to lie prone. The boat had been trapped by enemy machine-gun fire. The men paddling had gone over the side swiftly, leaving Garman with the wounded. But then, as the boat with the wounded had started to drift toward the German-held side of the river, Garman had slipped overboard and under intense fire, with German slugs plucking at the water all around him, he'd pushed the boat back to safety. Even Patton was astonished at such bravery on the part of a man whose comrades had deserted him. He asked the young soldier why he had done it. Garman (in Patton's words) 'looked surprised and said, "Well someone had to, sir!"'

It was the stuff of which legends were made. And that gray wet day in February Patton created a legend of his own. Under the cover of a thick smokescreen, his jeep raced across the pontoon bridge constructed by the engineers of the 5th Division. Suddenly the hard-pressed infantrymen were surprised to find in their midst no less a person than the Commanding General of the Third Army, spick and span in his lacquered helmet and custom-made uniform, complete with famed pistols. It was 'Ole Blood an' Guts' himself! Word started to spread that Patton had swum the Sauer single-handed.

As the soldiers' newspaper *Stars and Stripes* reported later: 'A fighting front is the breeding place for wild stories. Here is one from this sector. Out of the misty night appeared General George S. Patton, Jr. "Call back the boats!" he screamed. "They make too high a silhouette. *We will swim!*" The boats turned in midstream. The GIs climbed onto the west bank. They hesitated. The general acted. He waded deep into the river and struck out with a powerful crawl. Halfway to the other side, he turned his head and waved. The inspired troops dove in and swam across.'[12]

That same day Patton and General Irwin inspected the West Wall through which the 5th Division had just broken. Most of the bunkers captured had been taken from the rear and Patton observed to Irwin, 'Now I know the Germans are crazy.' Then he added bitterly, obviously thinking of the role Eisenhower had given his Third Army while Montgomery planned his great attack on the West Wall for the morrow, 'No more crazy however than our own directives from on high to maintain an "active defense."' Shaking his head ruefully, he said, 'You know, there are times when I'm sorry the word "defense" was ever invented. From the Great Wall of China to the Maginot Line, *nothing . . . anywhere . . . ever* has been successfully defended!'[13]

2

That day, General Crerar, commanding the First Canadian Army, called the war correspondents to his tactical headquarters at the Dutch town of Tilburg. There he secretly briefed them on Montgomery's plan to breach the West Wall. The First Canadian on Monty's northern flank would attack over a six-mile strip of land between the

River Rhine and the River Meuse, not far from the Dutch town of Nijmegen.

'This operation may be protracted and the fighting tough and trying,' the Canadian told the correspondents. 'All ranks are confident, however, that we will carry through to a successful conclusion the great task which we have been given the responsibility and honor to fulfill.'[14]

Crerar sounded more confident than he was. The Canadians had had an unlucky war so far. After over two years of inactivity in England, their first big operation was the débâcle of the Dieppe landing in 1942 which had resulted in nearly a whole Canadian division being wiped out. They had not fared much better in France two years later and the ponderous staff work of the First Canadian Army had allowed many Germans to escape from the trap of the Falaise Pocket in August 1944. Again their casualties had been heavy too. By October 1944 the 2nd Canadian Division had lost 8,211 men and the 3rd Canadian 9,263, the highest casualty rate in Montgomery's Army Group at that time.

Montgomery was not pleased with Crerar, for he knew that Canadian manpower was running out (only volunteers served overseas) and any further great blood-letting could well bring about a political crisis in Ottawa. All the same, Canada had to be shown that the great dominion was still taking an active part in the war. But although it seemed as if this army which was going to have the first crack at the West Wall in Montgomery's great set-piece attack was Canadian, it was in practice mainly British (even in Canadian outfits, twenty percent of the men were British-born). For it was Horrocks's XXX Corps of three British divisions, plus the firepower of two further ones and several armored brigades, and two Canadian divisions, which would make the main attack.

Here Horrocks had the problem of turning the northern

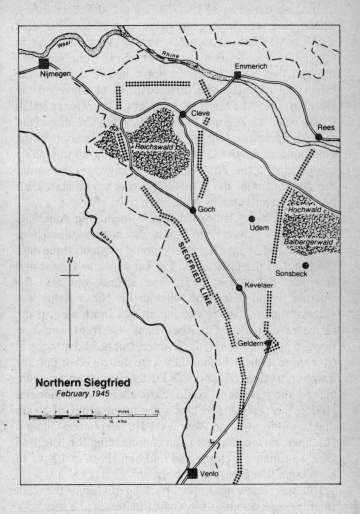

Northern Siegfried
February 1945

end of the West Wall. To the southeast there was the forbidding darkness of the *Reichswald*, the state forest, where pinetrees were planted so closely together that visibility was limited to a few yards. He would have to attack this head-on along a road which ran from Nijmegen through five miles of low country before it began the three-mile ascent to the fortified town of Cleve on the German side – the home of Anne of Cleves, Henry VIII's fourth wife. It was going to be tough. What Crerar had not told the correspondents that day was that as soon as the German commander General Schlemm started to rush up troops to stop the First Canadian Army from the south, the Americans of the US Ninth Army would start their attack sixty miles below Nijmegen.

'Big Simp' – to distinguish him from another American officer called 'Little Simp' – was also not sanguine about his chances that day. His attack would jump off three days after that of the Canadians. He knew just as Crerar and Horrocks did that not only the enemy, but also the weather would determine whether his Ninth Army was successful or not in the coming attack. In his case, if the Germans destroyed the Roer dams, his front would be flooded by millions of tons of water. But he had no control over those dams, whether they were destroyed or not; for it was up to General Hodges's First Army to capture them before the Germans could blow them. And General Hodges's attacking divisions were running out of steam that day in front of the West Wall. He telephoned General Huebner, now promoted from commanding the 'Big Red One' to running a corps, and told him shortly: 'I have to have them [the dams] by tomorrow.'

Huebner knew that the attacking division, the 78th Infantry, was about at the end of its tether; he needed a fresher outfit. 'I've got to use the 9th Division,' he told Hodges.

'I want those dams in the morning,' Hodges repeated. 'How you get them is your business.'

Huebner thereupon telephoned General Craig, commander of the 9th Infantry, and asked him just how soon he could move.

Craig replied, 'In short order!'[15]

Now they waited – the Canadians, British, and Americans – that fateful night of February 7th/8th, wondering whether the morrow would see the final defeat of Germany's vaunted Great Wall. Leslie Atwell attached to the 78th Division noted in his diary, 'This is the part of the war I have dreaded most . . . I have always thought the Krauts would fight like devils for every inch of German soil . . . I dreaded this Siegfried Line.' Later, after his captain had told the men they were going to attack the Siegfried Line on the morrow, Atwell prayed suddenly, 'God, don't let this be a slaughter. Help them. *End* this. In my imagination I saw them running, being hit, reeling back. But I couldn't pin my mind down. I was hearing the voices of English men and women in the smoky little parlor of the pub in Stone singing, "We'll 'ang our washing on the Siegfried Line." '[16]

A British tank officer who had moved up into the battle area that day was not so fanciful. All the same, as he viewed the *Reichswald* in the dusk, he too was not so happy with the prospect of what lay before him. 'In the valley clustered the houses of a few scruffy villages which marked the Dutch-German border and beyond loomed the solid forbidding bulk of the *Reichswald*. It was not a pleasing prospect and as the rain poured down we could imagine what the mud was going to be like on the low lying ground before us.'[17]

Major Fergusson of the Black Watch, an infantryman who would end the war by having fought on three continents, felt much the same that day: 'At last it was the Siegfried Line and many of us felt a new fear. There was just a hope that the coming battle might be the last of the war. The enemy would not lightly yield the Siegfried Line. He might well make his last stand in it!'[18]

Lieutenant John Foley, commander of a troop of Churchill tanks, viewing the front that day wrote that 'the *Reichswald* looked sombre and uninviting, the black trunks of the big trees seeming as solid as if carved from granite.' His companion said, 'There it is. That's the objective for the first day. The Germans think that the forest is an anti-tank obstacle, maybe it is, too. But you never know until you try. Personally I think we should be able to operate in there, providing we pick our trees carefully.'[19]

Another officer was not so sure. Knowing that they had to breach the outer defenses of the West Wall before they even entered the forest, he said, 'We've got to reach it first.'

Later Lieutenant Foley briefed his troops on the plan for the morrow. The only thing that seemed to puzzle them was, as his senior non-com put it, 'why we're starting [the attack] at half-past ten in the morning instead of the usual crack of dawn or nightfall?'

Foley told his men that it was indeed a gentlemanly hour to start a battle and then, yawning, said with feigned sangfroid, 'Oh well, I'll probably sleep until nine-ish, a leisurely wash and shave, some breakfast, and then Heigh Ho for the Start Line.'

As Foley ruefully commented later, 'It was a nice dream while it lasted.'[20]

Now Montgomery's concentration was complete. He had nearly half a million men hidden behind the front. Everywhere the trucks, the tanks, the guns, the soldiers were packed into the houses, the fields, the lanes, the few roads. As Brigadier Essame later described it, 'The tension could be felt – the kind of feeling which runs through the crowd before the Derby.'[21]

As the night wore on, there was the drone of heavy bombers of the RAF heading for their targets behind the German front. Men waiting for the order to attack told each other with satisfaction, 'Bomber Harris is out tonight.' Later they would be cursing that same Air Marshal Harris, head of the RAF's Bomber Command, as they fought their way through the rubble that his bombs had made of the towns of Goch and Cleve.

Now the infantry prepared to move out: the men of the 51st Highland Division, known throughout the Army as the 'Highway Decorators' on account of their habit of painting their divisional sign 'HD' on any object big enough; those of the 15th Scottish, a tough no-nonsense division which had already seen plenty of action; those of the 53rd Welsh, and those of the 2nd Canadian Division. They were all confident. This might well be the battle that would end the long bloody war, at the start of which most of the infantrymen had been schoolboys in short pants.

One minute to five on the morning of February 8th: all was silent, tense, dark, the only sound the dripping of the raindrops from the dreary trees. Five o'clock – and the greatest bombardment of World War Two thundered into tumultuous, crazy life.

'It was a fantastic scene, never to be forgotten,' the historian of the 4th/7th Dragoon Guards wrote later. 'One moment silence and the next moment a terrific ear-splitting din, with every pitch of noise imaginable. Little bangs, big bangs, sharp cracks, the rattle of machine guns and the ripple of Bofors intermingled with the periodic swoosh of a rocket battery. The night was lit by flashes of every color and the tracer of the Bofors guns weaving fairy patterns in the sky as it streamed off toward the target.'

Lieutenant Foley recalled, 'I was nearly blasted from my blankets by the deafening barrage of noise. The ground shook with the fury of the cannonade and the walls of the sixty-pound tent whipped in and out like a sparrow's wings.' That was the end of the long sleep he had envisioned for himself and he sat up and conversed with his men 'by means of a mixture of shouting and sign language.'

'It should be a walk-over by half-past ten [the time when the barrage would end and the attack commence],' someone shouted hopefully.

Foley wasn't convinced. He knew the 'Germans had a peculiar aptitude for emerging unscathed from the fiercest bombardment.' Still, he told himself, 'It was an encouraging thought.'[22]

Far away to the east General Schlemm, the commander of the German First Parachute Army, heard the barrage too. In fact, it woke him out of an exhausted sleep. He seized the phone immediately and called his army group commander. 'I feel it's the big push,' he told him. It was, and it was coming exactly where Schlemm had expected it to come back in January when he had taken up his command: through the Reichswald Forest to the north.

Yet the bombardment was so tremendous that the waiting German infantry were temporarily paralyzed. Prisoners told their interrogators later that the barrage had created 'an impression of overwhelming force opposed to them which, in their isolated state, with no communications, it was useless to resist.' Another soldier wrote in a letter captured later, 'When Tommy began his attack, he started such a terrific artillery barrage that we took leave of our senses. I shall not forget my experience in the *Reichswald* for a long time.'[23]

Now it was ten twenty-five. A line of yellow smoke shells started to hit the *Reichswald*, the signal that the time of assault had come. Ten thirty. It was H-Hour!

The Scots, the Welsh, the Canadians swarmed forward into the drifting smoke of battle, disappearing among the shattered trees of the *Reichswald*. Behind them came the tanks.

'Dead on the dot of ten thirty,' Foley recalled, 'we emerged from our wood and headed for the *Reichswald*. In front of us the Black Watch moved purposefully forward, little groups of men hurrying over the ground, while others spreadeagled themselves behind what cover they could and fired their rifles and Bren guns calmly and methodically.'[24]

Everything seemed to be going smoothly. There was hardly any German resistance. The men, moving into the forest where the trees lay shattered and limbless, winkled the deafened bewildered field-grays out of their holes with scarcely a shot being fired.

Foley rattled past a company commander of the Black Watch, quietly smoking his pipe. 'With his little cane and red hackle at the side of his cap, he might well have been taking a Sunday morning stroll down Aldershot High Street, except vicious little spurts of dust were cracking about his heels.' He raised his stick in greeting when he saw the tanks, completely indifferent to the bullets kicking up the dirt all about him. Foley called to him, 'Look here, aren't you being shot at?'

'Oh never mind that,' the infantry captain answered, 'it's only got nuisance value.'

The tanks rolled on. Suddenly Foley heard a noise 'like a small boy dragging a stick along some iron railings, and a line of sparks dotted the side of *Avenger*' (Foley's tank). 'They've woken up!' Foley shouted and dropped inside the turret just at the same instant that the Black Watch 'melted into the landscape.'[25]

Now the real battle began.

Colonel Lindsay of the Gordons was advancing through the smoke when he heard the pipes of the Camerons of Canada, which told him he was leading his Gordons in the right direction. Suddenly there was a loud bang and one of his officers, by the name of Danny, dropped to the ground.

Lindsay knew exactly what had happened. They had blundered into a minefield. 'Everyone stand still, exactly where you are!' he bellowed over the racket. 'Danny, how bad is it?' he added a moment later.

Lindsay knew the young officer had either a broken ankle or the whole foot blown off – what the medical officers called a traumatic operation. Danny needed help at once. At the top of his voice he called to the Canadians for stretcher-bearers, telling Danny a little later, 'Never mind, Danny, the moonlight's lovely [the area was illuminated by 'Monty's Moonlight'] and I'll get you a bar to your MC [Military Cross] for this day's work, you mark my words.'

Three-quarters of an hour later the first Canadian medics came on the scene and promptly started stepping on mines themselves. But in the end Colonel Lindsay managed to get his trapped men out of the minefield. Four of the leading company's officers were now dead or wounded, and as Lindsay formed the survivors up and marched them back, he was 'dead tired and felt none of the elation to which I was entitled when I reported to Brigade that the road was now clear.'

Foley felt no elation that midday either. Leaving behind the Black Watch which had just run into a minefield made up of the deadly 'deballockers,' he surged ahead with his troop of Churchills. Suddenly one of his fifty-ton monsters disappeared in a spout of flame-tinted smoke and a cloud of dust.

'He's hit!' Foley cried instinctively, forgetting he was still on the air, then he formed the rest of the tanks in a square around the most seriously wounded survivor, a man named Riley. While he waited for the medics to come up, Foley attended to Riley himself.

'The lower half of his right leg was a tattered bloody mess of khaki, tank suit, woollen sock and raw flesh. I couldn't quite make out what the polished white plastic was in the middle of it, and then I felt slightly sick when I realized it was his shin bone.'

Foley looked down at Riley's blue-chinned face and unemotional eyes. 'Hurt much?' he asked.

'Only when I laff,' Riley replied dead-pan.

'You'll be back in Blighty before morning, Riley,' said Foley's NCO Sergeant Robinson. 'Dead lucky, eh?'

A flicker of a smile appeared in Riley's transparent eyes. 'Shake the ol' woman, that will. Last time I wrote 'ome, I told 'er I'd write from Germany. She'll wonder what the 'ell 'as 'appened when she gets a telegram from the War Office.'

It was starting to rain, huge cold drops that beat down cruelly on the heads of the advancing infantry. Everywhere vehicles began to get stuck in the thick mud of the battlefield. The forward infantry of the 3rd Canadian Division were marooned in the villages they had already taken when the Rhine overflowed. The 51st Highland Division was cut off from supplies to the rear, and that afternoon only one Weasel managed to get through the mud bearing a load of 500 tins of self-heating soup intended normally for commandos. It was the only hot food that the infantry of the whole of Horrocks's XXX Corps received that day.

Still the infantry pressed on. Firing over the heads of the advancing Scots, Foley's tankers watched their advance as if they were viewing one 'of those old news-reels of World War One. Khaki-clad figures with fixed bayonets charging across open ground; one or two of them throwing their hands into the air and dropping dramatically to the ground, while others quietly folded up as if their bones had suddenly turned to water.'[26]

Young Captain Woollcombe up there with the Scottish infantry felt proud of himself at that moment: 'We were the first British unit to breach the main belt of the Siegfried Line.'[27] Solemnly the battalion's regimental sergeant-major, who had waited a long time for this moment, 'ceremonially hoisted a quantity of washing on the Siegfried Line.'

But Woollcombe's strangest memory of that moment of glory concerned 'a solitary German woman – how she got there goodness knows – at the height of the assault, hurrying along a track as fast as she could from the danger. A middle-aged frau in black and the first enemy civilian one had seen. Beside her a British soldier in full battle order was carrying her suitcase!'

And it rained and it rained and it rained.

Settling down for the night, worn and weary, Foley listened to the rain drumming on the steel of the turret hatch above his head and knew the way ahead would be 'a proper mess' the next day. His crew were more interested in the extra rum ration that they were entitled to on account of the bad weather.

'This should square things for a rum issue, eh, sir?' one of them suggested hopefully.

'Depends how long it lasts,' Foley answered.

'Sounds as if it'll last for a couple of days anyway,' the crew man said.[28]

In fact, apart from two isolated breaks, the heavy rain was going to last exactly nineteen days.

* * *

Two days after Montgomery's great set-piece battle had run into the one element he had not allowed for, war correspondent R. W. Thompson set off to visit the Canadians in the Siegfried Line, now calling themselves the 'Water Rats,' just as Monty's Eighth Army men in North Africa had entitled themselves the 'Desert Rats.'

It was a strange journey as Thompson traveled through the flooded fields in an amphibious armored vehicle, the Buffalo. As he wrote, 'It is an odd sensation to know the elaborate defenses in depth, the minefields, the barbed wire, the machine gun and mortar nests, and all the deadly devices of an ingenious enemy, six feet beneath your feet . . . It is an odd sensation, in fact, to sail over the Siegfried Line and beyond deep into the Reich.'[29]

The Canadian crew had only land maps to 'sail' by and felt happiest in deep water, gliding through the branches of trees and beside the tops of telegraph poles. Finally they reached their destination and 'made land' at a small village where a platoon of Canadian infantry had been marooned for two days with little food and no heat whatsoever. They welcomed the 'Noah's Ark,' as the crew were now calling their vehicle, and dug into the rations greedily before the Buffalo passed on to find more marooned survivors of the great floods. As the Canadians somehow formed up for another attack that dawn, with the sun beginning at last to climb the gray horizon, Thompson noted, 'Enemy jet planes swoop in to harass us, but these men cannot be disturbed by anything from air, land or water. As I churn back toward Wainwright Beach [the name the crew had given to the Buffalo's staging area] across the Siegfried Line, I am glad land is at last in sight for them . . .'[30]

3

At last land was in sight for the Allied infantry along the whole length of that dreaded wall. Private Atwell, following the 78th Division, walked up a soaked track that same day and saw his first pillbox. In its indistinctness, he thought it looked like the 'curbed stone top of a prehistoric ruin.' He and his companions were overcome by the uncanny atmosphere of the place and one of them cried angrily, 'Fer Chrissake, someone say something!'

Later Atwell and the rest went to bed down in the abandoned bunker. But while his comrades snored, Atwell couldn't sleep. He listened to the 'wild sighing through the pinetrees and I lay watching the ghostly mist pour in. Echoes of German voices seemed to linger, giving commands and the sad tune of "Lili Marlene" that they must have hummed or sung, writing homesick letters. All the German dreams that led them on to war, all the myths, all the hours of standing guard – the room held the cries and remembrances. I fell asleep hearing the pines sigh sadly in the rain.'[31]

Sergeant Giles of the combat engineers, also following the 78th Division through the shattered Huertgen Forest, found himself in the West Wall that same night. As he wrote to his wife, 'I think it is rather historic and worth mentioning that tonight some of us from HQ squad are bivouacked in the middle of Adolf's famous Siegfried Line and in one of his damned pillboxes.'[32]

The men hadn't wanted to sleep there because they felt they were not supposed to and the place might be booby-trapped, but they were engineers after all. So after clearing the place, they decided: 'Hell – let's be historic. Let's make this damned thing our home for the night.'

Their reward? A bad case of lice for each man. Souvenir of the lately departed *Wehrmacht*.

Others, such as the greenhorns of the 76th Infantry, had been right in the middle of the West Wall for nearly three days now and they had still not fought their way out of what the divisional history called 'rats' nests,' with as many as forty pillboxes per square mile, one every forty yards. In addition, those heights opposite the Luxembourg town of Echternach contained per square mile no fewer than a hundred other fortified positions, trenches and the ever-present minefields. One GI brought up as a reinforcement on the morning of February 11th, viewing the battlefield from the Luxembourg side of the River Sauer, exploded with understandable reaction, 'Holy Jesus, what a detail!'

That morning a full-scale attack, planned by a lieutenant colonel no less, was going in against one pillbox which had held up the 76th Division all the previous day. A full-scale barrage from one whole artillery battalion fell on the place for fifteen minutes. This was followed by a mortar stonk, which ended as a pallid green flare sailed into the sky to hang there momentarily before hissing down like a falling angel. It was the signal for the assault squad to go in.

As they rushed forward, the leading troops touched off a cunningly concealed tripwire. Mines started to explode everywhere. The lieutenant leading the assault staggered. He was hit, but he recovered and continued running forward. Now the infantry were twenty-five yards away from the obstinate pillbox. The machine guns covering their rush ceased firing. It would have been too dangerous to continue. The men were on their own now. A private rushed forward and dropped a satchel charge against the door of the large front embrasure. He pelted for cover as the satchel charge exploded with a great roar. But when the smoke cleared, the watching infantry could see that only part of the iron door had disappeared. It still barred their entry. Another volunteer rushed forward to deposit a second satchel charge. It failed to explode. A sergeant ran out, ignoring the lead plucking at the dirt around his flying feet. He tossed two grenades through the hole that the first charge had made.

That did it. The whole crew of fifteen men came running out, hands high in the air, crying a fearful '*Kamerad! . . . No shoot please!*'

The infantry who had cracked the pillbox were too weary even to think. They slumped down, as if they were the vanquished and the Germans were the victors. An officer came up and ordered the captured Germans to start clearing away the mines around their pillbox. The whole operation had taken one hour and fifteen minutes and had cost two men wounded. *And there were forty pillboxes to each square mile of German territory!*

By February 13th, Patton's Third Army had crossed the Our–Sauer line along its whole length from near St Vith in Belgium down to Echternach in Luxembourg. In the north Colonel 'Buck' Lanham's 22nd Infantry had finally captured Prum, its objective back in those heady optimistic days of the previous September. Now there was only a handful of the veterans left. Irwin's 5th, Patton's favorite division for a while, had taken all its objectives, and the green troops of the 76th Division were so firmly entrenched in the West Wall that the Germans now were incapable of ever throwing them out again.

Slowly the fighting died out, and the weary men, who six days before had assaulted the river line and the West Wall beyond, now began to come down from the hills. On the Luxembourg side of the River Sauer the divisional brass watched as Lieutenant Richard Bluhm brought in those of his men who were left. As the 76th's divisional history noted, 'All that could be seen in those dirty whiskered faces, in the sag of wet shoulders, in the shuffle of mudcaked feet, was the weariness of men who had lived with continuous danger, little food and less sleep for nearly a week – complete utter fatigue.'

Another platoon came in and one weary GI called out, 'Hey, did you hear about Lieutenant Mears?' Thereupon he told anyone prepared to listen in that fatigued conglomeration of begrimed humanity about how Mears had led Company K through machine-gun fire that came 'so fast it was like solid steel.' Then single-handed, armed only with a jammed carbine and a grenade, Mears had attacked a pillbox and forced the six Krauts inside it to surrender. 'Gosh, what a guy!' the GI breathed in awe.

But most of them were too exhausted to listen to tales of battlefield heroism. They wanted food, hot water and, above all, sleep. All were waiting for them; even their Christmas mail and packages had finally reached them. Now several hundred grimy soldiers trekked to an open field next to a Luxembourg village where a Quartermaster shower unit had been set up. Stripping naked in the drizzle, dropping their uniforms in the mud – they would get clean deloused ones at the other end of the shower line – they filed into the tents and surrendered their skinny dirty naked bodies to the benison of hot water and soap. As Sergeant Philmon Erickson sighed pleasurably, 'I had to travel through France, Belgium, and most of Luxembourg to get a chance at hot water and soap, but boy, *it was worth it!*'

One day after the fighting on the Third Army front died down, General Patton took his first leave of the campaign. One after another, the members of his staff had broken down under the strain of the last seven months of fighting, even the Third Army's senior doctor, yet the 60-year-old Commanding General, the oldest of them all, seemed to thrive on the stress of battle. Even now Patton's motives were not related entirely to relaxation in Paris, where he had chosen to spend his leave. His main concern was to ensure somehow that, now that Montgomery's campaign in the north was in full swing, the Third Army would not be ordered to halt in position; he wanted to continue the battle for the three-river line, although he was now facing some of the toughest and most rugged terrain in southwest Germany where a handful of determined men could hold up whole regiments.

Together with his personal aide, French-speaking Colonel Codman, Patton traveled in style to Paris in Field Marshal Goering's captured auto-rail train and established himself in the luxurious George V Hotel. The leavemen's first stop was the Folies Bergères, where 'les girls' put on a special show for Patton. Codman, who had served in France in World War One, as had Patton, thought it was the same show he had seen in 1918.

Thereafter the Commanding General was received by Madame la Directrice Derval, who put a motherly hand on his arm and said in halting English, 'Please remember, General, from now on whenever you are in Paris, should you feel in need of a little repose' – she broke into French, '*enfin du calme – ne vous faites pas prier; venez aux Folies Bergères. Ici vous êtes chez vous.*' ('Or some peace – don't wait to be asked. Come to the Folies Bergères. You can make yourself at home here.')

To which Patton replied, a grin on his long face, 'Jesus, I'm not *that* old!'[33]

Next morning after champagne cocktails with Marlene Dietrich – Patton's 'favorite Kraut' – and Ernest Hemingway who was preparing to leave Europe, Patton left to go hunting with General Hughes.

Codman stayed behind with Hemingway to discuss books and the fact that a trigger-happy American sentry had shot la Dietrich's driver in France recently. Later he returned to his hotel to find that Patton had come back from his hunting much earlier than was expected and was now in bed with a case of suspected food poisoning. But although Patton was in some pain, he was quite satisfied with the results of his 48-hour leave to the French capital. During the course of the hunt, before the stomach pains had become too severe to bear, he had obtained that which he had come to Paris to obtain – another armored division from Eisenhower's SHAEF Reserve. He was going to be given General Morris's 10th Armored for a single operation; thereafter the division had to be returned to the SHAEF Reserve at once.

No wonder Patton was happy, for Morris's 10th ensured that he could now launch the third phase of his 'active defense,' as Eisenhower's staff officers present at the hunt were now calling the activities of the Third Army. Without telling Hughes and the rest what he had in mind for the 10th, Patton left Paris in Goering's train with the firm intention of breaking through the West Wall on the River Saar and capturing the key railhead-and-road town of Trier, 'old when Rome was young,' as its citizens boasted. Now he had the means to complete his 'rock soup' operation and Montgomery be damned. As Colonel Codman commented in a letter to his wife in Boston, 'The inside story of this operation [the attack on the West Wall toward Trier] will, I think, shed an interesting light on the General's implementation of "active defense." '[34] It certainly would.

4

In the north everything was going wrong. The battlefield
had turned into a swamp. The key highway from
Nijmegen to Cleve had become inundated and a monu-
mental traffic jam had developed. South of Montgomery's
First Canadian Army, Simpson's Ninth US Army was also
beset by water. The River Roer was rising and the tall
bald-headed Army Commander thought that the Germans might have blown the dams, for there was still no
news from Hodges's First Army which had the task of
capturing them.

Simpson was plagued with doubts. Montgomery's
attack had drawn off the main body of General Schlemm's
First Parachute Army. Now he was faced by only four
weak German divisions. But dared he risk his men getting
bogged down, even isolated by a massive flood of water?
He polled his corps commanders. All but one of them
urged the postponement of Ninth Army's attack. Simpson
told them he would give them his decision at four o'clock.

All afternoon he wrestled with the problem. His engineers had told him that the dams had not been breached
and that the water was occasioned by a 'run-off' from the
River Roer. Should he take a calculated risk, Simpson
asked himself. Just before four o'clock he learnt the river
was still rising, but only slightly. What if he called off the
attack and the Roer did not overflow its banks? It would
probably mean the end of his career. He agonized and
vacillated. Then at exactly four o'clock, something told
him, a kind of inner voice, 'Postpone the Ninth's attack.'
He did.

*   *   *

It was fortunate for the Ninth that he did. For Craig's 9th Infantry Division of the First Army had still not reached the dams. The Germans retreated painfully slowly, fighting for every inch of muddy German earth. Five hours after General Simpson had made his fateful decision, at exactly nine o'clock that night, the men of Craig's 309th Infantry Regiment groped their way through the darkness to the largest of the German dams, which held back 81,000 acre-feet of water. In battalion strength they rushed the powerhouse. By midnight, harried by German machine-gun fire, a platoon of combat engineers were racing along the top of the dam itself, heading for an inspection tunnel. Their way was blocked by a blasted spillway. The engineers didn't hesitate. With tracer hissing all about them like lethal fireflies, they slid two hundred feet down the steep dam face to reach the tunnel's bottom exit. To no avail.

The Germans had already destroyed the machinery in the powerhouse and then blown up the penstocks. Now the ice-cold water was rushing out steadily, hour after hour. The Roer valley would be flooded for another two weeks.

Horrocks was on his own. Simpson's Ninth would be unable to move; he would face the full force of Schlemm's First Parachute Army mired down in terrain no better than that which the young subalterns, who were now the British and Canadian divisional commanders, had experienced in the dreaded trenches of World War One. And there was worse to come. Soon the water released from the shattered dams would be spilling into the River Meuse. By midnight Horrocks realized that calamity had struck: the low ground below the *Reichswald* was flooded. His Canadians, Welshmen, Scots, and English infantry were now going to fight one of the most grueling, punishing battles of the war, while the Americans stood on the sidelines as helpless spectators.

* * *

Major Brodie of the 5th Seaforths of the 51st Highland
Division, who had already suffered multiple wounds back
in Normandy, was now leading his company in an attack
on a monastery on the outskirts of the German town of
Goch, a central West Wall position. At the head of his
men he rushed the place, clambering up the big steps
under machine-gun fire. 'One poor chap was shot down,'
he recollected later, 'but the rest of us arrived safely . . . I
threw a smoke grenade, but it bounced back and burst a
foot or two from me so that I was quite badly burned on
each hand and in the face.'[35]

Still the Seaforths pushed on. A German officer surrendered. One of Brodie's non-coms asked, 'Can we have
him, sir?'

Brodie asked what he meant.

The non-com pointed to the latest recruits to the
company, a bunch of eighteen-year-olds, and said they
hadn't killed a German yet. Brodie was shocked and told
the much-decorated non-com to ensure that the German
officer and the other prisoners now flooding out of the
monastery were taken safely to the rear.

The Major and his men pushed on into the suburbs of
Goch, now burning merrily. He was hit in the throat with
grenade fragments, 'which tickled a bit, but did not hurt
much.' He and the survivors were struck by a mortar
barrage. Again Major Brodie was wounded 'in the leg and
one or two other places . . . Nothing serious. However,
being hit does sting a lot at the time and is rather a shock.'
Eventually, covered in blood, Brodie decided he was
getting delirious and had better see a doctor. Walking
back to the dressing station through the shell-shattered
streets, littered with the dead in their soaked khaki and
field-gray, he was hit yet again, by a shell fragment which
cracked a bone in his foot. He finally arrived at his
destination, 'looking a pretty bloody sight, looking worse

than I was. Everyone was far more sympathetic than I deserved.'[36]

In the end he was evacuated. But Major Brodie's misfortunes for the day were not yet over. The jeep bearing him back skidded into a ditch full of icy water. Philosophically, the sorely hurt Major Brodie thought the icy water 'probably did my foot good.' He woke up again in England.

Lance-Corporal Wingfield of the Queen's Royal Regiment did not escape the battlefield that easily. He had been wounded with many others of his platoon attacking a great anti-tank ditch the night before. That dawn, he and the other wounded lying in shell craters all about had been abandoned as their fellow infantrymen had been forced to withdraw.

Suddenly advancing Germans were everywhere. '*Tot* [dead],' one of them grunted, stepping on the corporal's badly wounded abdomen.

Suddenly several things happened at once, as Wingfield recalled. 'A Vickers cut loose from behind. The tracers flared three feet overhead, stopped and went on again. One of the men's boots was right by my head when the burst started. A horrid sound, midway between a cough and a belch, and a body fell heavily across my legs, quivered, thrashed and lay still. His Schmeisser toppled across my shoulders and clouted me over the ear.'[37]

The German counter-attack faded away to be replaced by British artillery fire which started to 'walk backward,' clearing away the rest of the Germans but also falling on the wounded.

Wingfield screamed for mercy, crying to God and demanding '*No more! . . . No more!*' A shell landed right among the wounded, and another, and another. 'Their concussion threw me this way and that, forward and backward. The earth heaved. It shook. I seemed to bounce like a ball. I turned a complete somersault and landed on my knees with a crash. I buried my face in the ground. I closed my eyes. I daren't look any more.'[38]

Finally the barrage ceased and the stretcher-bearers started to creep out in no man's land looking for wounded, crying 'Here we are, mate. The sheriff's bleeding posse always gets through!'

One of Wingfield's old mates was first to find him. 'Glad to see you're out of it, Corp,' he said and then added greedily, 'Can I have the tin of soup you've got clasped to your manly bosom?'

Wingfield laughed and gave him the tin of self-heating soup. A little while later he found himself in the advance dressing station. His uniform was cut away and he was bandaged up temporarily and then placed on a Bren-gun carrier to be transported to the rear. To his alarm he found he was accompanied by a padre wearing a steel helmet.

The chaplain saw his expression and said, 'Don't worry, boy. I'm not with you in case you die on the way! I'm just coming down to the CCS to see the rest of our boys. You're our last customer.'

Wingfield relaxed. He had been lying out in no man's land, with two tracer-bullet shots through his hips, for seven hours. Now, as the carrier bore him (as he expressed it sarcastically) on 'a moving feather-bed,' he knew he was leaving the battalion for good. '*I was out!*'[39]

The rain was beginning to get the men down. For some it was worse than the actual fighting.

John Foley, fighting the pillboxes of the West Wall the best he could with his Churchills and supporting flame-throwing tanks, wrote later: 'After ten days of rain we were beginning to feel the effect. Wet through, plastered with mud, half-deafened by gunfire, we were getting irritable and short-tempered with one another.'[40]

Occasionally, though, there was a ray of light in the gray gloom. One afternoon Foley's troop crossed the Dutch-German frontier yet again (they kept crossing it throughout the battle).

This time they were confronted by a striped wooden pole barring the road. Foley's driver asked what it was and the officer, eyeing the first German civilian he had seen since the battle commenced, said it was a border marker. The occasion was too good to waste on Smith 161 (his last three army serial numbers, to distinguish him from all the other Smiths), the troop's humorist. He leaned out of his driver's seat and said perfectly straight-faced, 'We on the right road to Berlin, mate?'

The elderly civilian tugged his grizzled moustache and equally straight-faced answered, '*Berlin, ja, ja . . . immer gerade aus*' (Berlin, yes, straight ahead).

'And I thought the Germans had no sense of humor,' another crew member said as the tanks started to rumble forward once more.

Thompson, the war correspondent, reached Goch that day and noted the few civilians wandering around the steaming rubble of their homes in a daze. A priest approached the correspondent and asked if he could hold a service. Thompson told him it was no use. Most of his flock was now buried beneath 'all this lath and plaster that once gave form and pattern to the shapeless mass of Goch.'

Now Goch was taken, and Cleve too. The Canadian infantry of a French-Canadian regiment rushed the village of Moyland which barred the way to the small town of Calcar, Horrocks's last objective before his XXX Corps faced the final German defensive line called the 'Hochwald Layback.'

There the French-Canadians of the 3rd Canadian Division fought for four solid days, facing one counter-attack after another from four fresh paratroop regiments thrown into the battle by General Schlemm. Finally, on the morning of February 22nd, they broke through to Moyland to meet a reception they had surely not expected in the middle of that lunar landscape, where the dead lay everywhere among the shattered trees and in the waterlogged fields.

Out of the cellars of Moyland Castle, built in the eighteenth century, emerged the ancient Baroness Steengracht von Moyland, who protested that the Canadians had taken no notice of the white sheets of surrender she had ordered hung all about her castle. The French-Canadian infantrymen told her that they had grown exceedingly wary of white flags of surrender.

The Baroness sighed and accepted their explanation. In the old Army, she said, they would not have done such things: she supposed it was these 'dreadful SS people.' With that she retired back to her cellars, where R. W. Thompson spotted her a few hours later, sitting 'silent with her thoughts, perhaps with the pageant of the years and the distant past like a sumptuous tapestry of brilliant color in her mind. All these things that she will never see again. All these things of a dead world.'

As he left the battle to return to Brussels for a welcome rest, Thompson noted, 'On a grand piano of lovely mellow tone, amidst the ruins of the drawing room of the great lodge at the crossroads of Moyland, a young French-Canadian officer is playing the *Warsaw Concerto*, the vivid dramatic music of a world crashing in flames. Through the desolation of the trees I had a last glimpse of Moyland Castle with the white flag drooping at its round tower.'[41]

* * *

One day later Calcar fell and Horrocks could say in a personal message to his weary, mud-caked troops, dated February 23, 1945: 'You have now successfully completed the first part of your task. You have taken approximately 12,000 prisoners and killed large numbers of Germans. You have broken through the Siegfried Line and drawn on to yourselves the bulk of the German reserves in the West. A strong US offensive was launched over the Roer at 0330 hours this morning against positions which, thanks to your efforts, are lightly held by the Germans . . . Thank you for what you have done so well. If we continue our efforts a few more days, the German front is bound to crack.'

But this hope was not yet to be fulfilled. The Germans and the West Wall had plenty of fight in them yet.

5

At three thirty on the morning of February 23rd, Simpson's Ninth Army finally attacked, while further south Hodges's First Army assaulted the main control center for that part of the West Wall, the frontier town of Dueren. Attacking as they did before the floods had altogether disappeared, the Americans caught the Germans off guard and their casualties were surprisingly light – under one hundred men killed in all four assault divisions.

That morning von Rundstedt telephoned General Schlemm and told him, 'The Americans have crossed the Roer . . . after a forty-five minute bombardment. They have crossed the river on a front of twenty-two kilometers.'

'That's bad news,' the little paratroop general said.

'I agree,' Germany's most senior soldier replied.

All that day the two generals followed the Americans' progress anxiously. Next morning Schlemm telephoned von Rundstedt and told him, 'We must at all costs prevent the enemy junction. My paratroopers are holding back the Canadians. Have you enough men to hold the Americans?'

Von Rundstedt said he had not.

'Then I suggest taking two armored and one infantry division away from me and sending them south.'[42]

Von Rundstedt agreed. Schlemm putting down the phone now concentrated on warding off the new attack just launched by Crerar's 2nd Canadian Corps against the Hochwald Layback position. This time it was a mainly Canadian effort; three Canadian divisions and two British ones taking part in it, in an effort to blast a huge hole in Schlemm's line and pour in the armor.

But in spite of the massive artillery and air support which Crerar had obtained – so that to General Essame who took part in the battle it seemed as if he was back fighting in 'the muddy fields of Passchendaele and the shell-torn slopes of Vimy Ridge' of World War One – Schlemm was not going to give up easily. He turned the new battle into a fierce courageous slogging match of attack and counter-attack.

Sergeant Aubrey Cousins found himself in command of the four surviving members of his platoon just as Schlemm's paratroops commenced a new attack. He ran through the thick of the enemy's fire to a stalled tank. Seating himself calmly on the turret, he directed the gunner's fire against the advancing paratroops in their camouflage tunics and baggy trousers. They broke and ran for the cover of the woods. But they came again. This time Cousins directed the driver to drive his Sherman right into the mass of the paratroops, and he sent them reeling back in confusion.

Now Cousins went over to the counter-attack. He and the handful of Canadian infantry rushed the nearest houses and turfed out the Germans, killing twenty and capturing many more. At last satisfied he had done enough, he consolidated the positions captured and went back to report to his commanding officer. He was shot by a sniper as he did so. He was posthumously awarded the Victoria Cross.

He was not the only Canadian to receive that highest of all awards from the Crown in those grim days of the last week of February 1945. Major Tiltson of the Canadian Essex Scottish led his company across five hundred yards of open ground, clambering over ten feet of barbed wire to finally attack the trenches held by the paratroopers. He was wounded in the head. Still he continued in the fore of his company. He silenced a machine-gun-post with grenades and pressed on into the second line of defense. This time he was hit severely in the thigh, but he refused to allow himself to be evacuated and directed the Essex Scottish in hand-to-hand fighting in order to clear the trenches.

Now the Germans counter-attacked. Tiltson organized the defenders, now one quarter of their original strength, beating off the attack. He was hit again. But lying in a shell hole he continued to fight back, refusing all medical aid, until finally the Germans gave up and Tiltson handed over command of the handful of men left alive to his one remaining officer. Tiltson survived, but his incredible courage, which gained him the VC, cost him both his legs.

R. W. Thompson, who was present at that last desperate battle, jumped on a tank 'because there did not seem to be any other fairly sure way to go on living,' and was told by its gunner: 'I wouldn't have their job [he was referring to the attacking infantry] for a pension. Compared with them it's a picnic for the rest of us. They're bloody heroes!'[43]

* * *

The young foot soldiers of both the Canadian and British Armies certainly did live hard that February. They existed on the cheap beef and fish of their Compo rations supplemented by 'hard tack.' Real bread was a luxury and when it did come up the line it was usually rationed out at one slice per man. The only luxuries the men were afforded were the seven cigarettes and the handful of 'boiled sweets' they each received daily, and above all their rum ration, half a mugful poured from the big platoon jar under the suspicious eye of the colour sergeant. The SRD (service rum, diluted) brought new fire to the skinny worn bodies of the teenage infantry, making their eyes water and causing them to cough, but as they invariably said later, 'It doesn't half go down good!'

Thompson, after an hour's sleep under a tarpaulin on that last day of February, rose and wandered about the positions of the British infantry who would attack that morning toward the village of Kurvenheim. 'I walked in the woodland, looking down in the dark slits. In each one two men huddled, facing each other, squatting with their backs to the ends of the slits, and their knees up together. They slept in their tin hats and wrapped in their greatcoats. One or two had got some straw from somewhere and made a bit of roof over the slit and they lay in some comfort. Last night, I knew, they had slept in much the same way, but not under fire. On the next night things might be even worse. So I stood a long time reflecting on all this while the sky filled with cloud and hid the three-quarter moon.'

At three thirty breakfast arrived. A young officer said cheerfully to the bespectacled correspondent, 'I bet you never thought you'd really enjoy a bowl of porridge at three in the middle of the night.'

Thompson agreed he hadn't. Then he watched as the young soldiers prepared to go and fight yet once again, 'with the red tracer hitting the roof of the building ricocheting and soaring high.' 'There is a kind of wonder in me,' he recorded for his readers that morning, 'and a sense of despair to make you know about them. Here is one with the heavy mortar tube on his shoulder. Another with a Bren over his shoulder. They pause and wait, and plod on, ready to fight, ready to charge with bayonets fixed, ready to die. I just want you to know about it.'[44]

6

The 10th Armored was not one of General Patton's favorite divisions. It was commanded by General Morris, who had graduated from West Point in the same year as Patton himself. Like Patton, Morris had fought briefly in France in 1918 and had been wounded there, too. But he did not possess the same fire as his illustrious contemporary. During the autumn fighting against the West Wall on the River Saar, the 10th had done well, but not brilliantly; still, it did know the ground like the infantry division, the 94th, which was now to be its running mate.

Now Patton was breathing down Morris's neck, knowing that if the 10th did not capture Trier soon it would have to revert to the SHAEF Reserve, and that would be the end of his attempts to keep the Third Army involved in the shooting war. Since February 21st, the 10th had been attacking the so-called 'Orscholz Line Position' of the West Wall, constructed as an east–west extension at right angles to the main Siegfried Line defenses. But its progress and also that of the 94th was too slow for Patton. In that last week of February while the Canadians were fighting their bloody and bitter campaign against

Schlemm's paras in the north, Patton went to visit his divisions on the River Saar – and his mood was bad.

Just before he had left for the front, Bradley had told him, 'Georgie, if you use the 10th Armored to take Trier, you may be sorry.' That was exactly what Patton was planning to do and every day that Morris delayed in achieving that objective made it more sure that SHAEF might recall the 10th.

At the CP of 94th Infantry, which was working in conjunction with the 10th, Patton gave its commander General Maloney a dressing down on account of the recent action the division had fought at Orscholz, telling him that his losses in men taken prisoner by the Germans were the worst he had ever come across. Speaking about that meeting long after the war, Harry McLaughlin said, 'He hated our guts. We lost 120 men in a bad battle at Orscholz, killed or taken prisoner, and he told our men in a speech that we were yellow bastards and that our losses in POWs were the worst of his career. He hated us with a passion!'[45]

From the 94th, Patton traveled on to the headquarters of XX Corps which was directing the attack through the West Wall toward Trier. There he learnt from General Walker, the bulky Corps Commander, that Morris had managed to lose the bridging train so vitally needed for the operation against Trier. He glowered at Walker and said, 'You should have seen it was in place. So should I. We have all three fallen down on the job.' Just before he left, Patton snapped to Walker, 'General Morris will lead his division across the river in the first boat, or, if necessary, *swim*!'

It was obvious to Walker's staff officers that Patton was letting the strain of attempting to capture Trier secretly, as it were, get him down. The old Roman city had to be captured soon or heads would roll!

*   *   *

On February 26th, XX Corps had still not captured Trier. Just north of the village of Zerf, the 10th Armored was violently attacked by the 6th SS Mountain Division. Morris for once reacted smartly. Assuming that the SS would attempt to stop him getting behind the West Wall from Zerf and attacking in a southeasterly direction, Morris ordered his troops to turn north. The trick worked. The SS attacked in the wrong direction and the 10th Armored began making progress once again.

That morning Patton marched into the headquarters of the 76th Division, now resting after its attack on the West Wall. According to the divisional historian, 'He strode brusquely into the inner sanctum, placed a huge fist on the map of Trier. That was all. It was an order . . . All efforts now were concentrated on making contact with XX Corps to the south.'

That night Patton called Bradley and told him the 10th was within five miles of Trier and asked him if he could keep on going. Now Bradley knew the secret. 'You either take Trier in two days,' Bradley told him, 'or you'll have to return the 10th Armored.' He then added he would stop Patton only if ordered to do so by higher authority – and he'd keep away from the phone for the next day or two.

On the 28th, the 10th had still not captured Trier. Patton decided to visit Morris. Codman, Patton's aide, telephoned Morris and the two of them agreed on a spot where Patton could meet the 10th's commander. Just as Patton's car reached the agreed spot, a military policeman directed it to another meeting place. Minutes later a heavy salvo of shells landed on the first spot, proving to Patton that the Germans were tapping the US phone lines and had planned to kill him.

They tried again later that day. After Morris had received his instructions, Patton and Maloney went to sample some Moselle wine, which turned out to be very poor. Just as the two generals were raising their glasses, a shell came 'almost as close to our heads as it could without hitting us,' as Patton explained later.

The near miss turned the officers' mind to religion. Thus during the trip back to Patton's Luxembourg head-quarters, one of his officers became so emphatic about his religious ancestry that he said, 'By God, General, my people have been Catholics for more than 3,000 years!'

Patton laughed. 'What – B.C. Catholics?' he asked.

'Yessir,' the officer said doggedly.

As Patton remarked later, 'I have told this story many times – and a few people have laughed.'

But if Patton was not satisfied with the speed of Morris's advance and now ordered Maloney, too, to make an assault crossing of the River Saar in the face of some of the West Wall's most formidable positions in order to aid Morris, von Rundstedt was worried by the unpredictable 'cowboy general,' as he called Patton.

In the north Montgomery's and Simpson's men were virtually completely through the West Wall and were about to enter the flat open country that led to the Rhine, ideal for armor. There, however, the aged Field Marshal still had Schlemm's formidable paratroopers to hold him up. In the south, on the other hand, there was little to stop Patton once he had broken through. He could race for the Rhine in a matter of days, barreling through the mostly second-line units opposing him.[46]

On the 25th, von Rundstedt asked Hitler for new directives for his command. Unless there was a general retreat across the Rhine, he signaled the Führer, the entire western front would crumble.

His desperate appeal was ignored. Two days later von Rundstedt put forward a more modest proposal: a withdrawal near the junction of the Roer and Maas rivers. Hitler sent him by return a curt personal message stating that no withdrawal could be sanctioned; the troops would have to stay and fight where they were. In a conference later he ridiculed von Rundstedt's persistent calls for withdrawal. 'I want him to hang onto the West Wall so long as humanly possible. Above all we must cure him of the idea of retreating here . . . These people just don't have any vision. It would only mean moving the catastrophe from one place to another.'[47]

Thus it was that General Maloney's 94th Infantry Division, the last of all Patton's Third Army to attack the West Wall, went into battle in that last week of February to experience the same terrible slaughter that the first US outfits had suffered the previous September.

Everything went wrong right from the start. On February 27th, the first companies of the 94th moved into the woods on the western bank of the River Saar which they would have to assault before they could attack the West Wall on the eastern bank near the Saar hamlet of Hamm. They had been told that the woods had been cleared of Germans save for a few stragglers. What they had not been told was that elements of the 10th Armored Division were combing those same woods for those stragglers.

Lieutenant Vinne, leading the company at point, blundered into armed men in the darkness which would cover their assault across the river. Tracer cut the night. Artillery howled into action. A regular fire-fight developed and Vinne was forced to withdraw his company with heavy losses. Only then was it discovered that the men of the 10th Armored and their supposed running-mate the 94th had been fighting each other! Vinne lost exactly half of his company in that tragic little battle between American and American. But there was worse to come.

At four o'clock that morning, two battalions of Colonel McClune's 376th Infantry Regiment started to cross the River Saar under cover of smoke. Their attack was to form a bridgehead between the largest of the West Wall bunkers facing them. The tanks of the 10th would follow, roll up the West Wall, and finally achieve the breakthrough that Patton so urgently needed if he were to capture Trier before the 10th was taken from him. But it didn't get far. The requisite number of assault boats failed to appear. Fog had formed further up the valley of the Saar and made it very difficult for the engineers to bring them up in sufficient strength.

So the attack was called off for the time being. As dawn broke, wet and foggy, some three thousand frustrated infantrymen lay in the woods opposite the site of the proposed bridgehead. They lay there all day, the fog refusing to lift, while on the heights beyond, the Germans in their bunkers had long since realized that the Americans must be going to attack in strength.

At four thirty-five that day, Colonel McClune, under pressure from division, decided he could wait no longer. He gave the order to cross immediately.

Once again the American chemical companies started making smoke to cover the crossing. But the thick brown smoke and fog offered no problem for the Germans. Almost immediately, the heavy guns in the second line of bunkers opened up with a tremendous crash, while the waiting tanks and assault guns added their fire to the thunder of the heavies. Meanwhile in the first row of bunkers, machine gunners systematically started to knock out the smoke generators, one by one.

Everything seemed to be in the Germans' favor, as boat after boat was hit, its occupants sent screaming and yelling for help into the fast-flowing Saar. A strong west wind blew up out of nowhere and began to drive away the fog.

Now the men in khaki in the middle of that shell-torn stretch of water were completely exposed to the full weight of the German heavy artillery.

It was too much for the GIs. They broke and started to chug furiously for the opposite bank, leaving scores of drifting boats filled with dead and dying behind them. Not one single soldier reached the eastern shore that day. Colonel McClune's attack was a total failure.

But McClune would not give up that easily. As engineers and medics pulled the scores of shaken, shivering soldiers of the first wave out of the water, he ordered a new crossing to be launched at nine thirty that night. Again everything went wrong. The fog returned. McClune postponed the attack till eleven o'clock.

Punctually the first companies pushed off, paddling their way through the thick wet fog, fighting the current which was very stiff now. A company under the command of Lieutenant Jacques was first to reach the opposite shore. He struck lucky. Slipping through the fog, he managed to capture a bunker whose commander had not expected the Americans to make a second attempt on the same day, especially after sustaining such losses.

Colonel McClune crossed with the second wave, but by now the Germans were waking up to the new danger. White tracer started to hiss across the Saar once again. Green and red signal flares whooshed alarmingly into the sky. Automatically the occupants of the bunkers began to give each other crossfire and thus prevent the Americans getting close enough to attack. McClune went forward personally to see what was holding up the advance. He was surprised by a German machine gunner and received a full burst in the body. He crumpled to the ground severely wounded. Before he passed out, he handed over command to Lieutenant Colonel Anderson. But Anderson could do no better than McClune, who now had been evacuated.

Now the dawn air was disturbed by a new and alarming sound – heavy tanks. The Germans were about to counter-attack. Just before first light they did so. Sixteen Panthers of the SS, laden with mounted infantry. They threw the Americans back into the cover of a small wood. More boats with reinforcements were rushed across under severe enemy fire to make up the 94th Division's losses which were mounting steeply by the hour. One whole company was wiped out in the water, but the rest, panting and wild-eyed, flung themselves down among their hard-pressed comrades and helped to hold off the SS attack.

Now as dawn spread a tentative light over the scene, desperate appeals for help began to cross the water, filled with the floating corpses of dead infantrymen. By midday, eight whole American artillery battalions had been drawn up on the western bank of the River Saar between the town of Saarburg and the village of Ayl. The formidable weight of their united fire descended upon the SS counter-attackers. 'It was a tremendous wave of fire,' one of the few survivors remembered later, 'that sent us running for our lives and turned the streets into rubble and ash.'

Now the Americans could advance again toward the bunker line. But behind them at the river, every attempt by the combat engineers to build a pontoon bridge to bring supplies and reinforcements across was destroyed by heavy German counterfire.

A desperate General Malone asked for air support. Just before darkness that long terrible day, the gleaming Thunderbolts came winging in low and at a hundred feet began attacking the bunkers with their rockets. Like flights of angry red hornets, the missiles flew toward the bunkers sunk deep in the earth so that only their concrete roofs showed. They made little impact. And each time the planes rose high into the air after the attack, their fat silver bellies were peppered by German small-arms fire. Not one dive-bomber escaped without hits.

That night all available troops on the eastern bank of the River Saar were ordered into an all-out attack on the bunker line. The lead company under Captain Standish managed to reach the railway line that ran through the bunker line. Heavy German fire forced him and his men to take cover. But not for long. At Standish's command they rushed the nearest bunker, men going down all the time, until finally satchel-charges thrust through apertures and doors forced the occupants to surrender. It was the first real success of the day. But further tragedy was to strike Patton's men in this last attempt to crack the West Wall.

Resting after their efforts in the growing darkness, the survivors mistook a large body of men marching slovenly along the railway track toward them for German prisoners. It was an error for which they paid directly. The Germans, who outnumbered Standish's survivors considerably, recognized the Americans first. They went into action at once. Bitter hand-to-hand fighting developed. There was some panic. Captain Standish disappeared. The Germans penetrated the newly captured bunkers. At one forty-five that morning there was a terrible explosion followed by screams and cries for help – then silence. By dawn what was left of Standish's men crawled back to the start-line. The Germans had destroyed the captured bunker and they were back where they had begun.

Three days later, Captain Standish was found, completely alone and half starved, in a state of complete shock.

The West Wall was living up to its terrible reputation. After seven months of battle for its grim concrete fortifications, Patton had still not taken Trier.

March

'Remember me when I am dead and simplify me when I'm dead.'

Keith Douglas, Royal Armoured Corps
(Killed in action, Normandy, 1944)

1

Thursday March 1st. R. W. Thompson watched the British infantry go in for the last time. He was present when an excited young second lieutenant reported to his colonel in a newly captured farmhouse that he had penetrated to the battalion's objective and knocked out a couple of spandaus. 'Well done, Norman,' the Colonel said. 'Absolutely first-class. Grand work!'

The boy was thrilled. He ran out saluting and the colonel said, 'He's a good officer. He loves it. Always out on these patrols.'[1]

Two hours later Thompson scratched Norman's name out of his diary because he was already dead, killed in action on his last patrol.

Now the enemy mortar barrage intensified as the British infantry put on more pressure. 'This mortaring is getting casualties all the time,' Thompson noted in his diary at nine o'clock, 'and every fifteen minutes there are masses of bursts all around us – I mean within a few yards. The Red Cross men are magnificent. Wherever the bursts are thickest they run. A corporal rallies them and leads them

getting the wounded out of the woods from the tree-bursts
. . . A boy, red-faced, wide-eyed with a kind of wonder
under his tin hat, a kind of reproach. Poor kid. His legs
are all shot up . . . The other boy on the other side is pale,
white, ginger-haired. His arm is in a mess. A young officer
comes in half-hopping. "It's going to be OK now," he tells
the correspondent.'[2]

Thompson pushes forward. A Bren-gunner is squatting
in a ditch. 'B Company lost all its officers,' he says. 'How
many came back, d'you know?'

Thompson tells him, 'I counted twenty.'

The Tommy thinks it's not too bad.

Further forward the rest of the King's Shropshire Light
Infantry attackers, followed for some reason by a stray
white goat, are pinned down. Private Stokes, armed only
with a rifle, dashes forward alone across seventy yards
of bullet-swept ground. Single-handed he captures the
nearest strongpoint and brings back twelve prisoners,
although he is wounded in the attempt.

He goes out again and again is wounded. Now he is
losing blood rapidly. He comforts his comrades and goes
in once more when they dash forward. Twenty yards from
the objective, firing from the hip as he staggers forward
with the rest, he is mortally wounded and falls. As his
comrades sweep past him, he raises his arm and cries,
'Goodbye!'

But now the survivors of General Schlemm's First Parachute Army, those who are still alive or not prisoners, are
beginning to withdraw. In the shattered town of Xanten,
just taken, Brigadier Essame of the 43rd Division orders
his staff to stand in respectful silence as weary, dust-
covered German paratroopers are brought by under
guard. 'This was not approved by the Press,' Brigadier
Essame wrote later. But their lack of approval didn't

worry the old soldier, for the 'German garrison of Xanten were very gallant men.'[3]

Now it was virtually over. After a month's hardest fighting under the most terrible weather conditions and against the prepared positions of the West Wall, the staffs began to total up the losses. They hadn't been light. The price paid by the First Canadian Army had been particularly high. The British part of it had lost 770 officers and 9,660 men; the Canadians 378 officers and 4,925 others, all battlefield casualties. Simpson's Ninth Army had lost just under 7,300.

Now the top brass swarmed onto the abandoned battlefield to inspect it before the final race to the Rhine. Eisenhower drove up in the rain to meet Simpson and discuss the fact that there were still eight bridges across the Rhine intact in his area. With luck he might be able to capture one by surprise.

Together Ike and 'Big Simp' drove by open jeep to visit the US division which had just captured the German town of München-Gladbach. On the way Eisenhower told the Ninth Army Commander, 'I want to tip you off. In a few days you can expect Prime Minister Churchill. What kind of automobile have you?'

Simpson replied that he had only a Plymouth. Someone in the rear apparently kept 'short-stopping' bigger cars meant for him.

'I'll take care of it,' Eisenhower said. Then he added, 'Another thing. Churchill likes Scotch. Be sure and have a good supply at hand.'[4]

As the two generals arrived at the newly captured Rhenish town, GIs were starting to recognize Eisenhower and call, 'There's Ike!' Eisenhower waved back to them and when the jeep stopped, the Supreme Commander walked through the ankle-deep mud to where some 3,000 infantrymen were gathered. He talked to them for about five minutes but when he turned to move off, he slipped as before at Aachen and sat down hard in the muck.

The GIs roared.

Ike took it in good humor. He struggled to his feet and, clasping his hands above his head, gave them the boxer's salute of triumph. The soldiers bellowed their approval.

Now the Great Man himself materialized, he who had done so much over so many years to ensure that this day would finally come. On the morning of March 3, 1945, Churchill arrived at Montgomery's headquarters to celebrate the Allied victory over the West Wall in the north. Together with Montgomery and Brooke, the Chief of the British Imperial General Staff, the Prime Minister's group motored in two Rolls Royces to visit Simpson, as Ike had warned him, at his headquarters in Maastricht. Behind them rolled the war correspondents to cover one of the most historic days of the whole long conflict that had cost so many lives.

At the Ninth Army headquarters Simpson asked the Great Man if he wanted to visit the men's room before he left for the front. Churchill said, 'How far is it to the West Wall?'[5]

Simpson was a little surprised, not knowing what was to come. He told Churchill it was about half an hour's trip.

Churchill beamed with that round unlined face of his which made him look a little like Buddha. 'I'll wait then,' he told Simpson.

At Montgomery's suggestion, Simpson sat next to Churchill. En route the cavalcade of twenty cars was overtaken by a speeding jeep. Ignoring all protocol, a messenger stepped out of the halted vehicle and handed the Prime Minister a small package. In a matter-of-fact manner, Churchill undid it and shoved his forgotten dentures into his mouth. He beamed at a surprised Simpson and the procession continued.

As they approached a bridge over a small ravine Simpson said, 'Mr Churchill, the boundary between Holland and Germany runs under the bridge ahead of us.'

'Stop the car,' Churchill commanded. 'Let's get out.' With the aid of his cane, clad in the uniform of a colonel of the 4th Hussars, the regiment he had joined as an eighteen-year-old in the previous century, Churchill stumped across the bridge. Then he climbed down the bank toward the river to a long row of concrete dragon's teeth.

There the generals lined up expectantly, knowing now instinctively what was in the Great Man's mind.

'Gentlemen,' Churchill announced delightedly, a huge grin on his cherubic face, big cigar tucked in the side of his mouth as he fumbled with his fly, 'I'd like to ask you to join me. Let us all urinate on the great West Wall of Germany!' Remembering the photographers now aiming their cameras so excitedly, he wagged his finger at them and called, 'This is one of those operations connected with this great war which must not be reproduced graphically.'

Field Marshal Alanbrooke, not always one of Churchill's greatest admirers, standing next to him at that moment, recalled later, 'I shall never forget the childish grin of inner satisfaction that spread all over his face as he looked down at the critical moment . . .'[6]

2

Now the pressure that Patton had been exerting on his divisions attacking Trier, and in particular on the 10th Armored, began to pay off at last. With the 94th and 76th

Infantry hammering away at the last fortresses of the West Wall on the Rivers Saar and Sauer, the tankers of Morris's 10th edged into the southeastern suburbs of the old Roman city. Under the command of Lieutenant Colonel Jack Robinson, a task force of Shermans and armored infantry captured a company of German infantry defending a railway crossing with four 57mm anti-tank guns, without having to fire a shot.

One of the prisoners revealed to the little colonel, whom Patton was later to call 'a brave son-of-a-bitch,' that it was his job to warn the demolition teams stationed on the two remaining bridges across the River Moselle of the approach of the Americans. They could then blow them and prevent any link-up between the 10th and the 76th Infantry fighting in a southeast direction toward Trier.

Robinson made a quick decision that night, while in the ruined city itself drunken men from the two *Volkssturm* battalions guarding it were raiding the cellars and celebrating the end of the battle for Trier. Swiftly he divided his force into two. One clattered off to the Römerbrücke, the northern bridge, which as its name implies was built by the Romans, while Robinson himself set off for the nearby Kaiserbrücke.

The men trying to seize the Römerbrücke in this bold *coup de main* were unlucky. It was blown right in their faces. Hearing the detonation and seeing the blue angry flame of the explosion ripping the darkness apart, Robinson ordered full speed. His Shermans raced down the shell-holed cobbled streets, while firing broke out on both sides from the ruined eighteenth-century villas. In the bright moonlight he now could see that his armored infantry were pinned down to his front, right on the eastern bank of the bridge. The little Colonel grabbed his turret machine gun and personally swept the far side of the nineteenth-century bridge with .50 caliber slugs, watching the tracer hiss flat across the Moselle. The firing slackened a little. Perhaps, Robinson thought, the Germans had had enough. He decided to risk it. He ordered a platoon of infantry and five tanks to rush across.

Six drunken and very scared Germans, who knew what their fate would be at the hands of SS execution commandos if they failed to carry out their vital mission, staggered out of their hiding places and tried to blow the Kaiserbrücke. Too late! The Americans were onto them. They raised their hands. They had failed and the Americans had an intact bridge across the Moselle.

More and more Americans started to swarm into the city now. By dawn, two tank regiments and the first elements of the 94th were combing the ruined evacuated city, digging out drunken German soldiers from the cellars and hiding places, 3,000 of them in all.

Patton was jubilant when he received the news. It meant that the West Wall defenses were completely broken, after nearly two months of severe fighting which had cost him no less than 42,000 battle and non-battle casualties. With Trier in his hands he could head up the Moselle to where that river joined the Rhine at Koblenz, his objective back in September 1944; or he could turn southeast, dash behind the West Wall defenses, still in German hands in the Saar, capture the Saar Basin and hit the Rhine below Mainz. Either way he could still beat Montgomery, who was not scheduled to launch his great set-piece Rhine crossing assault for another three weeks yet.

That day Patton had the world at his feet. When he received an urgent signal from SHAEF, just after he had been informed that Trier had fallen, ordering him to bypass Trier because it would take four divisions to capture it, he radioed back with relish: '*Have taken Trier with two divisions. What do you want me to do? Give it back?*'[7]

* * *

A little later, after Patton had been briefed by his staff about the confused situation on the Moselle, he barked in high good humor, in spite of the brusqueness with which he interrupted the briefing, 'You mean everything is as confused as hell and nobody is really sure where the Germans are! . . . Well, I'll tell you what I'm going to do. I'm going to drive through Trier and see how things are and then go and find out exactly where this damn war is today!'[8]

Thus Patton drove into the first big German city his Army had conquered, and one which had a long historical tradition, of which he knew much. His convoy sped past the little ghetto, the medieval Judengasse where Trier's most famous son, Karl Marx, had been born, up by the Porta Negra, the celebrated Roman gate ordered to be restored by Trier's last conqueror, no less a person than Napoleon Bonaparte himself.

The vehicles rolled the whole length of the city, through street after street of shattered, shell-pocked houses, for Trier had been under intermittent US fire since the previous winter, out to where he could glimpse the Moselle hills, still held by the Germans. Suddenly Patton yelled to his driver to stop. Up in front of him there was a mile-long column of stalled US vehicles, a perfect target for any remaining German gunners in those high hills, their sides planted with row after row of neat vines.

The cause of the jam was a great 155mm cannon trapped up ahead under a railway bridge. But the colonel in charge of the convoy was nowhere to be seen. Patton flew into one of his impressive rages. Halfway down the column he found the unfortunate officer. 'Listen,' he exploded, his face red with fury, 'you can blow up that goddamn gun, you can blow up the goddamn bridge, or you can blow out your goddamn brains – and I don't care which!'[9]

And with that, Patton ordered his driver to take him

back to headquarters, his high good humor soon restored. It had been a tremendous day for him. The question was now – what next?

That night Patton sat up late with his nephew Fred Ayres, killing a whole bottle of bourbon and smoking cigar after expensive cigar. He grew mellow under the influence of the alcohol, telling his FBI-man nephew how his men should enjoy everything they captured, including German women (unknown to the Third Army Commander, there would be quite a few incidents of rape among his men before the campaign was over) and how 'In any war, a commander, no matter what his rank, has to send to sure death, nearly every day, by his own order, a certain number of men. Some are personal friends. All are his personal responsibility. Any man with a heart would like to sit down and bawl, but he can't. So he sticks out his jaw and swaggers and swears.'[10]

After this interesting insight into his personal psychology, with the old wall clock already indicating three in the morning and the bottle almost empty, Patton got onto politics. 'Fred,' he told his nephew, 'we've got a president who is a great politician but goddammit, the man has never read history. He doesn't understand the Russians and he never will. From Genghis Khan to Stalin they haven't changed. They never will, and we'll never learn until it is too late. There's another thing people in our government can't understand. They can't even understand the Germans . . . Look at this fool unconditional-surrender announcement.[11] If the Hun ever needed anything to put a burr under his saddle, that's it. He'll now fight like the devil because he'll be ordered to do so . . . It will take much longer, cost us more lives and let the Russians take more territory. Sometimes we're such goddamned fools it makes me weep!'[12]

Thus philosophized the gray-haired General, whose willful independent strategy from now on would ensure that the bulk of the US Army swung southeast into the strategically unimportant Bavaria. Finally, putting out his last cigar, he announced, 'And now, by God, we can go to bed. See you at breakfast . . .'

3

The German Army that day was beaten. Unfortunately it did not know it. For nearly six years it had fought on all fronts over three continents and sustained some three and a half million soldiers killed. The morale of the survivors was not helped much by the fact that nearly half a million of their relatives, wives, children, mothers, etc., had been killed in the bombing raids flown by the RAF and USAAF. Soon the Americans would be on the Rhine and the Russians beginning the first phase on Berlin itself. Yet as the first troops of the US Seventh Army moved into their jump-off positions on that March 2nd, 1945, to begin the final attack of the war on the West Wall, the German defenders seemed as determined to hold on to their bunkers and pillboxes as they had seven months before.

It might have been the courage of despair, it might have been the threat that any abandonment of their position would result in dire consequences, or it might even have been some irrational belief that by fighting here they could still save Germany from defeat, that kept the louse-ridden, hungry, dirty men in field-gray behind their weapons waiting for the Americans to come. But stay they did, although their commander SS General Paul 'Papa' Hausser, the one-eyed SS general responsible for the defense of the last section of the famed wall in German hands, was well aware of the very real threat to his command.

Once Patton broke the German troops holding the line above Trier, he might well sweep *behind* the West Wall and cut it off completely. Accordingly he warned his superiors that if this took place, 'envelopment and annihilation of the First Army [his command] will be imminent.'

No one seemed to take much notice of his warning as the US Seventh Army started to reach the staging areas to his front and Patton prepared to cross the Moselle to his rear. Field Marshal Kesselring, since March 1st in charge of the whole of the West Front in place of von Rundstedt, paid little heed to it.

Kesselring, who had fought the long retreat of the German Army through the boot of Italy up to now, felt he might be able to do the same in the West. 'Smiling Albert,' as he was nicknamed by his staff behind his back, told Hausser ambiguously that there was a need for the 'retention of present positions,' but added that 'encirclement and with it the annihilation of the main body of the troops' should be avoided.

All that Colonel-General Hausser could make of this was that he had no authority to withdraw from the West Wall. Come what may, he had to stay there and make a fight for it.

On the morning of March 2nd, the men of the 70th US Infantry Division, belonging to General Patch's Seventh Army, which had fought its way up the length of France the previous autumn, were assembled in the French border cities of Forbach, Stirling-Wedel and Neu-Glass-hutte looking down from the heights there to the Saar basin below.

To Lieutenant Colonel Wallace Cheeves, commanding one of the battalions in the 70th's 27th Infantry Regiment, the valley looked like 'a picture of peace and contentment.' In fact, it was 'the front yard of hell,' as he phrased it later. 'We weren't just attacking another town, we were cracking the strongest net of fortifications ever constructed by the human race. Our job was to breach the famed wall and establish a corridor through which our armies could race to the heart of Germany.'[13]

All afternoon, the rumors went from foxhole to foxhole on the heights, which had been the scene of another great battle in the Franco-Prussian War of 1870, while the Americans were pounded by the infamous six-barrel German electric mortar, 'the screaming meemies.' To PFC Bealce, worried like the rest that there was going to be a great push through the Siegfried Line, it 'made a grating noise like the bark of a seal or like someone scratching his fingernails across a piece of tin. Then for several seconds everything would be quiet until it hit. The explosion sounded as though someone had struck a match in the Krupp Works. You'd think the whole mountain had exploded.'[14]

Then the tank destroyers with their heavy 90mm cannon started to nose their way forward to the infantry positions and the rumors thickened even more.

Just before darkness, company commanders and platoon leaders were summoned to their battalion CPs, and the GIs nodded to each other significantly. They were right. There *was* something in the air, something lethal.

By the flickering, hissing, bright-white light of the Coleman lamps, the battalion commanders explained that the whole division and its attached French troops would attack at first light. In the case of the 274th, two battalions would advance, leaving one in reserve on the Spicheren Heights. The officers of the reserve battalion, the 1st, breathed a sigh of relief.

That night the news was broken to the men. Some took

it calmly and went to sleep in their foxholes. Most couldn't do so and spent those hours of moonlight yarning with each other. PFC Bobby Hawthorne threw a poncho over his foxhole and read the New Testament by the yellow light of a candle.

By eight o'clock on the cool clear morning of March 3rd, the attackers were swarming through the trees to the start line below while the artillery started pounding the West Wall positions. Everywhere was noise and the usual confusion of a large-scale attack. The thunder of the guns, the roar and stink of the tanks, the orders and counter-orders, the jeeps whizzing back and forth.

And then suddenly the little khaki-clad figures were swarming out into the plain, alone and vulnerable. The first company were bogged down in front of a minefield, covered by a pillbox. The two support companies tried to outflank the German position. The anti-personnel mines, however, were a constant danger. One false step – the grate of the metal prong under the doomed man's foot, the hushed crack, a mushroom of earth and pebbles – and yet another maimed man would be lying on the ground writhing in pain or stunned to silence, staring in awed disbelief at his shattered limbs.

'The machine gunners were out in front supporting the leading platoon,' Sergeant Boughton recalled later. 'We were trying to work forward to positions where we could button up the pillbox. Lieutenant Rytting was up forward on reconnaissance, crawling around through mines as calmly as though he was walking through a potato field back home in Idaho. War was a game to "Riddle," as we called him. To him the only way to win was to get in the thick of it and play hard . . . That's what he was doing when he went after the pillbox. He went up so close that he got down on his hands and knees and started crawling. He hadn't gone very far when the ground seemed to blow up from under him. We saw his leg go flying through the air and his whole body leap up and then roll on the ground. The shock and pain almost paralyzed him. He never lost consciousness though. He just lay quietly on the ground and waited for the stretcher-bearers to pick him up.'[15]

It wasn't so easy. The wounded Lieutenant lay in the middle of a minefield. A medic named Kinsley finally got through and somehow managed to bandage up the mangled stump of the officer's leg. Then returning to get further aid, Kinsley too stepped on a mine and lost his foot. Another medic, Private Denning, found him sitting up trying to tie a tourniquet around his leg. He attempted to give Kinsley a shot of morphine to ease the terrible pain, but somehow he couldn't push the needle through the skin.

'Give me that thing,' Kinsley yelled and grabbed it from Denning's nerveless fingers. 'I'll give it to myself!'

In the end all the wounded were evacuated from the death trap, with Rytting, his face ashen with shock, pretty far gone. Yet before he was evacuated, he looked around the faces staring down at him and whispered faintly, 'You guys take it easy.'

Then he was hurried away. They never saw 'Riddle' again. To the very end Hitler's Wall was extracting its toll in blood.

The minefield and pillbox line had brought the whole attack to a halt. This was what the German artillery observers had been waiting for. They ordered the guns and mortars to open fire on this perfect target, thousands of men stalled in the open in broad daylight.

'Artillery, mortars, rockets . . . everything that the Kraut possessed was thrown at us,' Colonel Wallace Cheeves recalled later. 'The earth was ripped and torn and the whole area pockmarked with shell holes. The trees were sheared down to shattered trunks. All along the line we clawed into the ground, trying to escape the flying shell fragments. A thick black dry suffocating curtain of smoke hung over the whole area. Every few seconds another shell would explode with a murderous red flash and send death-dealing shrapnel *shrieking* among the prostrate troops. It looked for a while as though the attack would end before it began.'[16]

But the troops held their ground. These were different men from those of autumn 1944. There was no panic. They had become battle-hardened; rough, sometimes brutal young men, they were no longer ready to turn and run at the first sign of a setback. Besides, they knew from experience that more men were wounded turning and running away than when sticking to their positions, however dangerous these seemed. They had learned the hard way, just as their fathers had done in the Argonne in 1918.

A company armed with flame-throwers and white phosphorous grenades rushed forward to aid their comrades. They, too, were hit by the murderous enemy fire. They flopped to the ground, panting hard. Lieutenant Wilson in charge cried to his second-in-command, Lieutenant Beck, 'Beck, this is costing us lives! We'd better keep moving!'

As the German mortar bombs whined down upon them with their blood-chilling howl, the doughboys pushed on again, blundering blindly through some trees.

Another concentration of bombs hit the sorely tried infantry. This time Beck was hit by a piece of red-hot shrapnel. It set off the phosphorous grenade attached to his belt, which hissed into furious frightening life. His whole body was enveloped in a sheet of dazzling white flame. Men fell all around the terrible figure writhing there in the scorched grass. But Wilson could spare no time for the dead and dying. He had to save the living. He led the survivors across an open fire-break, slammed through a barbed wire entanglement, and collapsed into a small wood beyond, his lungs heaving like a cracked leathern bellows. But he had saved the rest of the company, for now the mortar barrage was falling behind them.

'I emptied my medical pouches that day,' T-5 Jimmie Owen, a medic, recalled later. 'I tried to take care of the worst cases first, but there were so many I hardly knew which ones needed help most. As soon as possible I got a line of walking wounded started back up the hill to the aid station. It was almost impossible to evacuate the serious cases. The casualty collecting point was in the edge of a wood clear at the top of the ridge. About two trips up that hill with a litter was all a guy could stand.'[17]

Many straggled back of their own accord, faces blanched with shock, eyes wild and wide. Some trembled and mumbled meaningless sounds. Others stared, as if outraged, at their torn limbs, wondering why this bloody indignity had to happen to *them*. A few were brave beyond words.

Medic Monroe Gable recalled meeting Master Sergeant Lewis Ripley staggering up the steep hill to the aid station, 'a crude bandage wrapped around a hole as big as an egg in his elbow. His face was ashen gray and he could hardly walk. But he refused to let me give him first aid or a shot of morphine. He told me to help the other boys first.'[18]

Thus the slaughter went on while the line moved forward once more, aided by tanks. But the Germans were fighting back with all they had; desperately, like men who knew they were condemned to death and had nothing to lose, they were prepared to take a few more of these brash young men in khaki with them.

As Sergeant McNeely, who was with Lieutenant

Wilson, later recalled, 'Mortar and artillery rounds were coming in as fast as they could be shot out of guns. We wondered how long they could keep it up . . . and how long we could stand it. As we got in closer we could hear rifles begin to fire. I knew we must be in closer now. Long bursts from our light machine guns and BARs cracked nearby – followed by answering bursts from enemy BURP guns. There were a lot of pillboxes in front of us to be blown and a squad of engineers was following close behind us loaded down with high explosives. If one of their shape charges were ever hit, it would have cleaned out an area of about a hundred yards.'[19]

Now new companies started to be thrown into the bloody conflict. Many of the men had been resting for the last week in the French border villages, having a good time with the *vin* and *m'selles*, practicing their very basic French from the official handbook given to every GI – '*Voulez-vous coucher avec moi ce soir, m'selle?*' was a favorite phrase, though it had little impact on the chaste maidens of rural Lorraine. They went into action cheerfully, almost light-heartedly.

One of the reserves attracted particular attention. Known as 'the Walking Pineapple' to his buddies, he carried three fragmentation grenades, a white phosphorous grenade, and a German fat-bellied flare pistol together with sixteen flares of different colors. 'Pineapples' he had in plenty, and those who were in the know gave him a wide berth. If he were hit, he'd make one hell of a bonfire.

Sergeant Robert Kirk with the new companies saw the casualties of the first attack streaming back on foot and in the litters. 'The sight of them was enough to take the heart right out of a guy,' he recalled. Now the first enemy fire started to fall on them. For a few minutes they tried to dig in, but soon gave up; the ground was too rocky. Besides, Private Tice came hurrying up just then with orders to start moving again.

'It was then that the Krauts saw me,' Tice recalled. 'I knew it was coming as soon as I heard the croak of the Screaming Meemie off in the distance. Everybody else heard it too and just stopped in his tracks and wondered if it was coming our way. Then it hit. The first rounds struck a trench where the second squad was waiting . . . The whole squad was nearly buried in the eruption of earth.'[20] The killing went on.

Now, however, US artillery, the feared 'Long Toms,' 155mm cannon, started pumping shells (they could fire them from five miles' distance) right over the heads of the infantry, forcing the German gunners in the bunkers to button up for a while. The foot soldiers took advantage of the chance and surged forward. The Germans either surrendered quickly or were killed at their posts. The infantry swarmed into the little Saar village of Brahn. For a while a minefield stopped them. Still they pushed on, filing one by one close to a high stone wall, which protected them against enemy shellfire and also, they thought, against mines. They entered the first houses, the typical dingy red-brick structures of this industrial area. They were empty. The infantry began to tell themselves the Germans had evacuated the place. They were beginning to strike lucky at last.

Sergeant Walker with one squad fired his rifle into the basement of the second house he encountered. The single shot was answered by yells and screams of pain. But no one came out. A Private Hay tossed a grenade in through the pipe of a stove which protruded from the basement window. Soot, stove and thirteen Germans, as 'black as the characters in a minstrel show' (as the regimental

history of 274th Infantry Regiment described them), came
bolting to the surface.

With this the infantry knew that their luck had run out.
The village was an integral part of the West Wall. It would
have to be fought for, house by house, just like the
bunkers had been.

4

As the weary Americans consolidated in the hamlet as
best they could, Sergeant Heinz Breuer decided that for
him the war was over. He started to crawl through the
shadows out of the eastern end of the place, ducking every
time a flare hissed into the darkening sky or a burst of
tracer cut startlingly across the battle-littered street. He
had told his little command – four sixteen-year-old boys,
several old men and a wounded young lieutenant, who
couldn't have been more than seventeen himself – what he
was going to do, but no one had attempted either to stop
or to follow him. Breuer, a big ex-miner in his early
thirties, did not know why nor, at this juncture, did he
care. 'I've had a noseful,' he told the weary, lice-ridden
collection of what he called 'cardboard soldiers,' crouched
in the cellar, 'I'm going home.'[21]

Now wounded in the right thigh, hand shattered, and
with a hole in his stomach through which his gut protruded
every time he took the pressure away, he escaped, giving
up on Hitler, the *Wehrmacht*, and the war. Sergeant
Breuer was going home.

In 1935 when the Saar had been returned to Germany,
Breuer had been a miner at a pit near St Wendel and a
staunch socialist. As soon as the Nazis came in, he had
been arrested and sent for a few months to a 're-education

camp.' The re-education had consisted of bread and water and beatings which had left him with a broken nose and a deep dislike of the brownshirts. Still, he had served them loyally enough. He had helped to build the same West Wall which he had been attempting to defend up to minutes before; he had served with distinction in Greece, Africa, and Russia and had been promoted to sergeant during the course of those long campaigns. In other words, Sergeant Breuer was typical of many Germans of his time. He fought because he had to and because he was German; it was his country he was defending, not the Hitler creed. He was fighting for '*mutti*' back in St Wendel and for his three kids, who he hoped fervently would never have to go through the same combat experiences that he and his father and his grandfather had undergone on this bloody frontier between France and Germany since 1870.

Crawling alone through that March night with every man's hand against him – for he knew, badly wounded as he was, if he were picked up by one of the 'chaindog' patrols[22] to the rear of the front, he might well be shot out of hand as a 'defeatist' or 'coward' – Breuer was a realist. Germany was lost, or at least Hitler's Germany was. Breuer wanted to survive.

But Hitler and the High Command did not seem to know that. Now the generals were awarding the Iron Cross by the basketful to encourage the soldiers to fight. Anyone who, after being cut off, managed to reach his own lines was automatically entitled to the high award. As the frontline commanders said after they had received the general order from Berlin, 'In that case every soldier who is neither dead nor a prisoner should receive the Iron Cross.'

But there were also plenty of threats to keep the men holding the line of the West Wall in the Saar. Hangings and shootings by summary courts of SS officers – 'the flying courts' as they were called by the scared soldiers – were the order of the day. Not only were cowards and deserters shot, but also any soldier who failed to blow up a bridge or made a withdrawal without a specific order.[23]

Propaganda too flooded the front, trying to keep the war-weary *landsers*, as the German infantry called themselves, in the line. The soldiers were told by leaflets and broadcasts from Goebbels's Ministry of Propaganda: 'All Germany's agricultural wealth will be placed at Moscow's disposal and planned famine will be used as a means of repression. German labor will be used as war reparation and thousands of slave laborers will be torn away from their families and deported to Siberia. German women will be carried away by human beasts, raped and assassinated. German children will be taken from their parents, deported and brought up as Bolsheviks. The German people, as such, will be obliterated and the survivors will have nothing to live for. The needs and sufferings of the moment are nothing compared to the extermination planned for us by our enemies. All Germany rises against this fate and will fight as one great National Socialist army.'[24]

But neither propaganda nor threats had much impact on the lone NCO crawling through the night that March. He had gone two miles, but just before he passed out (to be saved and looked after, surprisingly enough, by a Russian slave worker, a seventeen-year-old girl who had remained on the Saar farm when the German owner had fled), Breuer saw what he thought were 'baskets hanging from the trees to the right of the road.'

They weren't baskets; they were corpses of German soldiers who like himself had decided that there was no further purpose in defending the West Wall, and had been caught. By the light of a dying flare as he crawled ever further, Sergeant Breuer could just make out the sign attached to each man's grotesquely twisted neck – '*Turncoat . . . Traitor . . . Deserter . . . Folkparasite*' – and the fact that whoever had executed the nameless *landsers* had removed their boots. Perhaps, the absurd thought went through his distorted mind at that moment, 'they need them so that they can run faster themselves!' Five minutes later Breuer blacked out, leaving behind the old men, the boys, and the wounded lieutenant he had abandoned in the village to defend to their deaths the West Wall.

On the day that Sergeant Breuer made his lone escape, 'Papa' Hausser, who was no coward or a defeatist (at the age of 63 he had lost an eye in combat in Russia, and one year in France he had again been wounded severely and only managed to escape from the Falaise Pocket by the skin of his teeth), pleaded once more with 'Smiling Albert' Kesselring to be allowed to withdraw.

Kesselring, confident he would master the critical situation as he had done time and time again in Italy the previous year, told the SS General, 'These are my orders. You must hang on.'

Hausser put down the phone, then after some consideration told his staff to prepare a secret plan for withdrawal to the Rhine.

They asked the old general with the black patch over one eye, 'When?'

Hausser shook his head grimly. He had no answer to that. The West Wall, he knew, would hold a little longer in spite of all Patch's attacks. The question was – *what would Patton do?*

On March 5th, the day that Hodges's First Army seized its first bridge across the Rhine at Remagen, Eisenhower and Patton flew to Patch's headquarters at the Lorraine

town of Luneville. During the flight, Eisenhower praised
Patton and his Third Army excessively.

'George,' he said, 'you are not only a good general, you
are a lucky general, and as you well remember, in a
general, Napoleon prized luck above skill.'

Patton was well pleased with the praise. He laughed and
said, 'That's the first compliment you've paid me in the
two and a half years we've served together.'[25]

At the meeting in the eighteenth-century royal chateau
at Luneville, which served as Patch's headquarters,
Eisenhower mentioned that the West Wall was still standing in front of Patch's Seventh Army while Patton had
achieved his breakthrough. The Supreme Commander
turned to Patch and asked if it would be all right with him
if Patton attacked across the northern section of Seventh
Army's zone of operations. In this manner Patton could
cross the Moselle, cut through the Palatinate behind the
West Wall and hurry on to the Rhine.

Patch, whose men were fighting that desperate battle to
break through the Siegfried Line in the Saar, agreed
readily. Such a drive would be of the greatest help to his
operations there. 'Sure, Ike,' he said, 'we are all in the
same army.'

It was the decision that Hausser had feared ever since
Patton had captured Trier. Now if Kesselring did not
change his mind soon, his First Army holding the West
Wall was condemned to encirclement with no chance of
escape, destined to fight to the death. Those concrete
fortifications on the Saar might well turn out to be the
vaults they would be buried in.

5

The men fighting a grim battle of house-to-house combat in the Saar knew nothing of this, of course. The GIs battling in those grimy mining villages lived from minute to minute. They had no time to think of the grand strategy which might well mean in a few days' time that the bloody sacrifice they were having to make here would have been for naught; the German line would crumple of its own accord.

PFC Corrigan of Lieutenant Wilson's company recalled later what it was like to fight in those houses. 'We crossed the railroad tracks with guns blazing. When we got close to the house, the Krauts poked a white flag out of the window. When the guys saw it they only got sore. Everyone was for moving in and cleaning them out.'[26]

Wilson wouldn't have it. He wanted the Germans alive. The GIs called out to those inside to surrender and finally they came running out, 'three of the most frightened men I've ever seen.'

Wilson rushed the abandoned house with slugs still whining off the walls around him, for the next house was still in German hands. He signaled to Corrigan. 'I want you to holler in there,' he cried, 'and tell them to come out and give themselves up.'

There was no answer. They rushed the place. It was empty. Puzzled, they tried to figure out where the firing was coming from. Just then Sergeant McNeely ran toward them. Two shots rang out. He hit the ground, blood pouring from his nose and mouth. Then the alarmed GIs understood. The shots had come from a small pillbox built into the side of the next house so that the pillbox was hardly noticeable.

They decided to attack it. But how? The sniper in the pillbox, who seemed to be armed with a machine pistol, had the windows of the house where Wilson's men were crouching zeroed in perfectly, and was picking off every man who tried to get in or out. Indeed while Wilson was trying to work out a plan of attack, one of the last three remaining combat engineers (he had started out with twelve) was hit in the hip and collapsed moaning to the floor.

Wilson decided he could get a better picture of the situation from an upstairs window. Together with two soldiers he went up the debris-littered stairs to the second floor. To his alarm he saw down below some unsuspecting soldiers beginning to dig in. Ignoring the danger to himself, he leaned out of the shattered window and told them to run to the cover of the house at five-minute intervals.

Suddenly he jerked. He staggered back from the window. 'My God, I'm hit!' he cried, his voice full of disbelief. Abruptly he thrust out his legs, as if he were trying to brace himself, in a last desperate attempt to fight off death. 'Slap my face!' he commanded. 'Slap my face!'

A soldier dropped his rifle and struck him across his cheeks. To no avail. He dropped to the floor and with his last burst of energy, slammed his boots against a heavy oaken table, kicking it across the room.

'When I went upstairs,' Corrigan recalled, 'it was all over. I opened his shirt and found two small bullet holes just above his heart. There was not a trace of blood on the outside. He must have bled internally. I realized that sooner or later he would have been killed but now that it had happened none of us could quite believe it. I took the codes and overlays out of his pockets and looked at his AGO card. He was only twenty-one and as he lay there he didn't look anywhere near that. His hair was cropped close and he had no beard at all. He was just a kid, yet he proved himself to be the driving factor of the whole company. He was everything that could be expected of an officer and soldier. When he died the spirit of the company died with him.'[27]

There were a lot of Lieutenant Wilsons that grim March day.

By the sixth day of March, the Americans had completely penetrated the first belt of the West Wall, but here, in the most heavily fortified section of the whole 350-mile line (on account of the area's proximity to France), there were more to come. Not only that, but every basement and mine shaft, every slag heap and railroad embankment had been turned into a fortified position too. As the first week of March gave way to the second, a relentless slogging match continued in that grim industrial district, where men had to fight and die for every yard of ground.

It was basically an infantryman's war. Occasionally a tank would rumble up and help them out with a few quick shells from its 75mm gun before scuttling off to safety again; for the tankers knew that Germans armed with the one-shot *panzerfaust* (the German equivalent of the bazooka) lurked everywhere in the ruins.

Here a few determined Germans could hold up whole companies, and the capture of every single pillbox became a carefully planned operation involving the use of mortars, flame-throwers, a great variety of high explosives, and, in one case, a streetcar.

While held up by determined resistance from a pillbox located in the center of a mining village, the frustrated infantry searched around for some way of knocking the thing out. They knew it wouldn't be easy, for the village was located in a valley, with the village street running down and then up again toward the mine which had given its inhabitants employment before the war. Just below the mine the pillbox was situated so that it covered every area of approach.

'War is an excuse,' Tolstoy wrote in *War and Peace*, 'for men to wander around.' Thus it was while the stalled infantry 'wandered around' that they discovered a yellow-painted streetcar, its sides pocked with bullet holes as if someone had used it for target practice recently. For some time the young soldiers played with it, ringing the driver's bell and turning the tarnished brass handles which steered the thing, examining the blacked-out windows and the usual warning sign: '*Psst, Feind hoert mit!*' (Attention, the enemy is listening!) Then some genius came up with the idea of packing it with high explosive and launching it against the pillbox, which was conveniently located next to the streetcar line that ran through the center of the village.

Thus half an hour later, 'V-3,' as the happy expectant GIs were now calling it, was ready to go, with nearly a hundred pounds of explosive securely stowed away in its front and a score of hefty young men waiting for the signal to set it in motion.

Down below in the hollow, the young lieutenant who would lead the follow-up attack pumped his arm up and down rapidly three times. The infantry signal for attack.

'Heave!' cried the sergeant in charge of the 'launching party.'

With a will the young men strained. V-3 started to move.

'Put some beef into it!' the sergeant urged.

V-3 squeaked in rusty protest. Now it was near the edge of the incline.

'Come on, guys!' the sergeant yelled in delight. 'She's moving! *Come on!*'[28]

And then they were falling to their knees, trying to keep

their balance as the streetcar went over the dip. It started to gather speed at once, rumbling down the slope swaying alarmingly, while the young soldiers watched it open-mouthed, hoping that it wouldn't run off the tracks.

It made the bottom safely. Now it started to rumble up the slope beyond, slowing down appreciably as the watching soldiers cheered it on, urging it to reach the pillbox, while the attacking infantry waited for the command to assault.

Its progress grew slower and slower. It was down to walking pace now, as the incline became steeper. In a moment it would stop and begin to roll backward. The whole plan looked as if it was going to fail.

It stopped.

There was a loud groan of disappointment from the spectators. All their effort had been for nothing, it seemed, but their luck hadn't run out. Suddenly the German machine-gunner, obviously unsettled by the presence of the streetcar just in front of his position (perhaps he thought the 'Amis' were attempting to block his field of fire), let the front of the stalled vehicle have a burst of tracer. It was the last thing he ever did. The explosive erupted with a thunderous roar and the spectators ducked hurriedly as debris sailed everywhere.

When the smoke cleared, the whole front of the pillbox had been sheared off and the streetcar had disappeared. All that was left of it was a pair of buckled steel wheels slowly trundling their way down the littered street.

The infantry relaxed. That afternoon, at least, they wouldn't have to attack.

6

By the end of that second week of March, the infantry of
Patch's Seventh Army were approaching the last line of
the West Wall defenses, with the 70th and 63rd Infantry
Divisions again in the lead. Now the last reserves were
moving up across the French border into Germany and
the territory already captured by those who had gone
before.

That fine March day, twenty-four hours before the last
attack kicked off, they marched in their hundreds through
the little French border towns greeted by cries of '*Vive
l'Amérique!*' and '*Bravo!*' But the men who were going in
for the last battle were not impressed. They felt that the
same cheering civilians had greeted the Germans equally
enthusiastically five years before when they had come
marching in on May 10, 1940. Neither were they impressed by the German propaganda leaflets which lay
everywhere and proclaimed that the Siegfried Line was
held by bold brave men who had sworn that no Yank
would live to enter it. They tossed them aside and, as the
chronicler of the time has it, 'vowed they would hang their
washing on the Siegfried Line.'

But their commanders were not so sanguine. The
natural barrier of the River Saar, which had cost the men
of Patton's Third Army so dearly, lay in front of the last
line of pillboxes, and between the river and bunker line
there was a thick continuous line of dragon's teeth that
would make the going tough for any tanks which managed
to get across.

Naturally they didn't pass on their fears to the infantry
who would carry out the assault. They told them the

pillboxes were manned by retreads from the *Luftwaffe* who knew nothing about infantry fighting. But as Lieutenant Chappel of the 70th Division commented later, 'It made no difference whether they knew anything about infantry tactics or not. All they had to do was sit inside the thick concrete bunkers and pull the trigger of a machine gun. It was sure suicide to cross the fields swept by perfect enemy fire, but orders were orders and we were going to try it.'[29]

'My platoon jumped off first,' recalled Sergeant Rysso afterward. 'I had two squads forward and one back. As soon as we started to move, the Krauts threw over a lot of artillery and mortars, but most of it fell in back of us. PFC Condict was the first man over the knob of the hill in front of the Line. When he came back he was sweating and his face was pale. "It's going to be rough," was all he said. We kept going until the two leading squads were at the top of the hill. We could all see the dragons' teeth, pillboxes, dugouts and trenches from there. The hill was completely bare and we stood out in plain sight like sore thumbs. The Krauts couldn't help but see us. They waited until we were out on the flat ground in front and then cut loose.'[30]

Man after man went down. The Germans even fired at the manure heaps just in case they hid Americans. They called for artillery, but the shells bounced off the pillboxes harmlessly. All the occupants suffered was perhaps a headache. Tanks were sent up. One of them turned tail immediately when it saw the pillboxes. But the rest remained and slogged it out with the German 88mms. Not for long. After fifteen minutes, they informed the infantry trying to advance against the bunker line behind them that the ground was too soft and they couldn't get across the dragon's teeth anyway. So the infantry were once again left to deal with the West Wall themselves, just as they had been doing since the previous September.

Rysso ordered the survivors of his group to take cover. 'Once we had reached temporary safety, I started to reorganize the men we had left,' he recalled. 'Dunn [one of his men] made two attempts to go out into the field to get the wounded but was driven back by machine-gun fire. Then Newton the medic went out accompanied by Penland, Dunn, Boering, and Mann. Strange to say they drew no fire, even though they were plainly visible to the Germans. They found Palmer dead, Castro with a broken leg, and Jannick unconscious with a hole in his head . . . Cuervo and Condict were also lying on the ground badly wounded. Newton did what he could for the men. He gave them all a shot of morphine and then waited for the litter-bearers to come up.'[31]

What had happened to Sergeant Rysso's platoon that morning was happening to similar platoons of the 70th Infantry Division everywhere. The Germans, whatever their motives, were full of fight still and they were putting up a determined defense of the West Wall, although rumors were now spreading throughout the bunker line that the Americans had crossed the Moselle to their rear and were steadily working their way through the lonely Hunstrück Mountains which lay to their right flank, heading for the Saar.

That didn't help the wounded trapped in no man's land that morning as they found themselves being shelled by their own artillery.

Sergeant Penland lying out there with them recalled, 'Out of the corner of my eye, coming from the left, I saw two men supporting a third coming toward the shell crater [in which he sheltered]. I glanced about and recognized Andrews on the right, supporting Darling who had been wounded in the right thigh. I did not have time to tell who the third man was, but was later told it was Helaszek. I just got out the first word of warning, "Get down!", when a large-caliber shell screamed over very low and hit directly on the three men. I saw a tremendous flash of fire and a fearful cloud of black smoke. Pieces of men's bodies came flying through the air. The concussion blew off my helmet and threw me to the bottom of the crater, which was filled with mud and water. One man's horribly torn body flew over my head and hit in the water beside me. Newton was standing next to me, nearest the shell, and was blown into the water. I grabbed him to keep him from sinking under. He was covered with blood from the men who had been hit by the shell. I asked him if he was hit. He said he didn't know and crawled over to help another man who was pushing himself toward the water with only his legs. This was probably Helaszek who later was found dead in the hole. I looked around and saw just a man's chest and hands sticking out of the water. I grabbed to pull him out, thinking that possibly he might still be alive and was drowning. When I got him out, though, I saw he was mangled and dead so I let him slip back into the water . . .'[32]

Now Patton's men had fought their way through the veterans of the 6th SS Mountain Division, who had been holding the heights on the far side of the Moselle between Trier and Koblenz, and had made successful crossings of the river at a dozen places.

Resistance was crumbling rapidly. The heart was going out of the average German soldier, while the civilians were sick of the protracted struggle. In Guls, for instance, the GIs had to protect their SS prisoners from their own fellow-countrymen who wanted to lynch them; and at another crossing point, the Moselle township of Treis, they marched on the commander of the German troops and forbade him to blow the bridge there. He did so all the same and after the war when he returned to the area he was told swiftly he was not welcome and had better leave town quickly.

In the confused situation, General Gerber, commanding the German Seventh Army defending the Moselle area, was nearly captured and had to spend a whole day cut off from his men, hiding in a haystack as American tanks rumbled by. In the end he was reduced to directing what was left of his shattered army from a local post office, using the civilian telephone network as his sole means of communication.

In a letter to his wife that March, Lieutenant Fishler of the 4th Armored, Patton's favorite armored outfit, wrote, 'No German village is complete without a full set of white flags, although they are generally impromptu affairs such as tablecloths, napkins, shirts and grandpa's long winter underpants. If there are some German soldiers to contest our entrance, the reception is a little different at first although later it amounts to the same thing, except the white flags fly from the rubble. Personally I don't have a great deal of stomach for this town fighting business, even if they are Kraut towns, because it means that there are plenty of non-soldiers involved, but what is necessary is necessary, I suppose.'[33]

Private Atwell in newly captured Koblenz found that all was not fighting in the confused rubble of the ruined city. 'Infantrymen who had been in the cellars,' he wrote later, 'ran past drunkenly, firing anywhere and shrill, over-excited German girls, impatient of rape, ran after them through the shells and falling rubble ... A French newspaper photographer drove up in a jeep, brandished a revolver and staggered on drunk to take pictures. Someone played "Lili Marlene" on a piano. The Frenchman wanted to shoot somebody. He found himself aiming at an American soldier. In a living room up the street, drunken American soldiers bumped into drunken German soldiers, all armed, with "excuse me . . . pardon me." Don Stottard [a comrade of Atwell's] dashed into the street during a barrage and came across one of his men having sexual intercourse with a woman. Long streams of German prisoners came by, guarded by drunken Americans. Many of the prisoners were drunk themselves, their water bottles filled with cognac.'[34]

Now the German retreat was turning into a rout. The 26th Infantry Division, which was Patton's closest outfit to the last defenders of the West Wall, pushed along the road parallel to the eastern bank of the River Saar at a tremendous rate. As Lieutenant Maz Gissen of that Division recalled later, 'The stubborn retreat became a real rout. We pushed on as much as twenty-five miles a day. I came into Kaiserslautern at night with only two men, and couldn't find any enemy troops at all. Only Polish and Russian forced laborers, cadavers wandering around aimlessly about and suddenly creatures to be feared by the terrified civilians.'[35]

But all this was unknown to the men of the 70th and 63rd Divisions who were now preparing for yet another attack on the West Wall.

All day long on March 16th, the US artillery and tank guns pounded the German bunkers and pillboxes, followed during the night by extensive patrol activity, its aim to find out whether the pillboxes were still occupied. They were.

On the 17th, Colonel Landstrom's 274th Infantry Regiment took up its positions on the southern bank of the River Saar, ready for an assault crossing. That afternoon every gun in the regiment opened up at the enemy pillboxes and bunkers lining the far bank. Just before nightfall, the gunners saw someone waving a white flag from a church steeple which they thought was being used by the Germans as an observation post. But as soon as they lifted the barrage, the German machine gunners across the river opened up again.

Now the engineers started to bring up the boats for the assault crossing. Colonel Landstrom was told over the phone by his fellow regimental commander Colonel Conley, 'The Commanding General expects us to cross tonight. You are to select the time for the crossing. If you need any assistance, it is ready on call. If you are successful, the 2nd Battalion will follow you.'[36]

Landstrom was confronted by several of his staff officers who believed the Germans had really retreated, leaving a few fanatical machine gunners behind to cover them. Instead of a full-scale assault crossing, they argued, he should send over patrols only.

Landstrom did not agree. 'If we start across, we will complete it,' he stated. 'I am not in favor of patrols. Prefer to go all out. The time for crossing will be sometime between midnight and daybreak. We are still receiving fire from enemy 50 and 88mm guns. This points to the same resistance as before.'[37]

'The night of March 19th was quiet and peaceful,' Colonel Wallace Cheeves recalled after the war. 'The warming winds swept from the south and sent patterns of ripples twinkling in the starlight on the river. In foxholes along the shore the men looked up at the sky and waited.'[38] Soon they would be going for the last attack on the Wall that Hitler built . . .

Epilogue

'We who had fought this war could feel no pride. Victors and vanquished, all were one. We were one with the crowds moving silently along the boulevards of Paris; the old women hunting through the still ruins of Cologne; the bodies piled like yellow cordwood at Dachau; the dreadful vacant eyes of the beaten German soldiers; the white graves and the black crosses and the haunting melancholy of our hearts. All, all were one, all were the ghastly horror of what we had known, of what we had helped to do.'

US Captain Laurence Critchell,
101st Airborne Division

At dawn on March 20th, 1945, the 70th Infantry Division, followed by the 7th Armored Division, attacked across the River Saar to find that the Germans had quietly abandoned the West Wall in front of them a few hours before. With a few losses they continued that day right into the state capital of Saarbrücken.

Two days later, Patton crossed the Rhine a little above Saarbrücken at the small town of Oppenheim. With a force of six battalions, he took the German defenders completely by surprise and by dawn on March 23rd, he was pouring troops across.

Now Patton felt like a mischievous child who sensed he ought to be punished for having been naughty; for hadn't he spoiled the impact of Montgomery's great set-piece crossing of the Rhine in the north? At breakfast time, he telephoned Bradley who was just drinking coffee and said in a subdued voice, 'Brad, don't tell anyone, but I'm across.'

Bradley nearly choked on his coffee. 'Well, I'll be damned,' he spluttered. 'You mean across the Rhine?'

'Sure am,' Patton replied. 'I sneaked a division over last night. But there are so few Krauts around there they don't know it yet. So don't make any announcements yet. We'll keep it a secret until we see how it goes, eh?'[1]

The secret lasted two hours. At the morning briefing, Colonel Stillman of Patton's staff told the assembled newspapermen, obviously referring to Montgomery's tremendous preparations for his crossing, 'Without benefit of aerial bombardment, ground smoke, artillery preparations and airborne assistance, the Third Army, at 2200 hours, Thursday evening 22nd March 1945, crossed the River Rhine.'[2]

On the same day that Montgomery's attack was launched across the Rhine at Wesel, Patton crossed the Rhine himself at the pontoon bridge near Oppenheim. On the other bank, he appeared to slip, sinking to one knee before steadying himself with both hands. When he rose he held up those hands, filled with earth. 'Thus William the Conqueror,' he proclaimed to the watching correspondents with a smile.[3]

Later Patton wrote in his private diary, '24 March. Drove to the river and went across on the pontoon bridge, stopping in the middle to take a piss in the Rhine.'

Thus 'Ole Blood an' Guts,' the Conqueror of Hitler's West Wall from Prüm to Saarbrücken, passed into history . . .

The 'uneasy frontier' along which the West Wall ran did not come to peace so quickly after 1945. While the French, the British, the Americans, the Belgians, Dutch and Luxembourgers systematically blew up every remaining bunker and pillbox, as if they half expected a new army of Teutons to spring from the war-torn earth and man them yet once again, the starving locals on both sides of the frontier took their very lives in their hands to loot the canned food left in the ruins by the vanished soldiers.

Finally the engineers and their explosives departed. Still the border did not come to rest. Now local newspapers were calling it 'the sinful border,' across which bold, if crooked men, who weren't afraid to kill if necessary, transported their wares to feed the great black market which thrived in Occupied Germany.

The German customs men were ordered by their Allied bosses to fire on the smugglers, and in those same dragon's teeth which had brought Leander Doan's attack to a stop in September 1944, armored cars brought from US Army surplus stock and manned by smugglers fought it out with the customs men. After all, the Belgian and Dutch coffee they were transporting through the West Wall was worth a fortune on the German black market. In the Aachen region alone, between 1945 and 1950, forty smugglers and customs men were shot dead in such gun battles.

But the men who smuggled coffee and cigarettes through the West Wall in those years in their *smuggler-panzer*, as the ancient White scout cars and halftracks were called, weren't altogether bad. In that village of Schmidt, once the center of the 'Green Hell of the Huertgen,' where the 28th Division had bled to death, there is today a church called popularly 'St Mokka.' It was rebuilt after the war with gifts from the local coffee smugglers and its first post-war priest is reputed to have said in one Sunday's sermon, 'I pray night after night that you [he meant the smugglers] won't be caught, or that you won't have any further little gifts for our church.'

But by the early fifties, the uneasy border started to

achieve some sort of peace at last. Indeed, as if to symbolize the fact that the bloody past was finally being buried, one of the first recipients of Aachen's famed postwar prize named after Charlemagne himself, *der Karlspreis*, was that man who ten years before had ordered his generals to join him in urinating on the 'Great West Wall of Germany' – Winston Churchill!

It was a beginning. One year later the Americans, now under the command of NATO, started to come back to those remote Eifel townships where their fathers had fought and died. For over a quarter of a century now, Americans and Germans have lived in peace together there, as allies and friends.

At last, after the thousand years of war and terror that followed the division of Charlemagne's Empire, the uneasy border is at peace. The West Wall, as befits an anachronism from another time, has been placed under governmental protection as a national monument in some German federal states, while others have sold the remaining bunkers to private citizens, who have planted flowers where the 'Bouncing Bettys' were once so thickly sown, guarded by those jolly little garden dwarfs so beloved by the Germans as sentries.

'It is as great a mistake to return to old battlefields,' someone once wrote, 'as it is to revisit the place of your honeymoon or the house where you grew up. For years you have owned them in your memory. When you go back, you find the occupants have rearranged the furniture.'

How true. The West Wall bunker which once held up a whole battalion for a day, until some young man 'eager for some desperate glory' took it in the end at a cost of fifty percent casualties, is now simply a gentle mound in an Eifel farmer's backyard. Those dragon's teeth, upon which the Shermans were trapped to be pounded to death by the waiting 88mms, have disappeared into the firs and are covered with green mould so that they look like oddly regular rocks. Time, progress and the earth itself have drawn an almost impenetrable cloak over those scenes of desperate action where young men fought and died forty years ago.

But the Great Wall that Hitler built, ruined, covered with green mould, hidden in the new post-war pine forests, is still there – all three hundred and fifty long miles of it – as if daring Time itself to destroy its concrete heart. Visit it on some soft summer's day, hidden in the fresh green innocence of a pine forest, and one cannot believe the vivid personal recollections of murder and mayhem that once took place here. Was it here that that young Fusilier charged the guns and won his Victoria Cross? Did that young, unbearded, dying Lieutenant ask his men to slap him across the face here to prevent him from dying? Was it down this hill that the terrified young soldiers came streaming in panic with the great lumbering Tigers following them menacingly, snapping the trees as if they were matchsticks? *Did it all really ever happen just a mere four decades ago?*

It did. Here, young men from half a dozen nations fought that winter and were grievously hurt and died in their thousands, hundreds of thousands.

For the military historians the history of that terrible winter is mere chronology – a series of moves and countermoves made by omnipotent generals sitting in remote headquarters. They may wear different uniforms and speak a different mother tongue, but they have the same backgrounds, the same training, the same ideals, the same terrain maps. For them it is an impersonal battle of wills, matching their moral strength and tactical ingenuity against their unseen opponents on the other side of the line.

But war for the soldier who does the fighting is not like that, especially for the infantry who fought the Battle of the West Wall. War for them was a tragedy, made up of the dramas and disasters of many humble little men, who were not consulted on the length of the preliminary artillery bombardment, the proper manner of isolating the battlefield, the appropriate time to throw in the reserves and so on.

That winter the GIs, the PBI (poor bloody infantry), the 'stubble-hoppers' were ordered simply, without explanation, to attack, capture, and, if necessary, to die in the attempt; just as their opponents were ordered, in the time-honored phrase, 'to defend to the last man and the last bullet.'

More often than not, they did just that. For that reason, I should like to dedicate this book to the memory of those young men, whatever their nationality, who fought and died in The Battle for the Siegfried Line.

Wittlich/Eifel, Summer 1981

Notes and Sources

Introduction
1. Quoted in *Le Monde*.

Book I: 1944 – September
1. SHAEF Review of Intelligence, September 1945.
2. Ibid.
3. Quoted in Flowers, *The Taste of Courage*.
4. Ibid.
5. Meyer, *Panzergrenadiere*.
6. SHAEF Review of Intelligence, 1944.
7. Flowers, op. cit.
8. Woollcombe, *Lion Rampant*.
9. The three cantons of Malmedy, Eupen, and St Vith with their 70,000-odd inhabitants had been transferred to Belgium after World War One. With the exception of a few French-speaking Walloons, they were all native German speakers.
10. For this and the other Hemingway passages in this book, the author is indebted to Carlos Baker's *Ernest Hemingway* (see Bibliography).
11. Ibid.
12. From *Völkischer Beobachter*, September 1938 (author's translation).
13. Kenneth Strong, *Intelligence at the Top*.
14. In *The Siegfried Line Campaign*.
15. The details of what happened that night are unclear to this day. It seems, however, that Schultz's company was surprised by German half-tracks carrying flame-throwers. Only a few survivors – such as Fleming, who was posted to the rear of the company – were ever found.
16. Quoted in Baker's *Ernest Hemingway*.
17. Ibid.
18. The note is preserved in Aachen's Stadtmuseum.
19. See Whiting and Trees, *Die Amis sind da*.

20. Ibid.
21. Ibid.
22. Under the German system (unlike that of the US Army) reserve formations staffed with experienced NCOs and officers were always kept well to the rear ready to build up shattered formations at once.
23. From Bradley's *Soldier's Story*.
24. Ibid.
25. Von Rundstedt saw that von Schwerin did not end in those dreaded Gestapo cellars in Berlin. Instead, he was transferred to Italy, where he was given a corps. Surviving Allied imprisonment too, he lived on until 1980, often returning to the annual reunions of those portly white-haired old men who had once been his lean, keen 'Greyhounds.'
26. 'Throatache' was World War Two German Army slang for the lack of the Knight's Cross. On receiving that decoration, the 'throatache' was 'cured.'
27. Quoted in Essame's *Battle for Germany*.

October
1. In this and the following passages the author is indebted to Captain MacDonald's book, *Company Commander*.
2. Collected in BBC War Reports 1944.
3. PFC T. Stubbs, in a personal interview with the author.
4. From Merriam's book, *Dark December*.
5. From Atwell's book, *Private*.
6. From *The GI Journal of Sergeant Giles*, edited by Janice Giles.
7. Ibid.
8. From Eisenhower's book, *Crusade in Europe*.
9. The figures were never published, but it was estimated that there were about 100,000 US deserters hiding out in the ETO by Christmas 1944.
10. From *The GI Journal of Sergeant Giles*.
11. Eisenhower, op. cit.
12. This account of the occasion is based on the description in *The Way It Was* by M. Hemingway.
13. From W. Goerlitz, *Model*.
14. Essame, op. cit.
15. Model's body was kept hidden for several years after the war until finally his comrades thought it safe to give their late

Field Marshal a proper burial. Today he is buried in the
military cemetery at Vossenack.

16. Reported in *Stars and Stripes*, November 1944.
17. *Yank* magazine, November 1944.
18. Ibid.
19. From BBC War Reports 1944.
20. Flowers, op. cit.
21. Bradley, op. cit.
22. Ibid.
23. Whiting and Trees, op. cit.

November

1. One bright light was that the courageous aid men volunteered to stay behind with the seriously wounded.
2. Quoted in MacDonald, *The Battle of the Huertgen Forest*.
3. Ibid.
4. Ibid.
5. Ibid.
6. Ibid.
7. Whiting and Trees, op. cit.
8. This account of the dinner conversation is based on the
   description in *A Full Life* by Brian Horrocks.
9. Bradley, op. cit.
10. The 79th Division – or 'Funnies' as they were known –
    comprised a strange collection of armored vehicles used for
    all sorts of special tasks. The divisional commander was
    Monty's brother-in-law, who had been brought out of
    retirement for this purpose (he had previously been a lance-
    corporal in the Home Guard: a striking promotion).
11. Essame, op. cit.
12. Ibid.
13. Ibid.
14. Ibid.
15. Ibid.
16. Ibid.
17. Bradley, op. cit.
18. Ernie Pyle was a famous reporter at that time, later killed in
    combat.
19. This account is based on the description in Carlos Baker, op.
    cit.
20. *Stars and Stripes*, December 1944.
21. Quoted in MacDonald, *The Battle of the Huertgen Forest*.

22. Carlos Baker, op. cit.
23. Quoted by Carlos Baker, op. cit.
24. MacDonald, *The Battle of the Huertgen Forest*.
25. Ibid..
26. All German sources say that the forests around the village of Huertgen had no name prior to the arrival of the Americans; evidently it was they who first called them collectively 'the Huertgen Forest.' This was later adopted by the local Germans who now call it *der Huertgenwald*.
27. Quoted in MacDonald, *The Battle of the Huertgen Forest*.
28. Ibid.
29. Ibid.
30. Ibid.
31. Bradley, op. cit.
32. Ibid.
33. Whiting and Trees, op. cit.
34. MacDonald, *The Battle of the Huertgen Forest*.
35. Whiting and Trees, op. cit.
36. Quoted in Carlos Baker, op. cit.

December
 1. See *Decision at St Vith*, C. Whiting.
 2. Ibid.
 3. Ibid.
 4. Collected in BBC War Reports 1944.
 5. Ibid.
 6. Colonel Bremer, in a personal interview with the author.
 7. MacDonald, *The Battle of the Huertgen Forest*.
 8. Essame, op. cit.
 9. MacDonald, *The Battle of the Huertgen Forest*.
10. Atwell, op. cit.
11. Ibid.
12. It was later reported that advance German columns pushing into Belgium were handed 'green-colored envelopes' by the sleeper organization they had set up in the area when leaving in September 1944; the 'letters' contained information for the military men about the opposition they were likely to run into.
13. When Giskes told me the story of 'Freddie,' I doubted it. But reference to *Hansard*, the official publication of proceedings in the British Houses of Parliament, showed that in

1945 a Miss Eileen Wilkinson had asked Home Secretary Morrison questions about the 'spy in the Churchill family.'

14. Until he heard the radio news of the great offensive on December 16th, Giskes was very worried that he might inadvertently have picked Model's real objective.
15. Quoted in *The Bitter Woods* by John Eisenhower.
16. MacDonald, *Company Commander*.
17. Ibid.
18. BBC War Reports 1944.
19. Whiting and Trees, op. cit.
20. Ibid.
21. John Eisenhower, op. cit.
22. Ibid.
23. MacDonald, *Company Commander*.
24. Ibid.
25. Ibid.
26. Ibid.
27. Described in *Death of a Division*, C. Whiting.
28. Mel Brooks, in a *Playboy* interview, February 1978.
29. Strong, op. cit.
30. Troy Middleton, Commander of VIII US Corps, whose front in the Ardennes was now crumbling badly.
31. John Eisenhower, op. cit.
32. No figures of German casualties are available. All that is known is that 90,000 German POWs went into the cages of the US First and Ninth Armies during this period.

Book II: 1945 – January

1. R. W. Thompson, *Men Under Fire*.
2. Ibid.
3. Bradley, op. cit.
4. C. Codman, *Drive*.
5. *Daily Express*, January 1945.
6. Quoted in C. Whiting, *Bradley*.
7. Bradley, op. cit.
8. Ibid.
9. 'Penny ducks': something like a savoury hamburger made basically of offal.
10. Captain Moore, in a personal interview with the author.
11. H. St George Saunders, *The Green Beret*.
12. German Jews serving with the British Army were given the most British-sounding names possible, often those of

Scottish or Welsh origin (Griffiths is a Welsh name), and false identity papers in case they were captured; Intelligence feared the worst for them if they fell into the hands of their former countrymen.

13. Essame, *The Battle for Germany*.
14. Ryan, *A Bridge Too Far*.
15. Bradley, op. cit.
16. Ibid.
17. Ibid.
18. C. Whiting, *Patton*.
19. Ibid.
20. Farago, *Patton: Ordeal and Triumph*.
21. Ibid.
22. Patton was not the only general to circumvent Eisenhower's orders that month. De Gaulle – 'the military adventurer we brought with us in our baggage in '44,' as Brigadier Essame called him bitterly – told Marshal de Lattre, commander of the French troops in Ike's great force, 'My dear General, you must cross the Rhine even if the Americans don't agree. Matters of great national importance are at stake. Karlsruhe and Stuttgart await you.' When the French finally did get Stuttgart, Ike had to threaten to starve them out before they would relinquish the city.
23. M. Shulman, *The Other Side of the Hill*.
24. Ibid.
25. Ibid.
26. R. M. Wingfield, quoted in Flowers, op. cit.
27. MacDonald, *Company Commander*.
28. *The GI Journal of Sergeant Giles*.
29. Atwell, op. cit.
30. Ibid.
31. Johannes Nobuesch, *Zum Bitteren Ende* (author's translation).
32. Farago, op. cit.
33. Ibid.
34. Ibid.

February
1. Codman, op. cit.
2. Ibid.
3. Farago, op. cit.
4. *Divisional History of the 76th Division* (published 1945).

5. Ibid.
6. Ibid.
7. Ibid.
8. Ibid.
9. Ibid.
10. Fred Ayres, *Patton*.
11. Ibid.
12. *Stars and Stripes*, March 7, 1945.
13. Farago, op. cit.
14. *Daily Express*, March 1945.
15. John Toland, *The Last Hundred Days*.
16. Atwell, op. cit.
17. Ibid.
18. Quoted in Flowers, op. cit.
19. John Foley, *Mailed Fist*.
20. Ibid.
21. Essame, op. cit.
22. Foley, op. cit.
23. Quoted in Intelligence Reviews, March 1945.
24. Foley, op. cit.
25. Ibid.
26. Ibid.
27. Woollcombe, op. cit.
28. Foley, op. cit.
29. Thompson, op. cit.
30. Ibid.
31. Atwell, op. cit.
32. *The GI Journal of Sergeant Giles*.
33. Codman, op. cit.
34. Ibid.
35. Quoted in Grant, *The 51st Highland Division At War*.
36. Ibid.
37. Quoted in Flowers, op. cit.
38. Ibid.
39. Ibid.
40. Foley, op. cit.
41. Thompson, op. cit.
42. Shulman, op. cit.
43. Thompson, op. cit.
44. Ibid.
45. Harry McLaughlin, in a personal interview and correspondence with the author.

46. In fact, once Patton had broken through, it took his 4th Armored Division less than fifty hours to reach the Rhine.
47. Shulman, op.cit.

March

1. Thompson, op. cit.
2. Ibid.
3. Essame, op. cit.
4. Toland, op. cit.
5. For this account of Churchill's visit, I am indebted to John Toland's book, *The Last Hundred Days*.
6. Ibid.
7. Farago, op. cit.
8. Ibid.
9. Ibid.
10. Ayres, op. cit.
11. Overruling Churchill, Roosevelt had insisted that there should be no talking terms with the Germans: they would have to surrender unconditionally.
12. Ayres, op. cit.
13. *Combat: A Selection of Writings from Yank Magazine.*
14. Ibid.
15. Ibid.
16. Ibid.
17. Ibid.
18. Ibid.
19. Ibid.
20. Ibid.
21. Heinz Breuer, in a personal interview with the author.
22. The 'chaindog' patrols were made up of German military policemen, known as 'chained dogs' on account of the silver crescents, their insignia of office, suspended on a chain around their necks.
23. By 1945, it was estimated that nearly 16,000 German soldiers had been shot for desertion or cowardice in action. In the whole of the US Army only one man suffered that fate.
24. This particular item was published in several German newspapers in March/April 1945.
25. Farago, op. cit.
26. *Combat* (see above, note 13).
27 Ibid.

8. Whiting and Trees, op. cit.
9. *Combat* (see above, note 13).
0. Ibid.
1. Ibid.
2. Ibid.
3. McKee, *The Race for the Rhine Bridges*.
4. Atwell, op. cit.
5. Quoted in McKee, op. cit.
6. *Combat* (see above, note 13).
7. Ibid.
8. Ibid.

Epilogue
1. Farago, op. cit.
2. Codman, op. cit.
3. On landing at Hastings, England, in 1066, William the
   Conqueror slipped. Knowing that his men would regard this
   as a bad omen, he picked up two handfuls of earth and
   proclaimed: 'See, I have taken England with both hands!'

Bibliography

Leslie Atwell, *Private*, Popular Library, New York, 1968

Frederick Ayres, *Patton*, Little Brown, New York, 1972.

Carlos Baker, *Ernest Hemingway*, Scribners, New York, 1969.

C. N. Barclay, *History of the 53rd (Welsh) Division*, Clowes.

O. Bradley, *Soldier's Story*, Dell Paperbacks, New York, 1952.

W. Cheeves, *Snow Ridges and Pillboxes* (privately printed).

C. Codman, *Drive*, Atlantic Monthly Press, Boston, 1957.

Combat: A Selection of Writings from 'Yank' Magazine, Dell, New York, 1958.

H. M. Cole, *The Lorraine Campaign*, US Dept. of the Army, Washington, DC, 1950.

Dwight D. Eisenhower, *Crusade in Europe*, Doubleday, New York, 1948/Heinemann, London, 1949.

John Eisenhower, *The Bitter Woods*, Robert Hale, London, 1969.

Hubert Essame, *The Battle for Germany*, Batsford, 1969.

——*The 43rd Wessex Division at War*, Clowes.

L. Farago, *Patton: Ordeal and Triumph*, Astor-Honor, 1964/Granada, London, 1969.

D. Flowers, *The Taste of Courage*, Harper & Bros, New York, 1960.

John Foley, *Mailed Fist*, Panther, London, 1957.

Janice Giles (ed.), *The GI Journal of Sergeant Giles*, Houghton Mifflin, Boston, 1965.

W. Goerlitz, *Model*, DTV, Munich, 1978.

R. Grant, *The 51st Highland Division at War*, Allen, 1977.

M. Hemingway, *The Way It Was*, Scribners, New York, 1975.

Brian Horrocks, *A Full Life*, Leo Cooper, London, 1974.

Charles MacDonald, *The Battle of the Huertgen Forest*, Lippincott, New York, 1963.

——, *Company Commander*, Ballantine, New York, 1958.

——, *The Siegfried Line Campaign*, US Dept. of the Army, Washington, DC, 1963.

A. McKee, *The Race for the Rhine Bridges*, Souvenir Press, London, 1971.

Robert Merriam, *Dark December*, Ballantine, New York, 1947.

Kurt Meyer, *Panzergrenadiere*, Munin-verlag, Munich, 1960.

Johannes Nobuesch, *Zum Bitteren Ende*, Bibburg, 1979.

Cornelius Ryan, *A Bridge Too Far*, Simon & Schuster, New York, 1974/Collins, London, 1978.

J. Salmond, *The History of the 51st Highland Division*, Blackwood.

H. St George Saunders, *The Green Beret*, Four Square, London, 1959.

M. Shulman, *The Other Side of the Hill*, Collins, London, 1947.

Kenneth Strong, *Intelligence at the Top*, Cassell, London, 1968.

R. W. Thompson, *Men Under Fire*, Macdonald, London, 1945.

John Toland, *The Last Hundred Days*, Random House, New York, 1966/London, 1966.

Charles Whiting, *Bradley*, Ballantine, New York, 1973.

——, *Death of a Division*, Frederick Warne, London, 1981/Stein and Day, New York, 1981.

——, *Decision at St Vith*, Ballantine, New York, 1969.

——, *Patton*, Ballantine, New York, 1971.

Whiting and Trees, *Die Amis sind da*, AVZ Verlag, 1978.

Chester Wilmot, *The Struggle for Europe*, Harper & Row, New York, 1952/Collins, London, 1952.

R. Wingfield, *Hide and Seek in the Reichswald*, Hutchinson, London.

Robert Woollcombe, *Lion Rampant*, Leo Cooper, London, 1972.

A Short History of the 7th Armoured Division (privately printed).

Index